Gumbo Lilies

By Thelma Martin Anderson

Gumbo Lilies is dedicated to my daughters Deanna and Faye and to all my nieces and nephews: John, Judy and Dena Sanford; Kandi, Rex, Budd, Robin, Joe, Leslee, Kristen and Eric Woitte; Herbie, Linda, Hank and John Martin and Scott, Jean, Mike, Pat, Rodney, Randy, Jill, Kelly, Jess, Jay, Jennifer and Billie Martin.

Gumbo Lilies

Book Design by Deanna O. Peters

Manufactured in the United States of America

ISBN: 0-7392-0018-6

Library of Congress Catalog Card Number: 98-93952

Printed in the USA by

3212 East Highway 30 • Kearney, NE 68847 • 1-800-650-7888

Gumbo Lilies

Thelma Martin Anderson

Thelma Martin Anderson

Sagehen Creek Publishing
P.O. Box 311
Midland Avenue
Midland, South Dakota 57552

Introduction

Gumbo Lilies is the sequel to *Where Coyotes Howl* and begins where the first book left off. Our world was changing so fast we couldn't keep up with it. We were crawling out of The Great Depression. Rain was falling, and across the ocean the horns of war were blowing.

We had gone suddenly from the horse and buggy to the automobile traveling at speeds of up to sixty miles an hour. Some men forgot that automobiles had brakes and rammed through the walls of their garages or some farmer's gate.

It was a time when jobs were scarcer than hen's teeth and land was easy to get. A friend and I decided to buy some land, and we stuck to it like the beautiful Gumbo Lily sticks to a shale bank come hell or high water.

I am indebted to Ralph "Shorty" Jones for the title of this book. Thank you, Shorty. Thanks also to the librarians at the South Dakota State Library for invaluable information and to our own Karel Reimann of The Midland Community Library for all the help she gave me.

I also wish to thank everyone who contributed an anecdote for my book. I hope you enjoy it.

--Thelma Martin Anderson, Author

Chapter 1
Sun Flowers Blooming In The Rain

Cattle and horses grazed in pastures of brilliant green, green that cloaked our western South Dakota hills and valleys as they had not been clothed for many a year.

Midland High School graduation 1938 was over: "Climb though the rocks be rugged," a brave motto, "and may your valleys grow ever greener." The speeches were over. Twelve young people stepped forward to have Superintendent McNally hand each a diploma wrapped in genuine sheepskin.

And so the names were called: Kenneth Anderson, Orville Bentley, Willis Drew, John Gillaspie, Violet Hineline, Thelma Martin, Frances May, Ruby Muirhead, Harriet Olesen, Paul Sandbo, Margaret Seidler, Thomas Stalley.

Like the three little pigs, twelve young people struck out into the world to make their fortunes. Only we didn't have any sticks or bricks or even straw to build our houses, and the wolf was nipping at our heels. Most of us went home to our father's house where there was food on the table and beds in the bedrooms.

The horns of war were blowing and clouds, dark and ugly, gathered on the far horizon. France wasn't worried. She had the Maginot Line. England had the English Channel. And Hitler had war planes by the thousand and an insatiable desire for more land to conquer. We weren't worried either. An ocean separated us from

Germany. Our country wouldn't send soldiers to fight "over there" again, or would it?

I walked out of the auditorium, clutching my precious sheepskin and went home to milk cows and feed hogs, calves, turkeys, chickens, and assorted poultry. I bravely took pen and paper and wrote a letter to Pinky Anderson, proprieter of the B & M Cafe in Philip, asking him if he could use any waitresses. I signed my name "Yours truly, Thelma Martin." I affixed a three cent stamp, sent my letter off and waited for a reply that never came.

Brother Herb went to work for Griggs Davidson, herding sheep on the Davidson ranch west of the Nelson school. After lambing, Herb and Ole Kristenson built dams for Griggs. The Government was paying farmers to build dams on their land. Herb and Ole went out on sturdy, roaring F 20 Farmall tractors to pull tumble bugs and move dirt into draws from Midland to Ottumwa. Ponds appeared where none had been before.

Brother Hank went to a CCC camp in The Black Hills and helped beautify campgrounds for the government. Julian went to Aunt Amanda's place on Mitchell Creek. I stayed home, rode Darkie over Uncle Alvin's big pasture to check his cattle, milked cows and cultivated the corn that grew tall once more in Dad's east field. Once, I tipped the cultivator over and flew through the air like a bird, landing on my head on the hard ground.

Buddy and Mickey were our fishermen, supplying our table with tasty bullheads from the dam. They were ten and eight years old and took their job seriously.

The thirsty earth drank rain once more. The tiny fields on deserted homesteads were bare spots in a field of green. Not even weeds grew there. And then the sunflowers came, covering the bare earth with gold. Acres of sunflowers gleamed in the sunshine and nodded in every breeze. The prairie was transformed into a tapestry of green and gold, and I thought I had never seen anyhing so beautiful.

By July, farmers reported seeing grasshoppers gathered in restless, compact circles in fields and on the prairie. This phenomena was supposed to mean that they would take immediate flight. Aerial photographers reported that the air at about 4,000 feet was seething with grasshoppers, apparently flying north. We hoped they would land on the North Pole and freeze solid.

We planted a garden north of our house and raised radishes, lettuce, green beans, and peas, which along with the fish made a fine meal. We had potatoes growing, too. As summer wore on, blister beetles and grasshoppers nibbled on every green thing. Potato bugs made lace of the potato plant leaves. Aunt Mildred saw an ad in *The Dakota Farmer* for a sure fire potato bug killer for a quarter. She sent her quarter and received two 2x4x4 inch blocks. The instructions said: "Place potato bug on one block and squash with the other."

The Midland elevators were preparing for a bumper wheat harvest. Archie Joy built a new elevator that looked like a young sky scraper for $2,500. He was ready for harvest.

Spring wheat began coming to town in late July. Jake DeYoung, who lived about four miles northwest of Midland, reported his spring wheat weighed 60 pounds and made 12 bushels to the acre. Charley Nemec who lived northeast of town beat that with 18 bushels to the acre. The average was 5 to 7 bushels. Ten was considered good. Farmers hadn't learned to plant winter wheat.

Uncle Alvin Bertelson fell off his F 20 Farmall tractor and broke his wrist so he was working with a cast on one arm. He bought a combine, one of those towering galvanized machines pulled by a tractor, with another man riding the combine. Alvin drove the tractor and Dad manned the combine. That machine sure beat the old threshing machine.

Sister Julian went to work for Mrs. Eckwald who lived northwest of Steiens near Ottumwa. Eckwalds had a large grove of trees that you could see for miles--an oasis in the desert.

I was still home milking the cows. Buddy helped me haul water from the dam with the team and stone boat for the house and poultry. We had chickens, turkeys and guineas running about the farm and ducks and geese swimming in the dam. Buddy some times drove Star, hitching the black pony single on the stone boat to haul water. Star didn't mind, and Buddy was proud of his one horse outfit. When Dad worked late I milked eleven cows, unless Julian was home. Then she reluctantly helped me.

In August, the temperature hit 108 degrees, wilting vegetation and humans alike. Cattle prices were rising slowly. A bunch of seven hundred pound registered Hereford yearling heifers sold for $55.00 per head.

One warm day, Buddy and Mickey rode Whitefoot and Star down the trail to visit Aunt Tina. Buddy rode in the saddle on Whitefoot. He always got first choice. Mickey rode Star bareback and barefoot. As the horses trotted up the trail toward home, Mickey bounced on Star's broad back. Star's trot would jar your teeth. A jackrabbit jumped suddenly from the shade of a fence post. Star shied, and Mickey fell off, hitting the hard ground with a solid thud while the rabbit hopped away.

Buddy jumped off to help Mickey back on her horse. Mickey was upset. She stuck her lower lip out and said, "No." She looked at the fence. She could get on Star by climbing on the fence and leaping to his back, but she was barefoot, and the barb wire fence was sharp.

She headed up the trail, walking and leading Star, while Buddy rode beside her, trying to talk her into letting him boost her back on her horse. She steadfastly refused. Instead, she trudged home, leading Star, madder than a cat with its tail caught in the screen door.

Uncle Alvin was combining Dad's wheat while grasshoppers cut off the wheat heads ahead of the combine. They hadn't all left. The wheat only made about ten bushels to the acre. When he got through with the wheat harvest, Uncle Alvin raised the grade of our dam, and it never went dry again.

The speed limit on South Dakota highways was 35 miles per hour. *The Midland Mail* complained that "people are still trying to compete with trains at railroad crossings and pass other cars on hills and curves. Just because cars have more horse power doesn't mean people should have less horse sense." No yellow lines and no "no passing" signs may have been the reason South Dakota had 100 highway fatalities in one year.

A down pour in August slowed the combines and ran water into the ponds that Herb and Ole were building. Emil Nemec fenced out his eighty acres that was between our farmstead and the east field. He left us a lane so we didn't have to open any more gates. He built a dam across the draw which nearly filled with water. His pond was twice as big as ours and deep. Emil put a row boat on his dam so he could row out to deep water and fish.

We liked to swim in Emil's dam, using the boat to get past the sea weed to deep water where we could drop anchor and dive off the boat. Nearly every hot afternoon, we walked to Nemec's a mile east and got Florence to go swimming with us. We dived and swam where the water was clean and clear and no sea weed grew. The water was so deep I couldn't touch bottom, but we went down the anchor chain and touched mud.

One day Florence, Julian and I were swimming. Buddy, a husky ten-year-old, sat in the boat watching. He decided it would be fun to row away from us. He pulled up the anchor and rowed toward the far side of the dam. By the time we discovered what he was doing, it was too late to catch the boat. He could row as fast as we could swim.

Julian and I could have swam to shore, but Florence got tired and was close to panic as the row boat got farther and farther away. We finally convinced the little stinker that we meant it when we yelled, "Stop, we need to get in the boat." I swam to the boat and grabbed the gunwale, holding it until Florence got a hold on the side and scrambled aboard. Julian and I gave Buddy a sisterly lecture that turned his ears red. He never did that again.

The water in Nemec's dam stretched up one draw for a quarter of a mile and up another nearly that far, forming a Y. Gloria Saucerman, who was a couple of years younger than Julian, came to visit one hot afternoon. We went swimming in Nemec's dam and started to swim across the short end of the Y. Gloria paddled confidantly beside us until she tried to touch bottom. When her feet didn't touch mud, she panicked and started to flounder.

I held her up and said, "Just swim. Don't try to touch bottom."

"Keep paddling," Julian said. "We won't let you drown." Gloria dog paddled for shore. We soon came to shallow water and walked out of the water more relieved than we cared to admit.

C.O. Engman, the Midland druggist, bought some Thoroughbred race horses and graded a track on the flat north of Midland by the town well. He hired Tom Stalley who weighed a bit over a hundred pounds to be his jockey. After the Farmer's Picnic in August, there were horses races on Engman's track. Admission was fifteen cents. Three Thoroughbreds, owned by three different men, danced at the starting line. The starting gun banged. The horses tore down the track. Engman's bay flashed over the finish line a length ahead, and I wished for a race horse.

Cattle prices might have been looking up, but cream wasn't high. Our neighbor, Bill Crawford, said he took a can of cream to Midland and got enough money to buy enough gas to get home and back to town and maybe visit neighbors or go to a card party.

Midland had plenty of places to buy gas: Oscar's Service Station & Garage, Stub Joy's Standard Garage, Jake's Service and Schweigert's Texaco. As if that wasn't enough, Del Halvorson's White Eagle sold gas a block west on the north side of Main in a corner of what is now the city park.

Midland boasted two full fledged merchantiles: C. E. Murray's Store in business since 1906 was in The Frontier Bank building and The Midland Coop Store a block down the street. Murray's Store sold Hyers boots for $16.95, but I couldn't afford them. He sold hats and shoes and everything in between.

Engman's Drug Store had been sold to John Sturdevant. Almost anything one needed could be purchased in Midland. Dad bought his milk pails and cream cans from Davidson's Hardware. He sold cream and eggs to The Midland Co-op and bought groceries and bib overalls there as well. My folks didn't trade at Murray's Store except to buy ladies wear. Mom said Mrs. Murray had impeccable taste, and she was the buyer.

When fall came, Buddy and Mickey, in fifth and fourth grades, rode to Liberty School. Julian went to stay with Aunt Amanda and Uncle Walt for her Senior year at Midland High School. I, by some miracle, got a job. I went to work for Edith Gillaspie in Ottumwa, caring for baby Mickey while Edith taught the Ottumwa school. My friend and classmate for ten years, Frances May, went to Black Hills State College at Spearfish. I wanted to go to the University at Vermillion, but I had no money. I was about to earn some.

Edith lived in the teacher's cottage across the street from the school house. The small cottage had a kitchen, a parlor and one bedroom. My bed was in the parlor. The school house was a large square building with room for thirty students from grades one through ten. Now the large school house had one first grader, Lois Harry, and her teacher rattling around in it all day.

My job was to entertain four month old Mickey, cook dinner and wash diapers. I earned $2.00 per week. Edith pulled down about $60.00 per month. Teacher's salaries averaged between $60.00 and $90.00 per month in 1937. Mostly Mickey was a cheerful little red haired fellow, but one day, he wanted me to pick him up when I was preparing dinner. Mickey cried, but I ignored him and kept peeling potatoes. Mickey got his royal dander up. He howled and bellowed so loudly his mother heard him way over in the school house. She ran out of the building, dashed across the street and burst through the door. She picked up Mickey and wiped the tears from his indignant eyes. He stopped crying. "I was going to pick him up as soon as I had the potatoes on," I said.

"I don't like to have him cry," Edith answered. "If he cries, pick him up and let what you're doing wait." She handed me the now happy child and went back to the school house. I didn't let him cry again.

Ottumwa had shrunk from its heyday in Pioneer times to two businesses, three residences and a teacher's cottage. Jay and Lucy Decker had a grocery store and lived east of the school. The J.W.

Harry family lived south of the school. Lowell and Jimmie Maeder lived in the large, square Maeder house along the highway. Lowell operated a garage and service station beside the road. There was still a Methodist church and a Catholic church. The Methodists were all gone, but Father Sweeney from Midland had Mass in the Catholic church.

Ottumwa was founded in 1903 by brothers Cy and Harley "Foote" Thompson. The Thompson brothers had a general store. The store went through several owners before Jay Decker bought it. The Ottumwa of homestead days spread over the prairie with two hotels, a general store, a dance hall, a blacksmith shop, a livery barn, two churches, a school, a creamery, a saloon, a newspaper "The Ottumwa", and a number of residences. Ottumwa had stage service and looked for the railroad that never came.

The prairie stretched and rolled for miles in every direction. I watched the Harry boys, Clayton or Edwin, bringing in the milk cows at eventide, riding a bay horse. Sometimes I went to Decker's Store to get a can of peas. I walked a half mile north and went fishing in Lake Lucy, named for Lucy Decker. To the north, I could see Tom Gillaspie Sr.'s farm.

About a quarter of a mile south an ungraveled road went west past the Buchholtz and Thompson farms. Foote Thompson lived on his homestead south of Ottumwa. He went about with a piece of dirty sheet wrapped around his middle for a bandage. He had fallen off his load of hay and jabbed a pitchfork in his stomach. It was said that one could look into his stomach and see food churning about. He chose to wrap a sheet around himself and go about his business. His doctoring proved successful as he healed without problems.

Happy Wolf, a nice old man who was true to his name, lived in a dugout southeast of Ottumwa. One spring he kept an orphan colt in his house and fed the foal cow's milk from a bottle. His chickens roosted on the head of his bed. Happy turned the rooster and hens tails out before climbing into the bed for the night.Twice a week, he drifted down to visit the Heebs family, arriving around eleven a.m. He would say, "Now, I didn't come for dinner," but Mrs. Heeb always invited him to stay and eat, and he did.

Wanda Heeb herded the large band of sheep belonging to the Heeb's ranch. The sheep started grazing at sun up and often continued nibbling grass until ten o'clock at night before lying down to rest. Wanda put in a long day on the prairie, sometimes riding her horse, sometimes leading the animal and always accompanied by her faithful dog. Wanda had married Jim Heeb when she was seventeen and had been herding sheep ever since.

I worked in Ottumwa through September and part of October, earning enough money to buy two lovely dresses, one blue and one pink from the Montgomery Ward catalog. I paid $2.00 each for the dresses and still had $5.00 left when Edith fired me because Tom was laid off from his job at Archie Joy Enterprises. He came home and took care of Mickey, so I went home.

The Old Age Pension averaged $19.03 per month and Aunt Tina and Uncle Charley were both old enough to get a pension. On this bounty, they decided to go to Iowa to visit relatives. "Do you want to come with us, Thelma?" they asked. I sure did, so I packed a suitcase and hopped into the Model T with them.

Thelma Martin. High School graduation. 1938.

Buddy Martin, the fisherman, and his catch.

CHAPTER 2
Iowa

I slid behind the wheel of Aunt Tina's Model T coupe, and we headed south on the winding gravel road to Highway 16 on a crisp October day. Trailing us in Hank's Model T coupe, were my brothers, Herb and Hank and Clarence Petoske, called Pete or Smoky. The boys planned to get jobs picking Iowa corn.

We headed east on Highway 16. I had never traveled far from home before so the trip was a grand adventure for me. The Model Ts roared down the highway, going thirty miles an hour. Gradually, the buildings along the way began to look more prosperous. I marveled at a huge, round, red barn north of the highway. That barn now resides fifteen miles south of Midland as one of the main buildings at the 1880 Town.

We crossed the wide Missouri at Chamberlain and began to see white houses and more red barns. We stayed the night at a motel in Kimball. We'd made 225 miles in one day. By the time we reached Sioux Falls, the grass had turned to green, and the corn was tall, taller than any corn I had ever seen, with a huge ear hanging on every stalk.

The minute we crossed the Iowa line, I smelled pigs. I was amazed at the tall corn and grass as green as a well-watered lawn, not dry and brown like our prairie grass. The farms were tiny to me, mostly 160 acres with Holstein cows in the pastures and hogs of many colors in the pig pens. White houses, huge, hip-roofed barns and red outbuildings with white trim were shielded from the wind by groves of trees. We passed field after field of corn being picked by farmers who threw the ears into wagons as the horses plodded down the row.

I drove up a curving trail to Frank Schroader's house past a hundred honking geese. The white and gray geese were led by angry ganders that hissed at the car wheels and tried to chase the cars away. We parked beside a two story white house sitting on a gentle knoll.

The red barn had no haymow, but it had stanchions for ten milk cows. The brown and roan cows shared a large pasture with a herd of about twenty horses. The Schroader farm wasn't fancy, but it was large, over 320 acres. Many of the acres were swamp where wild ducks swam among the reeds and cattails. Pheasants lived in the corn fields. I had never seen pheasants in our part of South Dakota.

We were welcomed by Frank and Ula Schroader and three children. Their maternal Grandma Anderson lived with them. Leona (Lee) and Marian (Dolly) were close to my age. Both had red hair and blue eyes. Leslie (Buster) was eleven with innocent blue eyes that belied a mischievous nature. His curly hair was blond. In summer, he ran and played in fields and meadows all day. He was so tired when night came he sometimes went to sleep immediately after supper with Lee or Dolly guiding him upstairs to bed. One night, he went to sleep halfway up the stairs, draped over Lee's arm. He was still on his feet with his head on the step above.

Frank was Uncle Charley's nephew. He was a husky fellow and had been both a professional boxer and a professional wrestler. Lee was his hired man. She helped with the chores, milking cows, slopping and feeding hogs, cultivating corn, helping with the haying and picking corn.

The depression hit Frank as hard as it did most farmers. Hogs became worthless along with the corn they ate. In spite of this, Frank was gaining slowly. Iowa got rain and didn't have grasshoppers. He raised red hogs, kept a herd of milk cows and owned a pasture full of draft horses that he was breaking to work.

The corn picking was just underway. Herb, Hank and Smoky got work quickly. Hank went to work on the Fletcher farm which joined Schroader's. Fletcher milked Holstein cows and Hank helped with the farm work. He learned to watch out for the fierce Holstein bull, after the bull put him over the fence. Smoky went to work picking corn and was soon a hundred bushel a day picker. Herb didn't take to picking corn well. He was better on the scoop shovel.

Lee proudly showed me her saddle horse, Dan a brown and white paint. He stepped daintily out of the barn, a good looking horse built like a Thoroughbred. Dan was in his twenties so in horse years, he was an old man. That evening, Lee rode Dan after the milk cows. Since I was an old hand at the milking businss, I offered to help. We locked ten cows in their stanchions, and I grabbed a tin milk pail.

"You can milk that red cow," Lee said, handing me a milk stool. At home, we used old milk buckets for milk stools.I had to balance on this dinky one-legged stool while pulling and squeezing on the cow's faucets until they were empty.

Lee and Buster watched as I sat down beside the cow. Lee sat down and started milking. I grabbed two faucets and milk squirted into the bucket with a satisfying ping. I was squirting milk into my bucket, steady and fast when "Whambo!" the red cow lashed out with a powerful hind leg. She knocked me, bucket and stool into the gutter.

Buster and Lee laughed like fools. I got up, disgusted. The cow next door had scooted as far away as she could get. "That cow kicks," Lee said, still laughing like the chimp that stole a banana.

"I couldn't help but notice," I said.

Schroaders had harvested the produce from their garden, and I had never seen such abundance. The cellar under their house was stocked with pumpkins, squash,potatoes and melons as sweet as honey. The shelves groaned with canned tomatoes, peas, beans, corn and peaches. You could go through the outside cellar door and find a feast. In my country, The Government was still passing out beans, cabbage, flour, potatoes and prunes.

Uncle Charley and Aunt Tina had relatives and friends all over the country, and they visited all of them. They took me with them on one tour. We had lunch five times in one afternoon. Every where we went, those good Norwegian cooks spread coffee, lemonade, sandwiches and cookies before us. I was glad to get back to Schroaders. I didn't go on any more trips to visit cousins I had never seen before. When Aunt Tina and Uncle Charley went on another tour, I stayed behind.

Compared to South Dakota farms, the Iowa farms were like the pictures on our calendars. I found it almost unbelievable that they cut alfalfa two or three times in one summer. I came from a treeless prairie where the grass turned brown in July. Here cows grazed on pastures that looked like golf courses.

Lee liked to tell me how much better Iowa was than South Dakota. She said she saw a car with this sign on the back. "We came from Montana, the land of taxation. We went through Dakota, the land of starvation. We're going to Iowa to live on our relations."

We headed back to South Dakota about the time the geese were heading south. The green pastures gave way to the drab brown hills of South Dakota. When we crossed the Missouri River at Chamberlain, it was like entering a different world. The west really does begin at the Missouri River.

I was back home with no job in sight until Florence Nemec said, "Kathryn's hired girl is quitting and she needs someone to take care of Lowell. Do you want the job?" Kathryn Volmer was her sister. When Thanksgiving came, I went to Murdo forty miles southeast of Midland with Kathryn and Louie Volmer. They operated a grocery store on Murdo's Main Street. Both of them worked in the store. Their baby boy was ten-months-old.

Kathryn and Louie lived in a small house by the railroad tracks. A Spitz dog greeted us when we pulled up to the door. She was a pretty dog, snow white with her tail curled over her back. Their house had a kitchen, pantry, living room with a rug, and two bedrooms. Lowell's bed was in a hallway. Coal for the heater was outside in the coalshed.

My job was to keep the house clean, roll the washer and tubs in from the porch, wash clothes, hang the clothes on the line outside, iron, fix dinner and supper and care for baby Lowell. My wages were $4.00 per week. Louie always made breakfast: rolls from the store, coffee for him and Kathryn and milk for me. I thought the rolls were delicious. I wasn't used to such luxury. Louie brought meat from the store for dinner and supper, always four pork chops or four steaks. The dog got the extra piece.

Baby Lowell was a cute little fellow in his long white gown. They called him Lovey. I could see him growing up with Lovey attached to him like a cockle burr to a sheep's wooly hide. I called him Lowell. Soon Kathryn and Louie were calling him Lowell, too. Lowell was a happy baby except when I shut the folding gate between the living room and kitchen, and he had to stay in the living room. Then he grabbed the gate with both fists, shook it and howled. I fenced him out of the kitchen when I washed clothes.

I brought the washer and tubs from the porch, washed the clothes and hung them on the line outside to dry. There were no automatic washers and no dryers. I ironed shirts for Louie and dresses for myself and Kathryn. They were wonderful people to work for. Kathryn complained only once. She said, "Would you please stop dropping your shoes on the floor when you go to bed? I hear one shoe drop and then I hold my breath waiting for the other shoe to fall."

They had lots of company. Louie's parents came and Kathryn's brothers and sister, Nellie Iverson. Kathryn's brother, Skeeter, brought his fiance, Mary Ellen Anderson to play whist with Kathryn and Louie. Skeeter showed up some afternoons to take a nap. He'd say, "Call me at four o'clock." At four p.m. I'd say, "Skeeter, it's 4 o'clock." He'd say, "Okay," and a couple of hours later, he would get up and leave.

One night, Kathryn's younger brother Spike and a friend came for supper. The friend was a handsome young man with curly, brown hair. When Spike left, his friend stayed. He went into the living room and sat down with a magazine while I washed dishes. Kathryn and Louie were going to visit friends for the evening. As they walked past, Kathryn said, "He likes you," nodding toward the living room.

I finished the dishes and went into the living room. I picked up Lowell and sat down in the rocker. I rocked Lowell while the handsome boy looked at his magazine, both of us too bashful to say a word. Finally, in desparation, he laid the magazine down and escaped. I never saw him again.

I found entertainment by going to the school auditorium to play basketball on the Murdo Alumni Team. The girls high school basketball coach coached us and played too. We beat Draper's Alumni Team, but before I had a chance to play again, Kathryn quit work because she was pregnant. They took me home. I had worked two months, earned $32.00, and was out of a job again .

I was home in time for Christmas. In January, a four-inch snowfall blanketed the ground. A blizzard whipped through in February, but by March the snow was gone and the wayward wind sent dust scurrying from every bare patch of ground.

Our neighbor, Mrs. Crawford said, "Hilda needs a hired girl. Her housekeeper quit." Hilda was married to Claude Crawford and clerked at Murray's Store. They lived in a two story house about halfway up the hill on Millionaire Street. Millionaire Street was the western edge of Midland in 1939. Beyond that was a cow pasture with yucca plants scattered over the hill sides. Hilda refused to pay me $4.00 per week. She gave me $3.50.

Marjorie Ann Crawford was in the first grade. The household also had two teachers who shared a room: blond, willowy Marjorie Bloom and dark-haired Bonnie Carlson. Every day when she left for the store, Hilda said, "Don't let Marjorie Ann come to the store after school." After school, Marjorie Ann trotted into the house, the screen door banging behind her and said, "Can I go to the store?" I said "No, your mom said you have to stay here." Marjorie

Ann dashed to the phone and called her mother."Mom, can I come to the store?" A few seconds of begging and Marjorie Ann gave me a smug, little smile. "Mom said I could." She skipped out the door and trotted to the store.

My bedroom was upstairs, as was the one where Hilda, Claude and Marjorie Ann slept. The teachers had the downstairs bedroom. One morning, I tripped down the stairs, properly dressed in a clean dress. We didn't wear pants to work in those days, but we were looking for change. Claude sat by the table, drinking his morning coffee while Hilda prepared breakfast. Claude didn't work anywhere. He couldn't find work. Marjorie Ann and Claude watched me descend the stairs.

"Look at her pretty fat legs, Daddy," Marjorie Ann said. Daddy nearly choked on his coffee.

I worked for Hilda for a month and quit. I thought I had to work too hard. I made beds, swept floors, washed clothes, cooked dinner, supper, washed dishes, and ironed clothes. Since lunches were not served at school, Marjorie Ann and the teachers came home for dinner. Besides all that, Hilda wanted me to make pies and cakes. I didn't even have time to think, so I quit.

Eunice Nesheim worked for Hilda after that. When Marjorie Ann made her dash for the phone, Eunice grabbed her, paddled her rear and that was the end of that game. I don't think Eunice acted intelligently. I didn't care if Marjorie Ann went to the store. If she was bugging her mother, I didn't have to watch her.

Everyone in our family loved music. Whenever Herb was home, he and Dad played. Dad played melody on the violin and Herb played his banjo, the piano or whatever was handy. The rest of us listened. I wished I had an instrument to play, so on my nineteenth birthday, Aunt Tina gave me a mandolin. The little instrument with eight strings had fascinated me since Dad bought one for Herb. Herb didn't care for it, and he traded it off, but not before he and Cousin Hally had made it sing its way into my heart.

I rounded up all of Herb's cowboy song books and learned to play. I could soon play *Home On The Range, Red River Valley,*

Ghost Riders In The Sky, South Of The Border and many more. The difference between me and Herb was that I had to work at my music, while he could hear a tune, sit down and play it.

One day, Emil Nemec embarrassed me by asking me to play him a tune. Emil played the accordian and played it well. Dad grinned and said, "Go ahead, play him a tune." I stumbled through *Home On The Range* and escaped.

On a cool Saturday in March, Mom, I, Buddy and Mickey rode Freckles, Star and Darkie down the trail to visit Aunt Tina a mile and a half south of our place. We rode home and I dismounted to open the gate west of our house. I led Darkie through the gate. Buddy and Mickey followed on Star. Mom rode behind Star, even though she knew better than to ever ride behind the little beast. Star lashed out with both hind feet. He struck Freckles broad side. One hoof caught Mom midway between her ankle and knee on her right leg. She dismounted, stepped on her right foot and fell. Her leg was broken, a compound fracture with the bone sticking through the flesh. I rode to Crawfords to phone Dr. Studenberg and find Dad who was in town. Buddy and Mickey waited with Mom while the wind blew dirt into the wound on her leg.

After locating Dad and the doctor, I rode back home to Aunt Tina's house to tell them. By the time they had the Model T going, I was on my way home. We got there just as the ambulance was coming with Dad right behind it. Dr. Studenberg examined Mom's leg and sent her to St. Mary's Hospital in Pierre. Dad went along, and Aunt Tina and Uncle Charley stayed with us until Dad came home. He said that Dr. Riggs had set Mom's leg and she would be in the hospital for several weeks. Mom was unconsious when Dr. Riggs set her leg, and she told the nurses to "feed the scraps to the dogs."

On April 2, 1939, Julian and I, Alice Faye, Marjorie Douglas and Aldene and Shila Ellis were confirmed in the Midland Lutheran Church by Reverand O.H. Olson. Mom was still in the hospital. I wanted Aunt Tina and Uncle Charley to come, but he wouldn't take his Methodist body into a Lutheran church. Dad, Buddy,

Mickey, Aunt Amanda and Uncle Walt were there. We were confirmed and had our first communion.

One day, Aunt Tina told me that Myrtle Alcock was looking for a hired girl to work until Mahlon got out of high school so I had a job again. I tried to get Mrs. Alcock to pay me $4.00 per week, but she wouldn't give me more than $3.50 either. I worked for her for five days per week and went home weekends when Mahlon, a sophomore, came home from the dormatory in Midland.

The Alcock farm was on Little Prairie Dog Creek. Mrs. Alcock was a lovely lady. We had a lot of fun in spite of the fact that she suffered from cancer. The first thing I noticed when I walked into the kitchen was the pump organ against one wall. A rattlesnake about three-feet-long lay along the ledge above the keyboard. Anthony had skinned a rattler and stuffed the hide with salt. The reptile looked like it might slither off the organ any minute.

Lee Schroader came in March and spent three weeks with Aunt Tina and Uncle Charley. She didn't think much of my $3.50 a week job. "I can make almost that much in one day working in the vegetable fields," she said.

She invited me to come to Iowa in the fall and pick potatoes. She had a small .22 pistol that fascinated me. We weren't many years removed from the wild west. Zane Grey's novels danced in my head. When Lee went home, she left the pistol for me to play with.

On a Saturday in March, Lee and I drove Ham McCready's cattle from Uncle Walt's place where they had wintered to McCready's place up on the flat about ten miles northeast. The day was cold with a stiff northwest wind blowing. I had a small rip in one pants leg and that spot felt like it had frozen. I got off my horse and walked, but my horse was a bronc and didn't lead well. I pulled him most of the way. Lee rode part of the time, but I was so cold that I walked the whole ten miles.

I was glad to run those cows into McCready's corral. The sun was going down. I felt like an icicle, frozen clear through. Essie fed us supper, and then I sat beside the stove and shivered. McCready sold his cattle at auction March 21. He had lost his land to taxes, and Joe Nemec bought it for Jerry.

I enjoyed working for Alcocks. They had about thirty mostly Hereford cattle running down along the creek and a few milk cows. Anthony sold some red cows for $28.00 each while I was there and thought he got a good price. They had a gray saddle mare too old to ride, a bay saddle mare that was kept in the corral to round up the milk cows each night and three unbroken horses. Anthony said I could go after the milk cows each night. I was happy to get outside and ride. Melting snow had filled the lake beds with water and sent water running down Little Prairie Dog Creek. Melting snow had also filled the WPA dam west of the house.

One evening, I saddled the bay mare and rode down the creek after the milk cows. They were scattered among the Herefords, trying to get some of the green grass just beginning to show. I came to a lake of water, and my horse waded in to get a drink. She gulped a few swallows and flopped down in the water. I thought she had fallen in a hole. I dived out of the saddle and lit swimming. I didn't know how deep the water was so I swam until my feet touched bottom. I stood up and waded out, soaking wet from that cold water. The horse followed me across the pond which was only belly deep. I rounded up the milk cows and put them in the corral. Then I shivered to the house for dry clothes.

That horse got me in trouble more than once. Anthony let the other horses in the corral at night, and I let them out in the morning. He said to catch the bay mare first so she wouldn't run out with the others. One morning, I decided to let them out without catching her. I could cut them off and shut the gate in her face, I thought. Three horses ran out the gate, but the old gray mare was behind the saddle mare. I slammed the gate shut, too late. I had the old gray mare. The bay mare had escaped. I bridled the old mare and swung on her bare back. With a little luck, I hoped I could run the horses back into the corral before they got away to the far end of the pasture.

I put the old mare into a trot and cut across to head the

horses back to the pen. They tossed their heads and ran too fast for the old mare. She was not going to cut them off. I pulled Lee's pistol from the holster and sent a bullet across in front of the horses. To my surprise and relief, the leader wheeled around and headed home. They ran into the corral and I shut the gate. I caught the bay mare before I let the others out again. I never again let the horses go without having the bay mare tied securely to the fence.

Anthony churned butter in a green, three gallon, square churn and stored butter in a cool root cellar. One day, I started to churn right after breakfast and kept turning the crank till time to get dinner, but no butter came. Strange, because usually cream turns to butter in less than twenty minutes. Anthony came in for dinner.

"I'll put some salt in the churn. That will bring the butter," he said, dumping a tablespoon of salt into the churn. He turned the crank. All we had was salty whipped cream. I churned that cream off and on all afternoon, but no butter came. Disgusted, Anthony fed the cream to the pigs and brought in a new batch of cream. In no time, I turned a huge glob of butter into a bowl to be washed, salted and stored in the cellar.

One afternoon, Myrtle asked me if I wanted to play Chinese Checkers, the new rage. I said, "Sure." I set up the board with two sets of colored marbles. We had Chinese Checkers at home, and I was the expert. I knew all the good moves. I beat everybody. We sat down to play, and my blue marbles were soon all in her star point while she had red marbles still scattered over the board, far from home. I could have beat her every time, but sometimes I let her win, although I think she knew. One day, she said, "I'd rather play real checkers, but we don't have a board anymore."

"I'll make one," I said. "We can use buttons for checkers." (Everybody had a button box full of buttons cut from worn out clothing.) I colored squares on a piece of cardboard and counted out black and white buttons. We sat across the table from each other with the board between us. I'd played checkers all my life. I thought I was pretty good at this game, too, We made a few moves and were facing each other with very little space to maneuver in. I shoved a checker into her path.

"Oh, you want to play give away," she said. We began trading checkers and suddenly, I was trading two or three checkers for one until I didn't have any checkers left on the board. She whomped me good. We never played Chinese Checkers again. Every afternoon, we sat down and had a checker duel, and every afternoon, she trounced me. She didn't let me win even once.

Every Monday morning when I came back to work, I had to give Mr. Alcock a report on what was going on in the country round about. Not gossip, just what everybody was doing. He was interested in everything and everybody and he liked to visit. He was short, about five feet four, and he built his gateways and doorways to his scale. I had to duck my head to go through the yard gate and every barn door.

Mrs. Alcock's brother, Leo Sheeley, his wife Florence and four girls lived down Little Prairie Dog Creek on a farm. They came in a wagon with Leo driving an old team and had dinner with us every now and then.

Ora and Orland Keiffer and little Floyd came to visit one day. Ora had grown up at Alcocks after her mother died. Floyd was about three. He was playing by the corral and saw Mr. Alcock coming down the long hill south of Anker Olesen's place on his F 20 Farmall tractor. Floyd headed for the house at full speed, his little legs churning. He looked over his shoulder to see if the tractor was gaining. I caught him coming through the yard gate. "What's the matter, Floyd?" I asked.

He looked at the tractor roaring down the hill. "That monster is going to get me," he said.

"That's just your Uncle Anthony on the tractor," I said. "It won't hurt you." He watched the tractor like a hawk watches a rabbit till Mr. Alcock crossed the creek and stopped beside the corral.

One warm day in May, I took Mrs. Alcock fishing in the large WPA dam west of the house. We cast out lines on the water and waited for the corks to bob. Far across the water, a dark head emerged. An animal swam along the bank. The thing was dark brown, and we had no idea what it was. We watched the critter swim until it disappeared down the pond.

"What on earth was that?" Myrtle asked.

"I don't know."

"It certainly was huge," she said.

The animal was probably about the size of a medium-sized dog, probably a large mink or a beaver looking for a place to build a dam. The beast got bigger the longer we talked about it until, when Myrtle told Anthony about the strange creature it was the size of a yearling steer. Nobody figured out what it was or saw it again.

When Aunt Tina came to get me on Friday night, she often visited with Mrs. Alcock. Sometimes they sat and talked and tears rolled down their cheeks. I thought it a strange way to visit, but they both knew how sick Myrtle was. She died in September.

When school was out in May, Mahlon came home for the summer, and I was out of work again. Julian graduated Salutatorian of her class. Ruth Calhoon was Valedictorian. Mom was home, walking with crutches. Dad had brought her home in April after a month at St. Mary's Hospital in Pierre. The bones had not been set right, and the break was healing slowly. Dr. Riggs said, "You will never walk without crutches again." Mom didn't argue, she was just glad to be home.

She got home the week before her birthday which was April 26. Julian, Mickey, Buddy and I decided to have a surprise birthday party for her. We caught our horses and rode to Aunt Tina's house. She thought a party was a grand idea. Aunt Tina loved a party.

"I'll make the birthday cake," Julian said. At our house, birthday cakes were always angel food with seven minute frosting, and I didn't make them. Julian did. She baked the cake in the oven of the wood range and frosted it, decorating her masterpiece with pink flowers and green leaves while Mickey watched and waited to lick the frosting bowl.

I put dinner on the table, and Dad and Buddy came in to eat. As soon as we finished eating, Mom said, "Now let's have a piece of that lovely cake."

"I thought we could have cake for lunch," Julian said, quickly.

"I'm hungry for a piece of cake," Mom said. "We can have a piece now and still have some for lunch, so cut the cake."

Julian looked stricken. I didn't know what to say. Buddy and Mickey looked at Mom and didn't say a word. Dad grinned. "I'm too full for cake. We better save it for lunch."

"Oh, all right," Mom said.

About two o'clock in the afternoon, Aunt Tina chugged around the bend in her Model T. Mom didn't think anything of that. Aunt Tina often came to visit in the afternoon. We showed her the cake and wondered how we were going to get Mom to change into a nice dress.

Aunt Tina laughed. "Oh, I know how to do that." We followed her into the living room where Mom sat on the rocker. "Dena, put on that new dress you made before you broke your leg. I want to see how it looks."

"You've already seen it," Mom said.

"Yah, I know, but I want to see it again."

Mom got up, grabbed her crutches and hopped into the bedroom, grumbling about what a nuisance it was to change clothes with the clumsy cast on her leg. She hopped back wearing her new dress.

In a few minutes, Mrs. Crawford, Mrs. Hagan and children Wendell, Patty, Dick, Phyllis, Shirley and Florence Nemec arrived. Mom was thoroughly and completely surprised. We had a grand party, and Mom finally got a piece of her birthday cake.

Winter snow left enough moisture to green the grass and bring up the wheat. Rain in May kept the grain and grass growing. Farmers and ranchers looked hopefully toward a better year. But the grasshoppers were still here, chomping on the wheat and corn. Families were still leaving, driven away by a harsh land with too many grasshoppers and too little rain. Spring wheat averaged eight to sixteen bushels to the acre, better than nothing. I was wondering about another job, maybe in the Iowa potato fields.

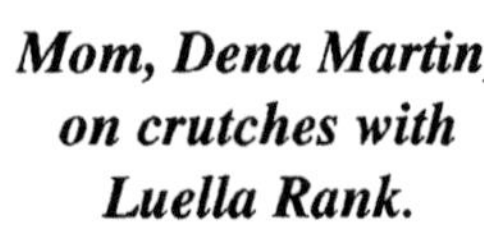

Mom, Dena Martin, on crutches with Luella Rank.

Me, my beloved mandolin, and Darkie.

Juliana Martin. High School graduation. 1939.

CHAPTER 3
Picking Potatoes

Julian wanted to go to college and learn to be a famous defense lawyer, but in June, a representative of Dakota Weslayan College in Mitchell came through the country, recruiting students. For $50.00 , in a year they would teach you to be a secretary. The college would find you a place to stay and a job to earn your keep.

Julian didn't have $50.00, but the man said he would take her horse. So Star became the property of Dakota Weslayan College. Mom said I could trade a horse and go, too. I had Whitefoot and Darkie, but I wouldn't part with either of them, not to be anybody's secretary anyway.

The college rep said for us to take Star to Kellar's auction sale on July 21, 1939, sell him and send the money to Dakota Weslayan. Kellar had a farm and store at what is now called The Twenty-one Mile Corner north of Midland. Then it was Keller's Corner; now it is part of the Sivage farms.

Since Julian had already gone to college, I had to do the dirty work of taking Star away from the only home he had ever known. I felt like a traitor as I rode the black pony up the road ditch beside Highway 14 to Kellar's Corner even though Star was an ornery critter, and I didn't like him much. Mom walked on crutches because of what he had done to her, but I felt sorry for him. He sold for $39.00, and I hoped he got a good home.

Julian left July 9, 1939 for Mitchell, South Dakota to attend

Dakota Weslayan College for a year. She was exactly two weeks shy of her seventeenth birthday. She went alone away from home for the first time in her life, into an alien world where she knew no one. She went into a room in a private home with a girl she had never seen before. She was a waitress at The Merchants Coffee Shop for her board and $1.00 per week plus tips which might be as small as a penny or nothing at all. She went to work at five o'clock every morning until October when the time changed to five thirty.

In twelve months, she came home only twice, and she hitch hiked to do that, standing on Highway 16 with her thumb in the air. Hitch hikers were a common sight on the highways, although they were mostly young men looking for some place to work.

In August, Aunt Tina and Uncle Charley had a disastrous fire that burned their house to the ground. They saw the glow of fire through their bedroom winddow. Uncle Charley jumped up, put his pants on backward and ran to the kitchen. The closed door was hot so he didn't open it. He was dashing frantically about when Aunt Tina came out of the bedroom.

Afraid he might do something foolish, she said, "We have to get the car away from the house before it burns, Charley." She grabbed a box of pictures that she had brought from the upstairs bedroom and ran outside through the east porch with Uncle Charley right behind her. He grabbed the mattress and bedding from the bed on the porch as he ran past. Outside, he dropped the bedding so close to the house that it caught fire and burned anyway.

Aunt Tina put the box of pictures on the seat of the Model T and got behind the wheel. She handed Charley the crank and turned the switch. He jerked up on the crank a couple of times and the motor caught. He jumped in the car, and Tina backed away from the house. Flames shot through the porch roof as they headed toward our place.

Uncle Charley pounded on the door, yelling, "Our house is on fire." Dad leaped out of bed and jumped into his bib overalls. Aunt Tina and Uncle Charley were telling him about the fire as I hurried

Mickey into her clothes. Buddy came out of the west bedroom.

We got in our Model A sedan and followed Aunt Tina and Uncle Charley home.We could see the glow of the fire on the southern horizon and as soon as we came over the hill, we saw flames leaping high in the dark night. Car lights were coming from every direction as dozens of cars roared toward the fire.

Dad pulled up a safe distance from the fire, and we watched in awe as the hungry flames devoured Aunt Tina's house and the accumulations of nearly a century of living. Actually, it was three centuries because her tiny wooden box made in 1640 went up in smoke. The house was gone by the time we arrived, gone except for the frame, that still stood, glowing red, the rafters shooting sparks like fireflies into the summer sky. Nearly everything they had was gone, but Aunt Tina and Uncle Charley had escaped unhurt.

People wondered what started the fire, teasing Uncle Charley about being so excited that he put his pants on backward. Grinning, Dad said, "No use getting excited. Can't stop a fire when she's going like that. I never got excited. I just put my pants on and came down."

Mickey, who was nine, pulled on Dad's pant leg. "Daddy, Daddy, why do you have your pants on backwards?" Sheepishly, Dad grinned, "Well, maybe I was a little excited."

Essie and Mom had helped Aunt Tina can 89 quarts of beef and fry down 13 gallons of hamburger-sausage patties for a summer meat supply in the spring. Many jars and crocks of meat were stored in the basement. When the ashes cooled, Uncle Charley poked around in the debris with a long stick. The jars of beef had all exploded and the crocks had broken in the heat, all except one. Those patties were still safe in that one crock sitting on the floor amid the ashes.

At the end of August, I boarded the train and headed for Iowa to pick potatoes. I hadn't worked anywhere since I left Alcocks in May, and I barely had money for the ticket. As I listened to the click, click of the train wheels, I was happy to be going east. The train stopped at every station along the way no matter how small. Between Midland and Pierre that meant stops at Capa, Van Metre, Wendte and Fort Pierre, five stops in just under sixty miles.

It was early morning. The great red eye of the train knifed through the dark as I stood on the station platform with my suitcase waiting for it to arrive. I went up the steps, found a seat and stayed in it for the next fifteen hours, no food, no drink, just the scenery going by.

I was happy when the brown South Dakota prairie turned to the green grass of Iowa. The train pulled into Sanford, Iowa about sundown and Lee, Buster and Frank Schroader hurried toward the station.

Schroaders had moved to a better farm west of the tiny town of Hayfield. Tiny towns in Iowa, like tiny towns in South Dakota, were shrinking. Pringle's Grocery Store, operated by a widow and her daughter Norma Jean, made up Hayfield. The new farm had a large two story house with an attic and a huge hip-roofed barn. Scattered about were hog houses, poultry houses, corn cribs and a granary.

The first thing Dolly said when I came into the kitchen was, "When are you going home? I'm going with you." Buster was excited about going to South Dakota, too, but they were worried about rattlesnakes. I assured them that I had never killed more than four or five rattlers a summer, but they were sure that the prairie was crawling with them.

It wasn't long before Lee introduced me to potato picking. Potatoes grow in the blackest dirt in Iowa, the peat fields. Peat gets under your fingernails and turns them black. The black dirt gets on your hide and itches. We got three cents per bushel for picking potatoes. The digger went down the rows and threw spuds out on top of the black dirt. Each picker had a half bushel steel basket. Gunny sacks were dumped at intervals along the rows. When your bucket was heaped, you and your partner dumped your spuds in a sack.

We started down the rows walking, but before the day was over, we were on our knees, paying homage to the mighty potato. We could average a hundred bushels per day each and that was as much money as I made in a week in South Dakota, if I had a job. When night fell, we were happy to go home, eat supper and fall into bed.

Morning always came too soon. We rose with the sun, still tired from the day before to go to the fields. The sun grew hot. Black dirt caked our faces and crept under our finger nails.

Two Mexican families picked in the same field. The fathers, picking together, went down their rows ahead of everyone. The digger went down a row, spitting out potatoes. We went down our rows, dropping spuds in our wire baskets. The beautiful Mexican girls sang and laughed as they picked potatoes. They taught us to sing "Evaba Mala", the bad weed, and they didn't mean marijuana. They sang about the miserable weeds they had to pull from the Iowa vegetable fields on hot summer days.

The Mexican families worked in the Iowa vegetable fields all summer, pulling weeds, thinning onions and carrots and picking potatoes. The mothers stayed at the camp, caring for children too small to work, washing clothes and cooking for the families. The Mexican girls took to potato picking better than we did. Maybe because they laughed more. We stooped and picked potatoes until our backs felt about to break, then crawled on our knees to rest.

When we had finished picking in that field, Lee and I found jobs in a field a couple of miles south of Schroaders. The potatoes were poor so we picked by the hour. The field belonged to a couple of brothers. About a half dozen pickers followed the digger. We heard some complaints about needing water, but we went down our rows, not paying much attention to anything except filling our baskets with the miserable, little potatoes. We were coming up behind the other pickers again when the father of the brothers came to the field with the water truck. He looked at us behind everyone and cussed us out for not keeping up.

The longer I thought about the injustice, the angrier I got. I said,

"I'm quitting. I won't work here anymore. Tonight is the end." When the sun went down, we turned in our baskets and collected our money. That evening, the brothers came to the Schroader farm and asked us to come back. "Dad didn't know you'd been down the field and were coming up behind the other pickers again," one of the brothers said, but we didn't go back.

During a lull in potato picking, Lee and I picked tomatoes for Fern Hefte on the Hefte farm northeast of Schroaders. Heftes had an acre of tomatoes to sell to the canning factory in Forest City, if they could get them picked. The tomatoes were large, red, luscious and cheap, about thirty cents per bushel. Fern said, "I'll give you four cents a bushel to pick tomatoes." She picked, too. We each had a wooden bushel basket to pick in. The day was hot. I picked tomatoes for three hours and made eighteen cents. The four little Hefte kids got in the way.

Fern threw a ripe tomato at me. The large, red globe splattered all over the back of my shirt. I zinged one back, and the fight was on. That was the most fun we had all week.

When the frosts of October whitened the pumpkins, Herb, Hank and "Smoky" Petoske showed up in Hank's Model T and went to work in the corn harvest. Saturday night and Sunday, they spent at Schroaders. We sat around the living room and sang cowboy songs. I had my mandolin, Herb his banjo and Lee played harmonica and Hawaiian guitar.

Frank and Ula liked having young people around. Ula enjoyed cooking for the kids that hung around, and Frank liked the help they sometimes gave him in the corn field. All of the Iowa relatives adopted us.

Ma Schroader cooked stacks of pancakes along with sausage, eggs and bacon for breakfast. One Sunday morning, Frank challenged Smoky to a pancake eating contest. They ate pancakes smothered with syrup, and we counted until they each had put away twenty pancakes. Frank laughed and said, "I'm done. I can't eat another bite." Smoky grinned and ate one more. He was the champ.

Potato picking ended with the coming of frosty nights so Lee and I decided to pick corn. We borrowed a wagon and Flash and Fly from Frank and headed for Hefte's corn field. We couldn't each pick a hundred bushels a day like Smoky did, but we earned more than we had picking tomatoes for Fern, a lot more. Flash and Fly trotted to the corn field as the sun brightened the eastern horizon. A pheasant rooster crowed. An answer came from a neighboring field.

The team turned into the field and headed down a row. The huge ears hung down, wet with frost. We stripped back the husks and tossed ears against the bangboard. They fell steadily into the wagon box. Our gloves got wet and our hands got cold. The horses moved down the row, gobbling corn as they went. I think horses love corn picking time. They eat all the corn they want, and the work isn't hard. Shoveling the load into the crib was the hardest. We came in about sundown, the wagon box heaped with golden ears, and had to shovel them all into the crib.

We stayed at Hefte's and slept upstairs. Lee had acquired another .22 pistol which she laid on the chair beside the bed at night. Fern sent one of the little girls up to wake us for breakfast one morning. I woke up with the child standing by the chair with the pistol pointed at Lee's head. She couldn't pull the trigger, fortunately. I told Lee, "You better put that gun away before you get shot."

We went downstairs to the smell of pancakes and frying bacon. Fern said, "You kids have to wait till Lee and Timmie eat so they can go to the field." We sat down to eat our delicious breakfast with four Hefte kids snitching our bacon as fast as Fern fried it.

Buddy and Mickey were riding to school at Liberty. Buddy had a new horse to ride. He called his gray horse Cloudy. Julian hitch-hiked home from college in October and in a few days, she hitch-hiked back to school. Mom's leg wasn't healing so Dad had taken her back to St. Mary's Hospital. Dr. Riggs was afraid he might have to re-break her leg. He put a cast on with a window so he could see the wound. The nurses put a cardboard box with both ends open over the cast. Mom waited for the decision.

Dr. Riggs worried about the infection which refused to clear up. He came to her room with a young intern one day. He inspected the wound and said, "The kind of infection we worry about is incurable and has a peculiar odor."

"Is that so, Doctor," the intern said, sniffing. "I have never smelled that type." There were no antibiotics then. Mom had the feeling that he would like to have her get the infection, so he could detect the odor.

Dad, Buddy and Mickey made the long trip on the winding, dusty, gravel road in the Model A to visit Mom a few times. The trip took several hours. Dad bought flowers and candy for Mom. Mickey couldn't understand why. It wasn't even her birthday, but she could hardly wait for Mom to open the box so she could have a chocolate. Mom was in the hospital for about three months before she finally came home without a cast. She still had her crutches. Dr. Riggs said she would always need them.

Because I was in Iowa working, and Julian was in college in Mitchell, nine-year-old Mickey was the cook. Uncle Alvin, Bob Crawford and Dad were working at our place one Saturday. Mickey peeled every potato in the house and put them on the range to cook. Dad came into the kitchen as she was setting the table. Mickey took the lid off the potatoes and discovered a couple of small, white worms that had boiled out of the potatoes. Horrified, she showed Dad.

He grinned. "Put them on the table anyway. The worms are cooked. They won't hurt anything. They'll just add a little more meat." The worms poured out with the water, and Mickey put the food on the table. The men sat down to potatoes, gravy and steak and ate heartily. Uncle Alvin told Mickey she was a fine little cook. Mickey ate, too, but she didn't eat any potatoes.

Mom came home shortly before Christmas. The wound on her leg slowly healed. She got along fine with her crutches and Buddy and Mickey soon learned how far those crutches would reach. We were all happy to have her home. She sent Julian five dollars. Julian was glad to get the money. She only had eight cents left in her tip bank.

When corn harvest was over, I was ready to go home. Frank Schroader drove me and visited Aunt Tina and Uncle Charley. Grandpa Herman Schroader, Buster and Dolly came along. They were disappointed, they didn't see a single rattlesnake.

The South Dakota prairie was dry and drab, a sharp contrast to the green pastures of Iowa. We went to the Bertelson ranch. Aunt Tina and Uncle Charley had moved there after fire destroyed the Calhoun house.

Grandpa Herman was fascinated with a long, flat hill he could see west of the house. He decided he would walk to the hill and climb to that intriguing flat top. He headed west. He walked and walked, but he seemed to get no closer to the hill. When he was so tired, he was afraid he might not make it home, he turned around and hiked back to the house. The hill was actually several miles west, south of the Linder place where Ronnie and Emily Sammons live now.

When Frank, Herman and Buster went home, Dolly stayed. Herb, Hank and Smoky came home a little richer. Our main form of entertainment was dances and movies. Bob Crawford had a Chevrolet sedan. He took me, Herb and Dolly to dances around the country in Midland, Hayes and Van Metre. Midland had a Thanksgiving dance, a Christmas dance, a New Years dance and a dance nearly every other Saturday. We didn't miss any. Everybody went to the dances. Little kids ran around the floor during intermission and went to sleep on the benches when they got tired.

The middle of December, a dreadful dust storm raged across South Dakota. People were still selling out and moving away. The empty houses were no longer claim shacks. They were houses with several rooms and often an upstairs, left to stand vacant and lonely on the prairie. Underneath, were cellars where mice peeked around abandoned fruit jars. They left outhouses, barns and chicken houses, forlorn and empty, where hens no longer cackled and roosters didn't crow at the morning sun. Bucket calves didn't bawl for milk as the sun reached for the western hills. The land was changing and perhaps we were changing with it.

Midland had a new look. The WPA had built new sidewalks all over town. Midland had a new doctor. Dr. Studenberg was gone. Dr. Brodie and his wife lived in the Midland Community Hospital, and his office was there. The hospital was across the street north of where the Reuben Vollmer Sr. house is now. Midland was proud of this modern facility, the best hospital between Pierre and Rapid City. Dr. Brodie delivered babies, set broken bones and performed operations of many kinds.

Midland still had its grocery stores and Sturdevant's Drug Store. Davidson still ran the hardware store. Bud Harman ran a pool hall. There were many cafes and Burkhart now owned the Midland Bar. Ben's Barber Shop did a big business on Saturday afternoon and evening. Midland had a motel, and Honey Russell built four cabins along the bank of Mitchell Creek.

Snow got deep during the winter. Buddy and Mickey rode Freckles and Cloudy to school. Tom Stalley, who broke Cloudy, had taught her to kneel, sit up and lay down. Buddy was proud of his trick horse.

Julian didn't get home for Christmas. For the first time in her life, she spent Christmas far from home. She found it hard even to buy a stamp to write home. I sent her a practical gift: *Evening In Paris* perfume.

We got piles of snow in January. Aunt Tina got deathly ill and was taken to St. Mary's Hospital in Pierre where Dr. Riggs removed her appendix. He said her appendix had ruptured some fifty years earlier, so she was lucky to live through the ordeal. Lee came from Iowa to help after she came home from the hospital, and Dolly went home.

Aunt Tina and Uncle Charley slept on a bed in the living room. A library table, flanked on either side by a comfortable, green Morris chair, stood between the two south windows. Uncle Charley put the barrel chair beside the bed for a night stand. He put his kerosene lamp on the chair so he could easily blow out the light at night and light it when he got up in the morning. He would put his false teeth on the chair, read his newspaper, lay it on the chair when he was finished, and then blow out the lamp. In the morning, he jumped out of bed and gathered up the newspapers.

He threw the papers into the kitchen range and put kindling and corn cobs on top. He lit the papers, and a merry fire roared in the stove, warming the kitchen. He went back to get his false teeth, and they were gone. The only thing on the chair was the lamp. He moved it and looked more closely.

"What are you looking for, Charley?" Aunt Tina asked.

"Oh, nothing." He didn't want to tell her. He searched on the floor, on the table, under the bed.

"What on earth are you looking for?"

Looking sheepish, he admitted that he couldn't find his false teeth. He had thrown them into the stove. They were burning with the cobs and wood. Uncle Charley had to buy new false teeth. He told us that he put his false teeth on a chair once and then forgot and sat on them. He said, "They bit me."

Thelma Martin (Front) Dolly Schroader (Back) on Darkie. 1940.

Bob Crawford and Thelma Martin looking at Lee Schroader's 22 pistol.

(Left)Uncle Charley Myrland in front of the Bertelson house. (Below) Branding on the Calhoun place. Herb looking for a calf to tackle.

CHAPTER 4
Little Farm On Mitchell Creek

I worked for a couple of weeks for the Garrett Rogers' family. They had a new baby boy, Robert, and Mrs. Rogers needed help for a while. Howard, 4, was also home. Velda, Marsha and Jerry went to school in Midland. The Rogers' family lived on his father's homestead two miles due north of Midland. Like his father, Garrett ran a small band of sheep, milked cows and sold cream.

At the Rogers' home, I had my first taste of mutton. My folks, being cattle raisers, didn't think mutton was fit to eat, but I found the meat at the Rogers' table quite good. I cooked, kept house, watered the buck sheep in his little pen, and rode the bay mare after the milk cows each evening.

The ewes were in a large pen where Garrett fed them hay. The buck lived by himself which made him crabby. He didn't have horns, but he had a wary eye. Howard went with me when I worked outside. One day, I carried a pail of water to the buck. I set the water on the ground and helped Howard over the board fence. I climbed into the pen. The buck backed away and watched us with mean little eyes. Howard stood with his back to the buck and watched me pour water into the small tank. The buck charged across the pen and hit Howard square in the back, knocking him flat on the frozen ground. I kicked the buck away, helped Howard up and wiped the dirt off his clothes. Between sobs, he said, "I was just standing there not doing a thing when all of a sudden, I felt some wool."

I never heard the Rogers' children use bad language in front of their parents. They were polite, nice youngsters, but when I rode after the milk cows, Howard sat behind me, hanging onto the saddle strings, bouncing along, repeating every obscene and profane word I had ever heard and some I hadn't.

I listened for a couple of days and said, "Howard, you shouldn't say those words." Howard stopped spouting obscenities, and we went on our way to find the milk cows. Never again did I hear Howard use bad language. A few years later, the Rogers' family moved to a farm east of Pierre. Their house and barn were moved to Midland.

After my stint with the Rogers', Dr. Brodie hired me to work in the hospital because Ethel Daly from southwest of Philip was there with a new baby boy, Mickey, born March 1, 1940. Mrs. Brodie was the nurse and Dr. Brodie's assistant. At that time, Doctors kept new mothers in bed for ten days. With sheets, diapers, white baby shirts and tiny white gowns to wash, Mrs. Brodie needed help.

Brodies were Jewish and didn't eat food that wasn't kosher.They also didn't eat with me. Mrs. Brodie fixed the meals, but she and Dr. Brodie ate their meal, then I ate mine, alone. Seemed like a strange arrangement to me, but I was well fed. Some farmers sold butter to the stores. Country butter was cheaper than Creamery butter. Mrs. Brodie bought both kinds. She asked me if I ate country butter. I said, "Yes." I'd eaten country butter all my life. She said, "I use country butter for cooking, but Dr. Brodie and I don't eat it on bread. You can have country butter on your bread." So I did, and she saved a few pennies.

I had the job of cleaning the operating room, the patients' rooms, dusting, sweeping and bringing the coal from the coal shed out back for the stoves. I learned to get all the dust balls out from under cupboards and beds.

My stay at The Midland Community Hospital was exciting. Mrs. Henry Reimann came in with acute appendicitis. Dr. Brodie, with only his wife assisting, removed her appendix. She stayed ten days and went home.

Accidents happened. Highway 14 came down cemetary hill, went around a curve and across the narrow Mitchell Creek bridge. Earl Schilling drove one of Archie Joy's trucks around the curve too fast and hit the bridge. The truck lit in the creek. Bernard Burns and Stub Joy were riding with him. Stub ended up with a broken wrist and was brought to the hospital, but Bernard wasn't hurt. Earl was treated and released. Dr. Brodie set Stub's wrist. In those days, the anesthetic was ether. People who have ether tend to vomit. I made up my mind then and there that I never wanted to be a nurse.

Snow fell all day and most of the night the day before I was to finish working in the hospital. A stiff wind blew. The March storm dumped about eighteen inches of wet snow on hill and valley, too much snow for anyone to drive to town and get me. I decided I would walk the two and a half miles to the Bertelson ranch. Since I wore a dress to work, I was wearing a dress, oxfords, and no overshoes. I wore a light jacket and had neither cap nor gloves, when I headed west, walking on the railroad track.

Walking between the rails, I slogged through the wet snow. My legs were sopping wet and cold halfway to my knees before I got a hundred yards. By the time I had walked two miles west, I was wet, cold and miserable. I turned south and headed for Uncle Alvin's house a half a mile away. The naked trees were dressed in coats of white, but their beauty was lost on me.

I trudged through the cold, deep snow and thought about the warm house and a cup of hot chocolate to warm my insides. I was cold clear through. Aunt Tina, Uncle Charley, Uncle Alvin and Lee were in the house, snug and warm, beside the fire. They would be surprised to see me.

As I neared the trees by the Bad River crossing, the snow was almost to my knees. I headed down the trail to the river and stopped abruptly. Dirty, gray water swirled past. Across the river, a few hundred yards away, was warmth, dry clothes and food. It may as well have been twenty miles. The sullen, swollen river was too deep to wade and icy cold. I yelled myself hoarse, but no one came with a horse to carry me across.

Finally, I turned and plodded the half mile back to the railroad bridge to where the pilings were stuck into barrels of cement. I climbed up a wet, slippery, snow covered barrel to the railroad bridge, crossed the angry river and slogged south again. I walked a mile around the river bend to the house.

I walked into the house, nearly frozen. They were surprised. "My goodness," Aunt Tina said, "I didn't think you would come home in this weather."

"Why didn't you holler," Uncle Alvin said."I would have come after you with a horse." I had already yelled myself silly and nobody heard me, but I was too tired to explain. I stood by the warm cook stove and shivered so hard that my teeth chattered.

Julian hitch-hiked home from college for Easter vacation, the first time she had been home since October. She told about waiting on two Mennonite couples. The men told their wives what they could have to eat. They even told their wives they would have chocolate ice cream when they didn't say they wanted any. Julian said, "I'm sure glad I'm not one of those women," but when she got married, I heard her husband tell her what to do and she did it.

April brought melting snow that greened the prairie and made the roads muddy, ample moisture to start the spring crops as soon as the farmers could get into the fields to plant. Bad River ran several times. Aunt Tina and Uncle Charley often drove to town, then had to leave their Model T on the far side of the river and wade in to get to the house. Aunt Tina didn't like to wade because the rocks hurt her tender feet.

"I'll carry you across," Uncle Charley said, once. "Get on my back." He was seventy-five years old and she was a fair chunk of a woman. He rolled his pants legs above his knees and started across, a stout walking stick in one hand and Aunt Tina piggy back, hanging to his neck. Water rushed and tugged, swirling around his knees. He stopped in midstream and steadied himself against the strong Bad River current, leaning on his trusty stick. He went on and deposited her safe and dry on the other side.

One afternoon, they went to town and came home to find the river too deep for the car to cross. Aunt Tina parked the Model T on the meadow. They waded the river and walked to the house. The next morning Bad River was raging. Uncle Charley looked toward where the Model T was parked. About a foot of the top stuck above the rampaging water that flowed a quarter of a mile wide across the meadow.

Bill Elrod sold automobiles in Midland. Aunt Tina bought a green 1933 Chevrolet coupe from Bill. It was the last car they owned.

When my job at the hospital ended, I was out of work again. Lee didn't have a job either, and neither of us had any prospects for getting work. We decided to pool our money and buy some land. We figured we could get some chickens and two or three brood sows, and we'd be in business. Lee had two cows, and I had two horses. We could sell cream and eggs to buy our groceries like everybody else did. Our dreams were large.

We poured over every real estate catalog we could find. There were plenty of farms for sale. County land could be had for fifty cents an acre.You could buy a thousand acres with buildings; house, barn, sheds, everything for $1200.00. We didn't have $1200.00 or even the down payment of $240.00.

Mom said, "Why don't you buy Charley's homestead?"

We hadn't thought of that. Uncle Charley lost his homestead on Mitchell Creek, a mile upstream from Uncle Walt's place, to The Rural Credit. Uncle Walt rented the homestead. He rented about three thousand acres north across Mitchell Creek because he could lease the land for five cents an acre and The Government Range Program paid him ten cents an acre for each acre he controlled. The guys that run the government weren't any smarter then than they are now.

Uncle Walt only had twenty cows. His problem was water. He had no dams and his good well had gone dry. He dug a well a half mile north which watered his livestock but didn't leave much to spare. Twenty cows were about all Aunt Amanda could pump water for anyway. Uncle Walt spent most of his time carpentering. They hauled water from the well on the flat for their house and the milk cows and Aunt Amanda's saddle horse.

The Rural Credit wanted $1.25 per acre and in exchange they would furnish a clear title. You paid 20% down and got five years to pay the rest at 3% interest. We could handle that. We were completely naive about the fact that 160 acres of South Dakota land, especially dry South Dakota land, wouldn't pasture much livestock. We didn't have much, two cows and two horses. The land cost $200.00, and we had the $40.00 down payment.

We walked up the creek from Aunt Amanda's house to look the place over. We saw deer tracks in the creek and could hardly believe our eyes. Deer weren't supposed to be in this part of the country. Antelope weren't either. Someone had seen four antelope and the sighting was so rare that The Midland Mail printed the story.

When we told Aunt Amanda, she said, "It must have been sheep. There aren't deer here." There weren't any sheep either, except Aunt Amanda's little flock, and they didn't get that far from home. A few years later, Mrs. DeYoung saw a deer in Cedar Canyon a half mile up the creek, and Aunt Amanda saw deer when she rode along Mitchell Creek.

We walked out of the creek and across a small meadow to the house. The house was gray because most of the tar paper had been torn loose by the wind and blown away. The porch had a broken pillar and the roof sagged in the middle. The living room and bedroom windows were broken. We could see blue sky through the roof and could have chased a cat through the walls. Rain and snow had rotted the floor boards, and we fell through the floor. The roof of the stone room had fallen in, but since the floor was of earth, the rain did no further damage. Clearly, the only room worth salvaging was the kitchen. By some miracle the windows, door and shingles were usable.

I looked ruefully at the black spot on the kitchen floor and wished Julian and I hadn't charred the floor that cool fall day when we built a fire in the ash pan to get warm.

The outbuildings weren't worth fixing except the unpainted chicken house sitting across the draw south of the house. The chicken house was as gray as the earth beneath it, but it was sound. The roof of Uncle Charley's dugout cow barn had fallen in. The dugout horse barn had large holes in the roof, and dirt sifted down on our heads. The buildings were sorry, but the location was beautiful. The buildings sat on the meadow with Mitchell Creek flowing to the north, then heading south past the house to the east. High hills rose on the north, west and south, protecting the homestead from fierce winter winds. Cottonwood, ash and elm trees grew thick along the creek.

The big problem was water. Mitchell Creek usually ran from melting snow in spring and whenever a pouring rain came in summer. When the hot days of July and August scorched the land, water holes dried up. The bullheads and catfish that had ventured up the flowing stream were trapped in the puddles and gasped their lives away in the drying pools.

We gave The Rural Credit $40.00 and were the proud owners of 160 acres of South Dakota land. We moved onto our homestead. We set up housekeeping without much to set up housekeeping with. No furniture. No dishes.

A rusty old bed sat in the bedroom. We put the bed spring in the attic, laying it across the ceiling two by fours. Uncle Charley gave us a sheet metal heater with a flat top for cooking. That little stove got red hot, but it didn't keep fire long. There was no ash pan. We scooped ashes out through a small door and some spilled on the floor.

Mom gave us a bed, a table, a couple of chairs, dishes and two black cats, a mom and a tom. Between Mom and Aunt Amanda, we got enough dishes, kettles and frying pans. Aunt Amanda gave us a three-burner kerosene cook stove. Lee built a nightstand from apple crates that looked like it came out of a furniture store. The stand had a magazine rack on each side and a drawer at the top. The stand sat beside the bed to hold the kerosene lamp Mom gave us.

When we got the bed made and the table, chairs and stoves brought in, the place looked almost homey, although we could see outside through cracks where the wallboard was falling down. A cottonwood tree towered high above the house outside the east window. If we looked out the south window, we saw the trail that angled up the hill toward Midland.

The heater stove pipes went through a hole in the wall into a brick chimney. We put the stove pipes up and started a fire in the stove. We stood beside the stove, getting warm while the cats inspected their new home. Tom sauntered up beside the stove and leaped on top. He yowled and danced about and tried to climb the stove pipe. The stove pipe buckled and came tumbling down. Tom tumbled with the stove pipe. Luckily, he jumped around too fast to burn his feet.

We wanted to plow some ground for a garden, but we didn't have any machinery. Uncle Charley gave us a three section drag and a dandy, six-foot disk that would almost plow the soil. Uncle Walt loaned us his old walking sod buster with one broken handle. Lee carved a new handle from an ash stick. She could carve axe handles and hammer handles so they looked exactly like the ones you bought in the store. Now we needed a team. We figured we could break our saddle horses to pull the machinery with the two sets of ancient harness Uncle Charley had given us.

We went to Dad's farm to get Darkie and Whitefoot. Mom loaned us Freckles to help pull the plow and Buck, her yellow roan gelding, for Lee to ride. We hitched Whitefoot and Freckles to the plow. The plow share was rusty, but Aunt Amanda said, "Yust start plowing. The plow will scour up and get bright after a few rounds."

I tied the lines behind my back, grabbed the plow handles and clucked to my team. The old mares turned their heads in and their tails out and looked at me. Whitefoot looked insulted. Freckles looked bored. She wanted out of the silly harness so she could go eat grass. Lee grabbed the bits and straightened the horses out before they could become hopelessly entangled. I drove and she lead the team until they started going in a fairly straight line. I walked behind, trying to keep the bucking plow in the ground. The plow share turned bright silver like Aunt Amanda said it would. I plowed about half an acre, disked and dragged the plot, and we were ready to plant our garden. Uncle Walt loaned us a garden planter, a contraption with a large wooden wheel, a furrow maker and a tiny bin to hold the seeds. Lee grabbed the handles and pushed the wheel down the row. Trying to keep the wheel going in a straight line, she went gaily down the row, planting lettuce, carrots, radishes and several rows of Navy bean seeds that she had brought from Iowa. We finished up with several hills of watermelons. We were going to raise lovely, sweet watermelons like Uncle Charley did.

We made crescent moon and star flower beds outlined by small stones and planted zinnias in them. We were going to raise lovely flowers like Lee's mother did in Iowa. The zinnias came up, grew a spindley eight inches tall and shriveled in the hot summer sun. The few small flowers that appeared shrank and died with barely a show of color. I didn't plant another flower seed for fifteen years.

The navy beans were the only things that grew. We pulled the plants and stored them on our open porch. "We can shell the beans when they get dry," Lee said. "They shell real easy. You just walk on the plants, and the beans fall right out." While we were in Iowa that fall, the deer Aunt Amanda said weren't around, ate the beans.

We often road horseback the six miles across the prairie to the Bertelson ranch. We rode out of the Mitchell Creek breaks onto the huge flat where the town well was. The horses had to dodge the mule ear cactus that covered the flat. In spring, the entire flat was gorgeous with red and yellow cactus roses.

We often stopped at the town well on the flat for a drink of cold water. We stopped once when Tom Jones and his cowboys, Mike and Martin Schofield, were getting a tank of water. Tom, in his courtly manner, offered us a dipper. We gladly accepted while Mike and Martin struggled to keep from laughing. We rode on our way, wondering what had tickled the Schofield boys' funny bones.

The next time I saw Mike, he said, "You want to know what me and Martin were laughing about up at the town well?"

"Yeah," I said. "What was so funny?"

"When we saw you coming, Tom said, 'I don't know whether to offer those girls a drink of water or a chew of tobacco.'" I didn't see the funny side of that, but Mike had a laughing fit.

Uncle Alvin drove a shiny, black Ford V8 sedan. He was climbing out of the hole the depression had left him in by summering his hundred head of good Hereford cows on the three thousand acre pasture west of Dad's farm. Dad borrowed money from the Federal Government and bought forty Hereford cows for $80.00 each. He, too, was pulling out of the terrible pit of depression and the dry years. He was fast becoming a rancher, phasing out the milk cows.

Those Hereford cows were the foundation of his cattle herd. They made the money to repay the loan on the farm. Mom and Dad were at last building the cattle ranch they had dreamed about for so many years. The Government rehab program picked a lot of farmers out of the dust and set them on their feet again.

Lee and I went to Philip with Uncle Alvin one day to get some parts for his machinery. He got stuck in the south bar so we sat in the fancy, black Ford and waited for him. Curt Anderson and Merle Heidler came out of the bar and saw us. They walked over to the car and introduced themselves. I thought Curt was the handsomest man I had ever seen.

He said he had seen Julian and me when he and Jack Hunt brought a horse to the Calhoun place for Uncle Alvin. I remembered, of course. That was three years previously. I was seventeen and Julian fifteen. We had sized him up pretty good, too, while we stood by the barn, slightly behind Uncle Alvin, pretending to look at the horse.

Curt said, "Jack thought Julian was the best looking, but I thought you were." I expect he would have told her the same thing, had she been the one sitting there at the time. They climbed into the back seat and invited us to give them a ride in Uncle Alvin's car.

Lee drove around and showed them the town of Philip and parked in front of the bar again. We hoped Uncle Alvin was ready to go home, but he didn't come outside. We watched the door and waited. Women almost never went into bars, unless their husband was in there, and they were mad enough to go after him.

The boys entertained us with brilliant conversation. Curt wore a spanking new pair of made to measure Blucher cowboy boots, which he proudly displayed. We admired his footwear, and I wished I had a pair of those marvelous boots. "Don't you have boots, Tim?" Curt asked.

"Nope." I shook my head. "Never owned a pair."

"Nobody should ride without boots. You can have my old boots. They're still good," he said. He was as good as his word. The boots showed very little wear. Uncle Alvin came out, ran our boyfriends off, slid behind the wheel and we went home.

Rob Olson, wife Hannah and daughter Agnes came from Iowa to visit Aunt Tina and Uncle Charley. Rob was Uncle Charley's youngest brother and owned a beautiful Iowa farm. Agnes was a school teacher. She was sure a rattlesnake hid behind every blade of grass. We encouraged her in that belief. Agnes didn't know how to ride a horse, but we persuaded her to mount Darkie. We thought it hilarious that she had to climb on a chair to get into the saddle. Once astride, she stayed long enough to have her picture taken.

Jean Ver Hoef, a friend of Lee's from Iowa, was visiting us. Jean wasn't afraid of horses, so she told Agnes more wild stories than we did. Jean was even taller than I with hair as yellow as flax straw, a tall, beautiful Dutch girl.

One day, I borrowed Hank's Terraplane. The Terraplane had one seat because the back seat had been taken out, and the top sawed off to make a pickup. The only thing left of the top was the windshield. We headed for the Bertelson place in the Terraplane. Road construction workers were widening Highway 14 west of Midland. I drove down into the ditch past a bunch of young men, digging in the dirt. They were shirtless. Their brawny chests glistened with sweat as they dug shovels into the earth.

"Get a horse," Jean yelled as we roared past. We sped to Aunt Tina's house. We came back a couple hours later. I slowed the Terraplane for the ditch and the car died right in front of those prespiring construction workers. Three mortified young ladies took turns cranking the Terraplane while the construction workers watched, laughing. Not one of those burly, young men offered to twirl the crank.

The Terraplane fascinated Buddy. He talked Hank into teaching him to drive the car. Buddy was about twelve years old. He drove the car over the prairie west of the house where there was lots of room. The acres of grass provided a fine place for practice driving. Buddy gave Mickey a ride around the pasture and offered to teach her to drive. Mickey was eleven and eager to drive Hank's car even though the pedals were a far reach for her feet.

She got behind the wheel, and they headed down the wagon trail toward what was left of the Calhoun buildings. Mickey breezed along the trail, steering mightily with the wind blowing her hair, enjoying every moment. She gripped the steering wheel hard. Dust rolled in a cloud behind the car, and a gate appeared suddenly in front of them.

"Hit the brakes! Hit the brakes!" Buddy screamed, close to panic. If she hit that gate, he'd never get to drive Hank's car again. Mickey slammed her foot hard on the brake pedal. The back wheels locked. The Terraplane did a screaming eleven right up to the gate, but didn't get a scratch.

Buddy moaned and shook his head. "Look at the skid marks." He jumped out of the car and looked at the fifty feet of marks behind the car. "If Hank sees that, he'll never let me drive his car again." He kicked at the skid marks and wiped the dusty trail with his hat till all traces of evidence were gone. Then he got behind the wheel and drove home.

July 12th and 13th, Midland celebrated its 50th Anniversary and the opening of The Stroppel Hotel's Hot Mineral Baths. Lee and Jean had gone back to Iowa to work in the vegetable fields. Julian and I got ready for the big parade.

I saddled Darkie and Julian saddled Cloudy, Buddy's horse, and we rode eleven miles straight south to Aunt Amanda's. We were excited. We had never ridden in a parade before, and we were thinking about the whopping $2.50 prize for the best dressed cowgirl. I knew I didn't have a chance. I was wearing boots and a hat. I had borrowed them from Forest Schofield. But my riding outfit was slacks and blouse, not good enough. We were hoping Julian would win. She didn't have a cowboy hat, but she was wearing Mom's boots, a white shirt and black riding pants. She was a well dressed cowgirl.

Midland's 50th was a grand celebration. Around two thousand people crowded the sidewalks from end to end of Main Street to watch the parade. Behind the color guard, Tom Jones drove his chuck wagon. His cowboys followed the wagon. We rode with a herd of riders behind the Midland Band, and were followed by colorful floats. Verna Lammon, riding her paint horse, won best dressed cowgirl.

After the parade, we rode our horses around to the different events. We watched the baseball game and the ladies kittenball (softball) game between Midland and Belvidere. A group of brawny men lined up on each end of a heavy rope for tug-o-war. They pulled and tugged until one group pulled the other over a line drawn in the dirt.

About sundown, Julian and I rode into the alley back of Oscar's Service Station. Verna Lammon loped past us on her paint. "Let's go through back of the hotel," she said, kicking Paint in the ribs. Paint plunged into full gallop. He ran under the clothes line, stretched tight between two poles. The clothes line peeled Verna over Paint's rump. She hit the ground like a sack of potatoes. She was shook up a bit, but the only thing badly injured was her dignity.

Julian and I put our horses in The Kingsbury Lumber Company yard and walked downtown. The Curl Amusement Company rides were spread up and down Russell Avenue and spilled onto the vacant lots east of Murray's Store. (That building is now occupied by The Frontier Bank, or officially The First National.) We rode the merry-go-round. Julian rode the whirling swings and the Octopus. I didn't. Those rides made me dizzy.

Pat Wachter talked me into riding the ferris wheel with him. I looked at the giant wheel with all those swinging seats and tried to get up my nerve to climb in one. "Come on," Pat said as another seat stopped at the bottom. I took a deep breath and climbed in the seat. Pat got in beside me. The gate was latched shut. The monster contraption began to move. I was stuck. I held my breath as the huge wheel turned. Just when I was getting used to the big wheel turning, it stopped, with us at the top.

I looked down from what seemed like at least one hundred feet to the people wandering around below. I could see seats below us with smart alecky guys rocking them to make the girls scream. Pat said he was going to rock our swing, and I panicked. "Please," I begged, "just sit still." I think I would have fainted if the swing had swung. Pat grinned, a wicked grin, but he didn't rock the swing.

We went to the movies and the dances. The Red Ramblers Orchestra played for the dance each night. Tickets were .75 for men. Ladies and children got in free. The Sturdevant Drug Store did a big business in ice cream and pop. The round, steel tables were crowded with people eating dishes of ice cream. Men could buy 3.2 beer in the drug store, too. Women could buy beer, too, but most didn't.

Julian hadn't been able to get an office job, so she went to work as a waitress in The Owens Cafe on the south side of Main Street. I didn't have a job at all so I decided to head for the vegetable fields of Iowa.

Uncle Charley Myrland on Darkie.

Jean Ver Hoef on Darkie.

Uncle Alvin Bertelson, Lee Schroader, Hank and Thelma Martin in front of the Calhoun house.

Charley Myrland homestead as Lee and I saw it when we inspected the farm.

Buddy Martin, wild cowboy wearing a Midland Basketball Jersey.

CHAPTER 5
The Vegetable Fields Of Iowa

I boarded the train in Midland in the wee hours of a day in August and went to Iowa. Lee and I got our first job thinning carrots at the Andresen farm where Lee and Dolly had pulled weeds from onion and carrot fields earlier in the summer. We went down those green rows on our knees, pulling out a couple of inches of carrots, leaving one carrot and pulling out more carrots while the hot sun bore down. The job was guaranteed to make you tired and leave you with sore knees.

Potato picking started in September. Once again, I watched red potatos roll out behind the digger. We filled our baskets, dumping them in endless rows of burlap sacks. Our money hoard increased.

On Saturday night, the Schroader clan and I crowded into Frank's car and went to Forest City eight miles away. Forest City was a fair-sized village, home of Waldorf College. The Winnebago River ran through town. Mom's Aunt Susan and daughters, Lenore and Murrie, lived there in a pleasant, white house shaded by oaks and maples. Mom had stayed with them and gone to high school in 1908. Every house had a green lawn and lovely flowers, especially asters and gladiolus, which I had never seen before. They didn't even have to water their lawns and flowers.

One Saturday night, Lee, Dolly and I wandered down to The Ford Garage and found a black Model A sedan. The paint was dull and the tires were poor, but the glass was all there, and the motor purred like a happy cat.

"We should buy this car," Lee said. "We'll need a way to get to the potato fields when Dad quits picking spuds."

We counted our money and came up with $35.00. "We don't have enough money," I said. "We need another ten bucks."

"We'll borrow the money from Dolly," Lee said with more confidence than I felt.

We looked at Dolly. She looked doubtful. "Come on, Dolly," Lee said. "We need a car to go to work. We'll pay you back as soon as we pick some more spuds." Dolly handed over the ten dollars, and we happily climbed into our Ford. Lee slid behind the wheel. Dolly and Buster got in the back.

Frank quit potato picking and started getting ready to pick corn. Monday morning about sunup, Lee, Dolly and I motored to a large potato field about eight miles east. A school house stood outside the north end of the field. We picked potatoes until sundown. The digger stopped. Everybody went home except us. We camped by the school house pump, thus saving our precious gasoline.

We had a couple of gallon syrup cans that we had brought our lunch to the field in. Lee went to a grove of trees to gather wood for a camp fire. Dolly and I scrounged some potatoes left by the digger and picked a few ears of corn from a nearby corn field. We built a fire and roasted corn and potatoes. We sat by the fire, eating supper and drinking water from the well.

By the time we had finished supper, darkness had descended. We decided it was safe to wash the itchy peat dirt off at the well. We took turns pumping and washing in the icy water. Clean and shivering, we piled into the Model A and tried to sleep. Sleep didn't come easily in our cramped quarters, and morning came too soon. As the morning sun turned the clouds a brilliant pink, the truck drove onto the field. We heard the tractor roar. Another day of potato picking had begun.

When the day was over, we went home to eat a hearty supper cooked by Ma Schroader. We didn't sleep in any more potato fields.

When pheasant season came, Lee's Uncle Delbert, Aunt Mae and cousin Bob came from Des Moines to hunt the pretty birds. Bob was about Buster's age. Uncle Delbert was Ma Schroader's brother. A tall, thin man, he could talk faster than anyone I ever knew. He sat at the table and spun one tale after the other, stopping occasionally to catch his breath. He rolled his own cigerettes and poured the tobacco out of the stub back in the Velvet can to smoke in his pipe. He didn't waste a pinch.

Frank had a handsome Greyhound named Tony. Tony was slate color with white feet, white face and a white chest. Lee immediately fell in love with him so Frank gave the dog to her. We decided to get another hound and hunt coyotes when we got back to South Dakota. Coyotes were worth about ten dollars besides the bounty.

I wanted a Russian wolfhound. We found a farm that raised Russian wolfhounds, but Russian wolfhounds were expensive. A pure white one like I wanted cost $30.00. I could have a dog with a large tan spot on each side for $15.00. I decided that for $15.00 less I could stand the spots. I handed over my hard earned fifteen bucks and led my dog to the car. I named him Stalin because he was Russian. Mom thought Stalin a horrid name, even for a dog. I guess it was.

Around the first of November, we loaded our hounds in the back seat of the Model A and headed back to South Dakota. Lee drove about thirty miles an hour for forty miles and a tire blew out. We jacked up the wheel, pulled out the tube and patched the hole. Lee forced the tube back into the tire. I hooked on the pump and huffed and puffed until the tube was full of air. On our way again and another flat. About every forty miles a patch melted off a tube, and we had to patch another tire. After a long four hundred miles and thirteen flats, we pulled up beside Uncle Alvin's house.

Buddy and Mickey were back in school, riding their horses to Liberty with Willard Burns teaching. Students came from every direction. The Hagan kids, Patty, Dick, Phyllis and Shirley lived about two miles northwest. George, Betty and Beverley Jean

Evans came from northeast. Gaylord Saucerman came from two miles south on Highway 14.

Mickey invited little Phyllis Hagan to come home with her and stay overnight. Phyllis climbed on Freckles behind Mickey. Buddy always rode Whitefoot with a saddle. Whitefoot wasn't lazy like Freckles. The next morning, Mom told Buddy he had to let the girls ride Whitefoot and use the saddle. Buddy didn't like that, but he bridled Freckles, and they headed for school. Buddy rode along, trying to figure out how he could get even with the girls.

North of Crawfords, the horses started down the incline into the creek. Buddy kicked Whitefoot's ticklish flank. Whitefoot squealed, bucked high, and the girls flew over her head. Laughing, Buddy kicked Freckles into a trot and rode on to school. Phyllis cried. Mickey got up, helped her on the horse,climbed into the saddle, and they went after Buddy.

Mickey sat in a daze until noon. The first thing she remembered was seeing Phyllis getting a sandwich from her lunch pail. She said, "Hey, why are you getting into my lunch pail?"

Phyllis looked surprised. "It's got my lunch in it too." Then Mickey remembered Phyllis had spent the night with her.

We never chased any coyotes with our hounds. Uncle Alvin said we could trap along Bad River for skunks and mink. The river was home to families of beaver, but Uncle Alvin trapped them when they came out of their dens along the river bank. Beaver hides were worth thirty to forty dollars each, and he knew exactly how to stretch the hide into a perfect circle nailed to the granary wall. He had to give the State of South Dakota half the hides, but he got a tidy sum for the hides he had left.

Skunks were only worth a dollar or maybe two, but Lee said a good mink was worth twenty bucks or more. Lee loved to run a trap line. She said she ran two miles on her trap line in Iowa before going to school. I didn't believe her. Where I came from, if you wanted to go two miles, you got on a horse. She really did run the trap line. We caught a few skunks. Uncle Alvin caught the only mink. We caught a big raccoon worth a couple of dollars in traps we set by a dead cow for coyotes. All in all, we didn't make much money trapping.

The only thing I liked about trapping was walking along the river when the early morning sun brightened the eastern hills. Fallen leaves crackled underfoot. A covey of quail might explode out of an ash copse and sail away into the dawn. Sometimes we shot a cottontail for dinner.

That fall, Aunt Tina wanted to get Uncle Charley away from his traps and his long walks into the rugged hills south of Bad River, so she talked him into moving to Midland. They moved into a tiny house on the east side of town close to Mitchell Creek. You entered the kitchen by the house's only door. The bedroom was an alcove barely large enough for a bed, no door for privacy, not even a wall between the bedroom and living room.

Aunt Tina didn't have much furniture since hers had all burned. She had a small table, a few chairs, a bed and stoves. She made a small cabinet and wash stand from an orange crate. She could make a lovely home anywhere.

Frances May Noble, now married to John Noble, was teaching at Lone Tree school on Little Prairie Dog Creek. Scott Lovald, from Midland High School days was teaching at Augustana College in Sioux Falls.

Lee and I were staying with Uncle Alvin, doing the cooking and house keeping. In December, Uncle Alvin and I took Lee to Pierre to catch the train to Iowa for Christmas. Julian was still waiting tables at The Owens Cafe, now moved to the old State Bank building on the north side of Main.

Uncle Charley bought a milk goat from Carl Nordstrom, a sassy nanny with long, curling horns, innocent brown eyes and a nasty temper. He also bought a tiny cream separator that sat on a table so he could separate the cream from the milk. Since you can't separate goat cream from goat milk very successfully, it didn't work well. Uncle Charley picketed his nanny on vacant lots so she had ample grass, and she gave an abundance of milk. When cold weather came, he sent the nanny goat to the farm, and we milked her.

Lee and I borrowed a two-man saw from Uncle Charley, bought a double-bitted axe and went out to our homestead to harvest down timber. We chopped off branches and sawed logs into stove lengths until we had a huge pile of stove wood and bigger muscles. We sold a truck load of wood to Jack Anderson. Jack and his wife, Myrna Blackmore Anderson, lived in a house on the north part of Russell Avenue. Lee, I and Jack threw the wood onto his truck. He gave us $8.00 and hauled the load to Midland to sell.

Ingwal Nelson and Gladys Rinehart of Pierre were married in 1939. One evening, Gladys called and invited us to come to their house and play cards. Snow covered the ground with some drifts fairly deep. Uncle Alvin said, " We'll drive down the river on the ice. That way we won't have to shovel through any snow drifts."

We got in the car, and Uncle Alvin drove onto the river. The Ford purred along through the soft snow in the river bed. We were almost to Nelsons when the back wheels broke through a spring. The wheels spun, but the car didn't budge. Uncle Alvin jumped out to look. "She's stuck tight," he said. "We'll have to walk the rest of the way." He never got excited or angry no matter what happened.

We walked to Nelsons. They had a lovely two story home with a Persian rug on the living room floor. We played cards for several hours. Ingwal teased Gladys if she made a mistake, and she got a bit huffy, which tickled him immensely. We walked home in the crisp, clear cold. The next day we drove the F20 down and pulled the Ford out of the spring.

Julian quit her job at The Owens Cafe and went to Pierre, March 1, 1941 to work in the Law Office of States Attorney Byron S. Payne. She rented a room, but didn't have enough money left to buy food until pay day. She found a second job working nights, setting pins in a bowling alley. Every night she stood behind the pins while bowlers threw heavy balls and knocked them down. (No automatic pin setters in those days.) She had to dodge balls and pop down quickly to reset the pins.

I worked briefly for Jimmie Maeder. I was back in Ottumwa

again. Jimmie was a nurse at St. Mary's Hospital in Pierre. She hired me to take care of her children and cook for Lowell. Lowell operated The Maeder Garage and Service Station.

Maxine was a charming four-year-old with curly, dark hair, and Donnie was a toddling red head. Jimmie stayed in Pierre during the week and came home weekends. She earned a phenomenal $25 per week. I thought she was making a fortune. I got about $5 per week, but I was happy to have a job.

Maeders lived in a large, two-story square house built by Lowell's father in Ottumwa's heyday. The house was a bit north of the garage. Ottumwa hadn't changed much since I worked there in1938. Jay and Lucy Decker still ran the grocery store. Lowell's garage got a few customers for either gas or repairs. He mostly sat in the garage all day, wishing for customers and watching the cars whiz past, heading down the dirt highway to Midland or Philip. The Catholic Church still held services.

I didn't see much livestock on the prairie that rolled and undulated to the far horizon in every direction. Tom Gillaspie Sr., Jimmie's father, had a few milk cows in a pasture north of Ottumwa. The J. W. Harry family still lived in the house south of the school. Harry's cows roamed around their pasture and were milked each night and morning.

Tuffy Harry worked with his father. A couple of miles south of Ottumwa, Wanda Heeb still herded the sheep on the Heeb ranch, heading the flock out before the sun rose to graze over the hills and valleys in search of the sparse grass. Long after sundown, she brought them back to bed down in the corral, safe from the coyotes that howled from every ridge at night.

Every evening, Tom Gillaspie Sr. drove his team and wagon across the prairie road to Ottumwa, bringing Jimmie's mother, Lela, to spend the night with us. When morning came, he came after her. Jimmie's job was soon finished, and I went back to Bad River again. There was plenty of work to do at the homestead on Mitchell Creek.

(Above) Calhoun place. Lee on Uncle Alvin's brown horse. Buddy on Cloudy. (Left) Lee's bucking barrel strung between Iowa's Black Walnut trees. Thelma Martin on board.

CHAPTER 6
Porky

Lee and I were as busy as two flies in a pop bottle when the weather warmed up, and the grass grew green. We saddled Darkie and Buck and rode the six miles to our rancho on Mitchell Creek, worked all day, then rode back at night. Tony and Stalin ran beside the horses and chased every rabbit they saw. Tony could scoop up a rabbit so fast the poor bunny didn't have a chance. Stalin was tall and aristocratic, but he didn't catch any rabbits. He roared full tilt after one of Engwal Nelson's calves when we were coming down the breaks north of Bad River, one day.

The calf bellowed and turned on the speed. Tail straight out behind, he ran for his life. Stalin gained with every jump. We yelled for him to come back. Tony watched. I could see that big hound grabbing the calf and killing it before we could stop him.

Stalin raced up the slope, his eyes intent on the fleeing calf. Suddenly, he hit a cat step and went end over end. He got up, looking confused, and I caught him. He didn't chase any more calves.

Lee and I took hammer and wrecking bar and tore the bedroom and living room off our house. We stacked the boards up for fire wood, saving the usable lumber. We cleaned all the fallen boards out of the stone room, leaving the rocks standing. We didn't know what we would do with it. We built shelves to hold our dishes and food, sugar bowl, salt and pepper shakers and a few cans of vegetables and syrup for our pancakes.

Sometimes, we stayed at our cabin several days and worked. One breezy spring morning, we rode up Mitchell Creek, and the hounds sniffed out a baby porcupine, hiding among dead leaves and tin cans left by some long ago homesteader. We dismounted, and I stirred the leaves with my boot toe as I looked at the small, black animal trying vainly to hide under the leaves. A tiny tail slapped at my boot toe.

"It's a baby porcupine," Lee said. "I'll bet it's the baby of the porcupine the Dennis' kids shot." The porcupine backed against an elm tree, daring us to touch him. He was a mass of needle sharp quills, all bristling. Tony and Stalin watched him from a safe distance.

"We can't leave him here to starve," Lee said. She reached toward the little ball of pins. He pivoted and slapped at her hand. "Wow!" She jerked her hand back.

"How are we going to get him home?" I asked. Lee shrugged.

While Lee watched the porcupine, I hunted among the discarded cans and found a syrup bucket. I looped my belt onto the bucket handle and dangled it in front of the little critter. Lee pushed him into the bucket with a stick. I jerked the can up, and he was caught as neatly as a mouse in a milk bottle. Quills scraped against the tin bucket. We rode home with the tin bucket dangling at the end of my belt.

I emptied the porcupine on the table. He backed up between the salt and pepper shakers with his back against the sugar bowl and glared at us. "What are we going to feed him?" I asked.

"I read in a magazine that porcupine milk is like evaporated milk," Lee said. "We could try some." She got a tin of canned milk and a spoon. She punctured the can and poured milk into the spoon. She held the spoon toward the little ball of fur and needles. The porky backed against the sugar bowl, and Lee pushed the spoon against his teeth. Milk ran down his chin, but some went into his mouth.

He stuck his tongue out and licked the milk off his whiskers. His little nose wrinkled. He sniffed. Lee stuck the spoon full of milk against his teeth agaim. He opened his mouth. Lee tipped the spoon, and milk ran into his mouth and down his chest. He slurped and looked for more. She filled the spoon again and emptied it into his hungry mouth. When he was full, we fixed him a box and put him to bed.

Porky loved canned milk. He grew fast. Soon he was big enough to crawl out of the box. He would waddle across the floor, saying, "Na, na, na," to himself until he got to our bed. He would grab a hunk of blanket, crawl into bed and chew our hair. We tucked the blankets up out of his reach. He tried to climb the nightstand beside the bed. Halfway up, he slipped and fell. Madder than a hatter, he stood up, grasped the stand with his little hands and shook it until everything fell on the floor.

Porky was frisky as a kitten. He danced around the house, kicking up his rear and popping his tail at imaginary enemies. The hounds watched him warily. Porky wouldn't stick a quill in a friend, but he accidently stuck my leg when he was doing his porcupine war dance. The quill barely broke the skin.

He had a mischievous sense of humor. He learned early that Tony and Stalin were afraid of him. He chased them about the house, making these giants move from one napping place to another.

Porky loved tender, green weeds, especially the round leafed button weed. He would grab foliage with both front paws and stuff his mouth so full his cheeks stuck out to where he could barely chew. His favorite foods were corn on the cob, apples and cookies. He sat on his haunches, grabbed the food firmly with both paws and ate. He learned to beg better than any dog. He sat up and mumbled, and if he didn't get some food, he motioned at his mouth with both front paws.

Lee had a small horse training pamphlet, published by Nellie Westerskow who lived on a ranch near Buffalo, South Dakota. The book contained some simple tricks to teach your horse. We decided that if Porky could learn to beg the horses ought to be able to learn a few tricks too. We taught Darkie and Buck to rear and paw the air like the Lone Ranger's horse, Silver.

Mom didn't approve. "Your horse will rear sometime when you don't want it to," she said. Uncle Alvin backed her up, but watching the movies and seeing Hopalong Cassidy rear his white steed and race away across the prairie was exciting. Mom and Uncle Alvin were at least half right. When Lee worked cattle in a pen with Buck, the excited horse reared while the cattle went every which way. Darkie never confused work with play. When she was supposed to cut cattle, she cut cattle. When asked to stand on her hind feet, she stood on her hind feet.

She learned to use that trick to her advantage. If an inexperienced rider got on her back, she might rear and scare the rider into dismounting. We thought it was funny. To us, it proved Darkie could use her head for something besides a bridle rack. I never taught another horse to rear. I decided Mom was right. Rearing was a poor trick for a working cow horse.

That didn't stop me from teaching Darkie to count, kiss me, and horse laugh. Buck didn't want to enrich his brain. He never learned to count or even do a decent horse laugh. Buddy and Mickey and their friends were baffled by Darkie. They couldn't understand how that horse knew that four minus two equals two. If they asked her to add, subtract or multiply, she always pawed the correct number of times.

Racing wasn't a good thing to do either, but race we did, although racing my saddle horse was a thing I learned not to do. Racing makes horses a little crazy. They love to test their mettle against another horse. Perhaps racing makes a horse feel wild and free. Darkie was always ready for a good run. She thought she could beat anything on four legs.

Lee wanted to see if Buck could beat Darkie. We lit out, almost flying across the prairie. Ears back, running flat out, Darkie pulled ahead. Her hooves thundered against the hard ground of the trail, and my cinch broke. I crashed to the ground. The saddle lit on my back. Buck dodged around me, but Darkie stopped. Lee skidded Buck to a halt. I lay on the ground and groaned. If I hadn't been a big girl, I would have cried. Another valuable lesson learned. Never ride with worn cinches or latigos.

Mom had a black two-year-old she wanted me to break to ride. He was built like a cottonwood log with fence posts for legs, but he was a flashy brute with his bald face, four white legs and white patch on each side. Darkie was the only horse I had ever broken to ride, and I was itching to get my saddle on a bronc. Lee was eager to help.

Uncle Alvin said we shouldn't ride a bronc with a bit, or he'd get cold jawed. He showed us how to make hackamores out of white rope and whang leather that we bought at Carl Nordstom's Shoe Repair Shop in Midland. Lee learned to tie the complicated hackamore knots, but I couldn't get the ends to come out in the right places. A properly adjusted nose band will come down on the horse's nostrils and choke him down some, if he doesn't buck you off first.

Uncle Alvin showed us how to scotch hobble Paint. Paint couldn't do much except fall down with one hind foot tied up to his neck. We sacked him out, saddled him and I got ready to ride.

Uncle Alvin gave us advice about riding, too. "You need spurs to ride a bronc," he said. "You can ride a pretty rough horse, if you turn your spurs in and hang on."

Lee had spurs. I sent for a pair of bronc spurs with offset star rowels, silver mounted on each side with a fish. When I set those rowels in a horse's hide, they didn't roll. I had also sent for contest stirrups, oxbow with one inch tread, a lot easier to hold than regular stirrups.

Uncle Alvin said in the old days, he saddled a bronc, put a blind fold over its eyes, mounted and jerked off the blind fold. A cowboy with any pride didn't pull leather. If the bronc bucked Uncle Alvin off, he tied one foot to the saddle horn and got back on. He said, "A horse can't buck very hard on three legs."

I didn't want to get on a bronc, sock in my spurs and say, "Go ahead, horse, do your worst." Then when he threw me forty feet, catch him, tie a foot to the saddle horn and mount again. I asked

Uncle Alvin if there wasn't some other method to keep from getting tossed.

"Well," he said, "You can tie a hind foot to his neck. He can't buck very hard with one hind foot off the ground either."

I didn't like that method any better. He said, "Some guys hobble the stirrups. They tie the stirrups together under the bronc's belly. You can stay on easier when the stirrups don't flop."

That sounded better, but when I told Mom, she said, "Hobbling stirrups isn't very smart. If the horse falls, you can't get away." So much for that idea.

She told about one of our neighbors who had a horse he couldn't ride. He decided he was going to show that bugger who was boss. He had his wife tie his ankles together under the horse's belly. He turned loose the reins, kicked the horse in the ribs, and that brute unwound. He bucked, pitched and bawled, stirring up the dust like a whirlwind gone crazy.

The guy sat up there and rode his bronc to a stand still. He couldn't do anything else. The horse didn't throw him, but he wished the bucking maniac could. By the time he got through beating around in the saddle, he didn't have any place that didn't hurt.

With Curt Anderson's boots, my brand new spurs with the star rowels and contest stirrups, I was ready to ride the strawberry roan's big brother, I thought, but not out on the wide prairie. However, if I was going to ride old Paint, I didn't have much choice. Uncle Alvin's round pole corral was falling down. His big corral needed repairs, and the cattle shed was falling down.

The depression had taken its toll. Alvin's whole place needed repairs. The wood granary on the river bank was solid, but the red paint had mostly peeled off. His hog houses and corn crib still stood with no sign that they had ever worn paint. His hog pen fences kept the cattle and horses away from the hog feeders, but let the red hogs roam free.

I decided to mount Paint on the open prairie and see what would happen. With Lee hazing on Darkie, we headed east across the pasture. When Paint saw all that open space, he decided to unload and head for greener pastures. He put his head between his knees and pitched. I grabbed the saddle horn in a choke hold and turned my spurs in tight. He crow hopped with Lee riding beside him, yelling like a Comanche. When Paint got tired of bucking, he followed Darkie back to the corral. I was still in the saddle, riding proud.

Uncle Alvin was ready with more good advice. "Lee needs a quirt. When he starts bucking, whack him on the rump, and he'll quit bucking and run." We didn't have a quirt, but we found a three foot piece of strap. Whenever Paint ducked his head, Lee cut him across tthe rear with the strap, and he ran.

Buddy was eager to see his big sister ride that bronco. He came for a weekend. I mounted Paint, and Buddy climbed on Darkie behind Lee. We headed east, horses at a walk.

"Make him buck," Buddy said. "I want to see him buck."

I didn't. I was riding carefully. The horses followed the wagon trail toward Nelsons. I kicked Paint into a trot. He bowed his head, left the trail and bucked toward the river with me hanging on with everything I had. Lee galloped up behind him and whacked him across the rump. He jumped about ten feet and lit running. He tore down the trail to the river with Darkie on his tail. Buddy clung to the back of Lee's saddle, yelling, "Make him quit."

The horses splashed across the river and scrambled up the other bank. Paint bucked through trees and brush, and I could hear Buddy, close to panic, "Make him quit. Make him quit," and Lee's "What do you think I'm trying to do?"

Paint bucked through four foot high buck brush and dogwood bushes to the river where there was no trail down, and the water was deep. He turned abruptly and bucked north, fetching up against a fence where he stopped, blowing like a whale. We headed south for a long ride in the Bad River Breaks. I took Paint home soon after for Buddy to ride.

We got more rain than normal in April so the pastures were greening. Herb went to work for Griggs Davidson, building dams with Ole Kristensen. The Government paid for the dams. Herb and Ole built more dams with Farmall F20 tractors and tumble bugs, making sparkling bodies of water for a thirsty land. Brother Hank worked wherever he found a job.

People were still leaving South Dakota. More empty houses appeared on the prairie, only now the houses were larger, often with bedrooms upstairs and cellars underneath. Country churches stood empty on the prairie, as well. People of faith no longer came to worship. This harsh land had destroyed their dreams and left them destitute.

Some people went west to work in the airplane factories. An ad in The Midland Mail said, "Airplane builders wanted: Men 18-25 not in the immediate draft to be trained and ready for airplane construction jobs in California. Minimum wage at .50 per hour. Tuition $89.50 includes text books. $50.00 paid with enrollment and balance of tuition out of pay while on the job." The time was fast approaching when factories would beg women to come and rivet airplanes together. Skeeter and Mary Ellen Groff from Murdo went to California where Skeeter worked in the shipyards. Their first child, a girl, was born in California. I should have built airplanes. Rosie the Riveter made a lot more money than I did.

Murray's Store advertised corn flakes for .09 per box. C.E. Murray was buying cream, poultry and eggs as was The Midland Co-op. The Co-op advertised Misses and Girls Two Piece Slack Suits. Married women didn't wear slacks, and nobody wore denim jeans to town on Saturday night, not even men and boys. Everybody wore their best.

My parent's neighborhood had empty houses, too. Bob Crawford operated his father's farm northeast of Dad's, but the Doud farm was vacant, the Roberts' family having moved to Washington. The Pat Hagan family still lived north of Crawfords, but the Hank Dennis' family had moved from the tiny house north of Liberty school to the Holden farm about a mile northwest of our place on Mitchell Creek. Emil and Florence Nemec had a new house on their place, adjoining Dad's on the east.

They built the house from an abandoned school house where children no longer ran and played, then trooped inside to learn the three R's plus history, geography and social studies. The Burns' family moved to Philip where Don Burns ran The Ford Garage.

Essie Curtis and her Uncle, Ham McCready, lived in a small house a couple of blocks north of Main on Midland Avenue. A railroad boxcar in the backyard was fixed for living quarters, but no one lived there. Essie worked in the sewing room. Eight women worked in this WPA project for women, cutting cloth into pieces and sewing the pieces into quilts for people on Government relief.

Aunt Tina and Uncle Charley moved out of the tiny house by the creek into a two-story monstrosity next to Oscar's Mobil Station. Clarence McKinley, young pastor of The Open Bible Church, was a frequent visitor. I met him there shortly after he arrived in Midland from Nebraska. Reverand Olson still pastored The Midland Lutheran Church, and Father Sweeney had the flock of St. Elizabeth's Catholic Church. Father Sweeney's rectory was the second house south of his church.

Aunt Tina's Chevrolet sometimes died as she slowed for a corner. One day, the car stopped in front of Father Sweeney's house. Uncle Charley got out to push start the stubborn auto. Father Sweeney looked out the window, saw the stalled car and rushed out to help. Father Sweeney was elderly and had a heart condition.

Uncle Charley said, "You better not push. You might have a heart attack."

"That's all right," Father Sweeney said, "It's not far up the hill to the cemetery." And so he pushed. Sometimes the car started, and sometimes Oscar Merkle pulled it to his garage with the wrecker.

Aunt Tina never lost her ability to think fast in an emergency. Her Chevy had poor brakes. Midland didn't have stop signs. One day, a huge Buckingham semi-trailer truck roared down Main Street. When Aunt Tina saw the truck, it was too late to stop. "I knew I couldn't stop," she said. "So I stepped on the gas and shot across in front of him." I expect the driver got a few more gray hairs, but had she done anything else, she would have slammed into the side of the Buckingham.

Along towards spring, Lee went to Iowa to get her livestock ready to come to South Dakota. I hired Fred Holden to go after the load. I hopped into the cab and rode along. He hauled a load of scrap iron to Sioux Falls on the way. People were gathering old iron stoves, horse machinery and junk car motors to sell to scrap metal dealers. Some guys took a farmer's old machinery before he was through with it. The United States sold tons of scrap iron to Japan so they could dump it on Pearl Harbor.

We arrived at the Schroader farm about dark and loaded out early the next morning. Frank gave us Flash and Fly, his small team of mares. Flash was bay with a blaze face, white hind feet and a stubborn streak a yard wide. Fly was all black and would have been a beautiful horse except she had no ears. Flash and Fly knew everything a draft horse needs to know and were gentle as baby lambs. He also gave us a red sow and a black and white spotted sow, heavy with pigs. Lee had three cows, a little Angus Jersey cross cow, she called Betty Ann, a black white-faced cow called Daisy and a red heifer. Frank thought we needed another milk cow so he gave us a black Angus. When we climbed into the truck cab, Dolly got in, too. She sat on my lap, and Fred scrunched behind the steering wheel.

We were glad to see Bad River and back up to the corral on the Bertelson ranch to unload. We hadn't even stopped to eat. None of us could afford to eat in a cafe. The cows, horses and pigs had been riding for over ten hours and were eager to walk on solid ground again.

(Right)Thelma Martin and Darkie giving Lee the horse laugh. (Below) Oscar Merkle getting ready to tow Aunt Tina's Chevy while Aunt Tina and Uncle Charley watch.

Porky Porcupine and black Tom.

CHAPTER 7
Iowa Cows, Horses And Pigs

Our cows, horses and pigs looked out of their pens at the rugged South Dakota hills far from the gentle, green meadows of Iowa. They drank from the river instead of a tank. We soon had baby calves and small pigs running around with Uncle Alvin's hogs, looking for mischief to get into.

We milked the three cows and Uncle Charley's goat and separated the cream in the small separator. With cream to sell, we had a steady, though small, income. Mom gave us ducks and geese and chicken and turkey eggs. We set turkey and chicken eggs under some of Uncle Alvin's setting hens. The ducks and geese liked the river, but when they swam, huge snapping turtles liked to grab the little feet paddling by. Then the poor duck or goose limped back to the barn yard.

We built small pens and shelters for the mother hens and their chicks. One of Uncle Alvin's red sows discovered that baby chicks and small turkeys were tasty and ate a bunch.We saved gilts from the broods of piglets and had eight brood sows. We were in the farming business, but our farm was starting to look a little small.

Betty Ann and Daisy birthed heifer calves. The black Angus had a red bull calf. The red heifer watched Uncle Charley's goat jump through a hole into the hog yard and eat ground barley. The barley was tempting. She forced her large body through the hole and ate ground barley until all of her stomachs were too full. She wasn't smart like the goat who stopped when she had enough. The red heifer was sick.

Lee said she could fix the heifer. She had watched the vet work on her dad's cows when they bloated from eating alfalfa that was wet with dew. "All you have to do is puncture the cow's belly with a trocar and let the gas out," she said, "and the cow is fine." A trocar is a sharp hollow tube. We didn't have one, but that didn't stop Lee. Without help, the cow would die. We tied her to a post. I held the rope while Lee punctured one of the heifer's stomachs with a knife, using a turkey feather for a gas tube. When the cow died, we lost one fourth of our herd.

In May, Julian took a South Dakota Merit Test with 500 other people, the hardest test she had ever taken: history, geography, English and math all rolled into one tough test. She passed with the highest score. She was sent to Mobridge, South Dakota and accepted a civil service appointment to Timber Lake, in the north central part of South Dakota, about a hundred miles north of Midland.

She worked in the courthouse for the Social Security Department. She was happily going about her work when someone checked her age. Julian was only eighteen, too young to work under Civil Service, too young even to take the South Dakota Merit Test. The powers that be did some quick paper shuffling and added years to her life. She went on doing her job, but she's been officially older ever since.

On the fourth of July, Willie borrowed his father's new Chevrolet and took me, Lee, Tom Stalley and Curt Anderson to the rodeo in Fort Pierre. Curt said he would ride an exhibition ride to get money to buy supper. Exhibition riders got $2.50 per ride.

We climbed into the grandstand and sat down. Curt headed for the chutes. We watched the saddle broncs buck across the arena. Then the announcer said, "Curt Anderson in an exhibition ride." The horse bucked and twisted with Curt spurring at every jump. Halfway across the arena, Curt shot into the air and landed on his hands and knees. The horse kicked him in the seat of the pants, boosting him on his way. Curt collected his $2.50 and treated us to steak supper at the Chuck Wagon Cafe. Lee and I ate T-bone steaks. We lived in an era when T-bones weren't bad for your health, weren't expensive and men always paid the bill--well almost always.

Willie had a .38 police revolver that fascinated me. I traded him some ducks for the wicked, little, black gun. Uncle Alvin said, "Let me see that gun. I shot a .45 Colt in the army." I handed him the gun. We were standing about fifty feet away from a telephone pole. "See that knot," he said. The knot was about the size of a quarter. I nodded. He aimed, pulled the trigger and "Bang!" the knot was gone. He didn't hold the gun with both hands either. I couldn't hit the side of his little barn from fifty feet.

In June, Buddy came to visit and brought Kenny Dennis with him. Bad River and Brave Bull Creek were rampaging from a three inch rain, and we ran out of bread. Of course, we didn't want to bake any. The boys offered to walk to town and get a loaf. I gave them a quarter and told them not to dwaddle in town because we needed the bread for dinner. They hiked around to the railroad bridge and walked down the track. They bought a loaf of bread and headed home. The sun was hot. They got hungry and ate half of the loaf before reaching the house.

Midland was gearing up for their Pioneer Celebration and Hot Spot Festival on July 11 and 12, celebrating 40 and 50 years ago and Midland's new enterprise, the "Stroppel Mineral Well Sanitarium" owned and operated by John and Violet Stroppel. The Midland Mail said, "water comes out of the ground 116 degrees and is loaded with health giving minerals." The Stroppel Hotel Hot Mineral Baths had been in operation for a year and those hot plunges were a great attraction. Cowboys took a hot dip on Saturday nights. Bathtubs in houses were a rarity so many people went to Stroppels for a hot, mineral bath. Today, the Stroppel Hotel has been in continuous operation for over fifty years.

Women were getting out their heirloom dresses, and men were growing mustaches, beards and sideburns. Men in the 1940s didn't wear whiskery appendages so the whiskers were a novelty.

Lee and I were going to ride in the parade. Lee said she was going to fix an outfit for me so I could beat Verna Lammon in the "best dressed cowgirl contest." She sewed the legs of my red slacks in so they looked like riding pants, but the riding pants in the western catalogs were gray gabardine with a leather patch on the seat. I had boots, spurs and a Stetson hat, but what cowgirl wears red pants? Because one could not wear Levis and be well dressed, I was stuck with the red pants.

Mickey, Buddy and Kenny Dennis helped wash the horses. Buddy and Kenny were riding in the parade, but Mickey wanted to carry Porky in The Kiddies Pet Class. We rode our horses into the river and shampooed them until they looked beautifully clean and shiny.

The half mile parade swung down Main Street between sidewalks packed with over two thousand people. The Belvidere Band led the parade followed by the cowgirls. Next came Tom Jones, driving his chuck wagon with the cowboys trailing. Faye Jones, dressed in a black riding skirt, white blouse and black hat, rode side saddle, looking the part of a well dressed equiestrienne of the 19th century. Tall, slim Joe Overman strode down the street dressed as Uncle Sam. Then came the many colorful floats.

Verna Lammon captured the prize for best dressed cowgirl again. She deserved it. She got enough money to buy twenty-five rides on the midway. The day was hot and by the time the parade was over, Porky was complaining. He hadn't won first prize, and he was thirsty. He said, "Na, na, na," in his most plaintive porcupine voice. Mickey gave him a drink at one of the sidewalk fountains, squirting the water on his hot little face, cooling him off. A lady standing nearby said, "Look at that. I wouldn't want to drink after that animal." Porky's little mouth hadn't touched the fountain, and Mickey was indignant. She didn't think Porky would want to drink after "that lady". She may have been right. Porky absolutely refused to drink milk from the cat dish unless we washed it.

I didn't win Best Dressed Cowgirl, but I won the potato race on

Darkie. For the potato race two barrels were set up at opposite sides of an arena. Potatoes were placed in the barrel opposite the rider. The riders took off with a lathe sharpened to a point. Spearing the potato, they raced back to the empty barrel dropping it inside. Whoever managed to transfer all the potatoes first won. Now, I had money for the merry-go-round, but I didn't have to pay for my rides anyway. Little Willie took me on all the rides I wanted to go on. He was ten years older than I and a successful rancher so he had a pocket full of dimes to spend, and I was happy to help him spend them.

It was a grand celebration. We watched the free street attractions featuring clowns, tap dancers and acrobats followed by the crowning events, a movie and a dance. Midland's Legion Hall was new then with six giant fans hanging from the ceiling to cool the dancers.

The Kool Cafe on the south side of Main had closed, but there were still plenty of places to eat. Owen's Cafe and Rapp's Cafe were the largest. Archie Joy was building a new 10,000 bushel elevator and offered top prices for wheat. When that elevator was finished, he would have three elevators, two in the middle of town and one on the south side of the railroad track, east of The Midland Co-op Elevator. The Midland Hospital changed doctors. Dr. Brodie left and Dr. L. L. Theberge took over the operation of the hospital with his wife as nurse.

The pastures were green from all the spring rain and so were the Russian thistles. The corn fields were tasseling, and the grasshoppers were chewing. They hadn't all flown away. My Russian wolfhound, Stalin, was growing, too. He was a powerful dog, almost as tall as a yearling steer. He walked across the living room and put his big head on Monica Waitman's lap, almost scaring her out of the chair. He was just being friendly. He wouldn't hurt anyone. We thought when winter came, we would chase those coyotes that howled on the ridges at night and harrassed our chickens, turkeys, ducks and geese. Tony and Stalin would take care of those pests.

Stalin took to traveling around at night. He ran down the river to Charley Zeiman's slaughter house and stole a chunk of beef. Mr. Zeiman didn't want to share his meat with a hound and complained. The back bedroom in the log part of the Bertelson house wasn't used anymore so I tied Stalin in that room at night, and whenever we were going to be gone. One day, we came home and found Stalin hanging outside the house. He had chewed a small hole in the logs with his powerful jaws until he had a hole big enough to crawl through. He squeezed through the hole, but the rope was too short for him to reach the ground, and he had hung himself.

Lee loaned Tony to Lloyd Heeb to run with his hounds after coyotes. Lloyd was going to teach Tony to hunt coyotes, but Tony jumped out of the pickup box and ended his hunting career before it started. Suddenly we were out of dogs.

Lee and I were sitting outside one day when a pickup pulled up. A man got out. He said his name was Bill Daly, and he had a Morgan stud that he wanted to sell. He didn't say that someone had told him there were a couple of naive girls on Bad River who would trade for anything with four legs and a mane and tail, but apparently somebody had. I didn't know Bill Daly from the man in the moon. Bill is what is called a scalper because he made his living buying, selling and trading livestock. He found a good pair when he drove into our yard, and he spent many happy years scalping us.

Bill introduced us to Laddie, the handsome Morgan stallion riding in his pickup box. Laddie was shining, solid black and eight years old. Bill said, "I heard you wanted a saddle stud. Laddie's a good one. Got him from Claude Ramsey." Claude Ramsey lived on a ranch west of Philip on the south fork of Bad River.

Lee's ears perked right up. She had the heart of a scalper. She just didn't have the money to pursue the career. I looked at Laddie and thought, "What a lovely horse."

"He's gentle as a lamb," Bill said. "Anybody can ride him." He squinted. "I'll take $45.00 for him." We said we didn't have

$45.00. Bill looked speculatively at our Model A. "That your car?" We admitted that it was. "I'll trade Laddie for the car." Of course, we traded. Who needs a car?

Laddie was as gentle as Bill said he was. When Buster came to visit, he and Buddy rode Laddie to town bareback. On the way home, they got to wrestling on his back over who was going to drive, and Laddie threw them off.

When Mickey came to visit, she brought Audrey Sturdevant. They rode across the river on Darkie and Whitefoot. Audrey came thundering home, hanging on for dear life, with Darkie going like a runaway freight car, straight for the corral. She tore through the gate and stopped. Audrey wasn't sure whether to be scared or angry, and Darkie waited patiently for her to dismount.

Uncle Walt's team was too old to do much work. He quit farming and let his farm land go back to hay. He bought a used F20 Farmall, hitched his horse mower and a rake to the drawbar and went out to mow hay east of his house on the flat adjoining the Howe's place where Gulbransons lived. Aunt Amanda rode the rake. She was wearing slacks and one of Uncle Walt's shirts. As the hay fell, she dumped the windrows behind the mower, until the mower plugged up, and Uncle Walt stopped the tractor.

Aunt Amanda got off the rake to see what the problem was. The power take-off grabbed her pants' legs and tore her pants off. To her horror, she saw Gus Gulbranson striding across the field toward them. Aunt Amanda grabbed her trousers, intending to put them on, and discovered that the power take-off had neatly ripped the inseam without tearing the pants. She slipped into them, climbed on the rake seat and draped the pants' legs over her own. She sat primly hoping Gus would say what he had to say and leave.

Gus strode up to the tractor. "Having trouble?"

"Mowers plugged up," Uncle Walt said.

Gus looked at Aunt Amanda. "Are you all right?"

She smiled, not moving a muscle for fear the pants' legs would slip. "Yah, yah, I'm fine." He studied her with a perplexed frown and kept asking if she was sure she was all right. She wished he would go home and let them fix their own machinery as she sat like a statue trying to keep the pants in place.

With fall approaching, Uncle Alvin's corn field across Bad River, adjoining Nelson's west field was filled with ears so heavy they hung down. Uncle Alvin looked toward his field and saw a herd of Jim Nelson's hogs headed around the fence into his corn field. Hogs are wont to stray when they aren't locked in a pen. Whenever Uncle Alvin's hogs strayed Nelson's way, someone called him on the phone and told him. He did the same when Nelson's hogs came his way. Uncle Alvin called Jim, "Your hogs are in my corn field, Jim."

"Vell," Jim said, "they should get fat then."

Lee and I were driving Flash and Fly back from our little rancho one day with Laddie tied to the wagon. As we drove across the flat we saw Uncle Walt's team, Snip and his fat, bay gelding that had never known halter or harness grazing about a quarter of a mile west. The bay gelding lifted his head. He snorted like a rifle shot and pranced toward the wagon. Laddie laid back and broke his rope. He thundered out to meet a horse twice as big as he was. The horses reared, squealing and striking. Laddie grabbed the bay's neck with his powerful teeth. He twisted and jerked. The bay went to his knees. With a final jerk, Laddie threw the big horse to the ground.

The gelding lay without moving. I thought Laddie was going to kill Uncle Walt's horse, and I couldn't stop him, but with a toss of his proud head, Laddie turned and pranced back to the wagon, tail streaming. The gelding wasn't fatally injured, but his dignity was badly rumpled.

Frank came after Buster, and we went home with them to work in the potato fields. The mighty potato had beckoned again. Ida Vollmer who lived on a farm in the Stamford vicinity came along. Ida left her Thoroughbred mare and colt that she had bought when Engman sold his race horses, with our horses. She wanted to try potato picking. Porky went along, sleeping on Buster's lap.

Schroaders still lived west of Hayfield. They always welcomed us with enthusiasm no matter how many kids trailed in. Ma seemed to enjoy cooking for us again. She made wonderful suppers--potatoes, gravy, meat, roasting ears from the corn field, tomatoes and carrots from her garden, and pie, cake and cookies from her oven. We worked hard, and we ate hearty.

We went to work in a large potato field east of Schroaders. Frank picked potatoes, too, earning extra money in the lull before corn picking time. The August days were hot. Sweat and black-dirt caked on our faces. We were always happy to see the water truck come down the row. The big flatbed truck brought out more gunny sacks for us to fill. The guys on the truck picked up the filled sacks and hauled them off the field. One blistering hot day, we watched-with parched throats as the water truck approached. The truck came almost to us, then turned back to haul a load of spuds off the field.

"Hey," Frank yelled, "we need a drink."

"Wait till next time," a potato loader yelled back.

Frank dropped his basket and took off down the field after the truck, but he couldn't catch it. Good thing. If he had one smart, young man would have been eating peat dirt for lunch.

One of the trucker drivers was a handsome young man from a neighboring farm. His brother loaded sacks of potatoes on the truck. We didn't know Ray and Cliff, but they introduced themselves. Cliff took a shine to Lee, and Ray stopped to talk to me every chance he got.

Another "Knight of the Potato Wars" had his eye on Dolly. He liked her so much that he threw a potato at her as she tipped up the crock jug to take a drink of water. The potato zinged in like a baseball headed for home plate, hitting the jug just as Dolly put it against her mouth. The heavy jug smashed against her teeth and broke one. She felt his affection clear to the top of her red head. The zinging potato didn't help his case.

On Saturday, Cliff said, "There's a Republican Rally in the Town Hall and a free dance tonight. How about you girls going with me and Ray?"

That sounded like fun. When we got home, we hurried to wash off the black dirt and don our best dresses. Ray and Cliff showed up in Ray's car, and we went gaily off to the dance. We walked into the hall. There weren't many people there, just a few ladies sitting on the benches against the walls.

Ray looked around, and his face changed color several times. You could have bought it for a nickel and got some change. A pretty, blond girl sat on one of the benches beside an older lady. Ray looked sideways at me and walked away. He walked straight to the pretty blond and sat down beside her.

Cliff grinned. "That's Ray's fiance. He didn't know she was going to be here."

He didn't know she was going to be here? I didn't even know he had a fiance. Ray didn't move from the pretty blond's side all night. He sat on the bench, acting exactly like he was only the driver for a bunch of kids wanting a ride to the dance. They just sat. They didn't talk. They didn't dance. They just sat. If I could have thought of a way to embarrass him even more, I would have.

By the time we finished that field, the leaves were turning color, and the days growing colder. We heard about a field north of Forest City that needed pickers so we hired on. We stayed with Lee's Grandma Andersen who lived in an apartment in Forest City. She cooked breakfast and supper for us. We took lunch to the field. We agreed to each put $2.00 per week in Grandma's fancy sugar bowl in her china closet to buy food. Grandma liked to have four girls around her table. She had raised two girls and two boys and was divorced, unusual in her day.

We rode to the field with another worker and paid him $1.00 per week for the ride. We earned about $3.00 per day, $18.00 per week, minus $3.00. That left $15.00 profit. The money added up.

Porky made himself at home in the large Schroader house. Ma Schroader liked Porky, but she was afraid of the harmless little animal. He often followed her around, talking in his gentle porcupine voice until she gave him a cookie.She tried to keep out of his way. Porky found the basket of apples in her bedroom. He loved apples. He would watch until he thought she wasn't looking, then waddle as fast as he could for the bedroom door. She would grab a newspaper and tear after him. He usually managed to climb into the basket, grab an apple and take a bite before she caught him. Then he would drop the apple, look at her with innocent eyes and clamber out of the basket. He knew she would give him the apple he had snatched a bite from. She always did before she shooed him back into the living room.

Porky also loved corn on the cob, preferably cooked. One Sunday night the supper table was crowded because Schroader's had guests. Porky smelled corn. He climbed up the back of Ma Schroader's chair. She didn't notice him until he was breathing on the back of her neck. Petrified, she didn't dare get up for fear the chair would tip over and crash him to the floor. Buster jumped up, took Porky off the chair and gave Porky an ear of corn. Porky sat up, grabbed the corn with both hands, and ate it. Frank laughed uproariously. He loved the little porcupine.

Porky slept in the attic at night. Buster often took him outside and left him in a patch of grass to forage during the day. In the evening, he carried Porky back to the attic to sleep. One evening, he couldn't find Porky. We all searched through the yards and in the tree lot, calling his name, but we couldn't find him. I hope he found wild friends to live with.

Lee introduced Ida Vollmer to Harney Whitmore, a young farmer friend. They liked each other, and Harney promised to come to South Dakota the next spring to visit her. Romance was in the air.

When potato picking time was over, Lee and I bought a Model A sedan from a neighbor of Schroaders for $45.00. The tires were a shade better than the ones on our first Model A. We got home without having to fix flats by the end of October. The trees along Bad River were dressed in Autumn finery, but the prairie was drab and brown.

We hired Gordon Stephanson who operated a garage in

Milesville to turn our Ford sedan into a pickup. Gordon cut the middle out of the car and welded the back to the front. We made a wooden box, painted it bright red and had a dandy little pickup with a box big enough to blow out the tires if we loaded it with grain.

I got a job washing dishes in The Owens Cafe. The Burkhart Saloon occupied the old Faubel Hotel south of Main Street. Darlene Burkhart waited tables in the cafe. I went to work at 5 a.m. and quit at 10 p.m. I was paid ten cents an hour, earning $1.50 for fifteen hours of washing dishes and making salads, half as much as I earned picking potatoes.

On dance nights, The Owens Cafe served midnight lunch and by the time I had washed all those dishes, the dancers were coming for lunch again. I could never wash dishes fast enough to get out of the cafe before the dance ended. Lee and Essie would tell me how much fun they had at the dance.I would like to have stuffed a dish rag in a couple of mouths.

Jim Nelson, Grandma Bertelson's cousin and neighbor of the Bertelsons since pioneer days, died in September, and another of Midland's earliest pioneers was gone. If there was anybody that didn't like Jim Nelson, I don't know who it was. His brother, Oluf Hauge, still ranched north of Powell.

Aunt Tina and Uncle Charley moved again, this time to the Flom house smack on the bank of Mitchell Creek on the north end of Midland. Uncle Charley got arthritis so severely he could hardly walk. Pastor McKinley of The Open Bible Church prayed for his healing. Uncle Charley recovered and was never bothered with arthritis again.

In spite of the grasshoppers and shortage of summer rain, Dad and Uncle Alvin raised a fair corn crop. Dad bought a second hand Ford pickup and a used Farmall F20 tractor. His work horses were too old to work anymore. He was going modern. One of Dad's neighbors had a large herd of red hogs ranging over the prairie. Hogs running loose find many good things to eat: roots, grass, grain lost in the stubble fields and the neighbor's corn.

The scrounging hogs found Dad's corn field. They rushed into this bonanza early one morning and began to feast. Dad drove to the field in his pickup and found it over run with hogs of many sizes. His own hogs were home in their pen. Dad roared onto the field, shouting, beeping the horn, and knocking corn stalks right and left. He rolled down the window and beat on the side of the door with his fist.

The squealing pigs ran for home. They tore down the rows with the pickup roaring after them. Dad laid on the horn and beat his fist red against the door. The hogs sped under the barbed wire fence and raced for home. Every morning, until his corn was in the crib, Dad drove early to the field. He never managed to hit one of the fleeing marauders, but he tried.

Uncle Alvin had a similiar problem with his corn field on the Calhoun place. He rode to the field one morning and found a herd of cattle gobbling his corn. He chased cows out of his field every morning until one morning, he beat the herd to their early morning feast. He saw them coming and loped over to head them back before they could scatter over the field. His horse galloped around, turned the cattle and ran smack into the owner of the herd, chasing them into the field. Uncle Alvin was so angry he turned the air blue, telling the farmer what he'd better do and what would happen if his cattle were ever caught in that corn field again. The cattle never returned.

Buddy and Mickey were riding to Liberty School in seventh and sixth grades with Berniece Blackett teaching, and Edwin May shining up to the teacher. A bunch of Hagan kids went there, too: Patty, Wendell, Dick, Shirley and Phyllis. George, Beverley Jean and Betty Evans came from the east and Gaylord Saucerman from the south.

Buddy was learning to drive Dad's pickup. One day, he and Wendell Hagan and Mickey went for a pickup ride in the west pasture. Buddy and Wendell sat in the front, and Mickey stood in the box. The breeze blew her hair, and she was enjoying the ride when Buddy suddenly wheeled around in a tight circle. Mickey flew twenty feet through the air and lit on her shoulders. She lay on the hard ground and groaned. Buddy drove back and jumped out of the pickup. "Are you all right?" He was almost afraid to ask. She nodded and got slowly to her feet. She felt like every bone in her body had jarred loose. Buddy let her ride in the cab on the way home, but Mickey hobbled around for two weeks.

Dolly Schroader went to New York state to visit her Uncle Haven and stayed to work in a resort in the Catskill Mountains. She came home the summer of 1942.

When Herb quit building dams for Griggs Davidson, he went to work for Jack Buchanan about a mile east of Midland where Morris and Barb Jones live today.

Lee and I bought ten broken mouth ewes (actually they needed false teeth) from Claude and Alice Harren. We figured if we took good care of the old girls they should each have two lambs to raise. We could get some bum lambs to raise on cow's milk, and we'd be in the sheep business. We forgot that Harren's sheep weren't like Aunt Amanda's pets. They were herding animals, used to being chased about by a herder and a fast dog. We brought our sheep to Uncle Alvin's ranch and locked them in a small shed back of the granary so the coyotes wouldn't get them. We locked Uncle Charley's ornery nanny goat in with the sheep.

The next morning, we opened the door to let the sheep and goat out to graze. The belligerent nanny stationed herself beside the door and lanced each ewe with her sharp horns as it dashed frantically for freedom. By the time we discovered what Nanny was up to, she had killed one ewe and scared what wits they had out of the others.

The sheep scattered along Bad River, searching for the large flock they'd been separated from. Lee rode up and down Bad River, looking for lost sheep. Aunt Tina brought Uncle Charley out to help. Uncle Charley located a ewe hiding in a plum thicket. The ewe was tucked into the thicket, hoping a coyote wouldn't find her before the herder who was supposed to protect her did. She stuck out like a mound of ice cream on a piece of chocolate cake.

Uncle Charley spotted the hiding ewe. He probably smelled her, too, because he claimed he could trail a fox to its den with his nose, and Mom always said you could smell a sheep a mile off. Uncle Charley sneaked, wary as a coyote, toward the rear end of the unsuspecting sheep. With a quick lunge, he grabbed a hind leg and dragged the ewe from the bushes. The ewe rolled over dead, the life scared out of her by the monster who had slipped up behind her.

Lee got our remaining eight sheep rounded up and brought them back to the shed. The stupid sheep didn't know how lucky they were. If they stayed around the buildings, they could find all they wanted to eat without fear of coyotes with sharp teeth and hungry bellies. They were lucky they weren't on a stock car headed for market.

Our small pile of money grew. We sold our two brood sows and the barrows, keeping eight gilts for next years pig crop. We sold our young turkeys and kept fifteen hens and two gobblers. We had money from picking potatoes, and I was saving most of my wages. I was the waitress for a few hours every afternoon when Darlene was off. Being a waitress was a cut above being a dishwasher. As a dishwasher, I made more money than Darlene, but I had to work twice as long to get it.

A telephone crew worked out of Midland, and a bunch of young men ate supper and sometimes dinner in the cafe. However, I could only watch them from the kitchen. Occasionally, I waited on them, if they came in for lunch in the afternoon. One afternoon, a rancher from the Ottumwa country stopped for lunch with a long geared friend. I was manning the cash register when he came to pay the bill. He handed me the money, took two nickel cigars from the box by the cash register and handed one to his friend. He stuck the other in his fat face, and they walked out without paying for them. I was flabbergasted. I stood with my mouth open, not even thinking to say, "Hey, pay for those cigars, you cheap jerks." I didn't dare tell Mr. Owens. He would probably have chased them down the street with a meat cleaver. Mr. Owens didn't take sass from the customers or anybody else.

We stuck our orders on a spindle in the window between the kitchen and the dining room. Mr. Owens told me not to put in supper orders until 5 pm, and he meant 5 pm not 4:59 pm. One afternoon, a couple of hungry truckers came in and ordered steaks and hash browns at 4:30. I took their orders and stuck the pad back in my apron pocket. They told me to put their orders in to the cook. They were hungry. I said, "The cook doesn't take supper orders until five o'clock."

The fuming truckers got up and left. Mr. Owens didn't care. If people didn't like the way he operated his cafe, they could go down the street to Rapp's. I was working in The Owens Cafe on December 7, 1941 when some one ran in and said,"The Japanese bombed Pearl Harbor."

The sneak attack on Pearl Harbor sent over two thousand American sailors to the bottom of the Pacific Ocean and brought the United States into war with Japan. The American Naval Base at Pearl Harbor was burning. Most of the planes were sitting ducks, destroyed before they could leave the ground. Fighter planes were torn to shreds. Within minutes, the Arizona and the Oklahoma were upside down, drowning four hundred American sailors. The Maryland, Tennesee and California were damaged, but fighting. The Pennsylvania was battered where it lay in dry dock.

Not a single Navy plane was air borne as one hundred and forty Japanese bombers swept over Pearl Harbor. A handful of Army pursuit planes roared into the sky and knocked eleven Japanese planes into the sea. Black smoke hung over the island as Pearl Harbor burned. Four battleships were sunk. Two thousand three hundred and seventy-five men died because the "Powers That Be" in Washington withheld vital information from Admiral Kimmel at Pearl Harbor, according to "And I Was There" by Admiral Edwin T. Layton.

Why the American sailors who heard the planes coming didn't

sound a warning is hard to understand. For reasons known only to God, Admiral Nagumo, when victory was his, turned his armada around and headed back to Japan. It was an error that would cost the Japanese dearly.

President Roosevelt no longer had to persuade the country to go to war. The United States was ready to fight. The Arizona became a monument to the men who died there. The Oklahoma turned belly up and slid beneath the waves. The United States found itself at war on this day that President Roosevelt thundered "would live in infamy."

Admiral Layton said, "The day wouldn't have lived so much in infamy if the powers that be in Washington had quit fighting long enough to warn Pearl Harbor the day before instead of sitting on their information until it was too late, and the American Navy was already destroyed."

Adolph Hitler jumped on the band wagon and declared war on the United States. Il Duce Benito Musselini of Italy joined with the Germans. President Roosevelt and Congress immediately declared war on Japan, Germany and Italy. American boys were called to the service in ever increasing numbers. My older brothers, Herb and Hank were among them.

Timmie set to ride the chestnut filly.

Washing the horses in Bad River before the big parade. Mickey and Timmie are in the river. Kenny Dennis has his back to the camera.

This horse is tearing the fence down faster than Timmie can fix it.

CHAPTER 8
A Country Gears For War

People were leaving South Dakota to work in defense industries on the west coast. Skeeter and Mary Ellen Groff from Murdo had been in San Francisco for a year where Skeeter worked in the shipyards. Their first child, a girl, was born on Pearl Harbor Day, December 7, 1941.

Our boys were jumping on the train and heading for Army or Navy camps all over the US. When his draft number came up, Glen Crawford, one of our neighbor boys and a schoolmate from Liberty, came home from Kansas and went into the Army.

Mom made a huge birthday cake topped with candles and an American flag for Hank's birthday January 30th. He was twenty-two years old. Herb and Hank went to Rapid City for their Army physicals in February.

February was unusually mild. One day, Lloyd Heeb showed up with a trail hound pup, a little ginger colored mutt appropriately named Ginger. Lee was estatic. She was going to hunt coons by the light of the moon with Ginger baying at her heels.

"He's got a nose on him, you know it," Lloyd said. "He can trail anything and stay right on the scent." He surely could. He could trail a car, a milk cow, a pig or a turkey hen to her nest where Ginger gobbled up the eggs. Lee and Lloyd were enthusiastic about the diminitive trail hound. He didn't look so great to me. He had a mangy patch as big as a silver dollar on his head. His little pot belly looked like he had swallowed a watermelon. I think Lloyd had been feeding the pup cornmeal when he needed milk. Ginger was to take the place of the magnificent Tony. Pretty poor substitute, I thought. Ginger turned out to be like the pup in the poem of the same name:

"Ginger was a scalawag, Ginger was a pup.
He got into the cellar way and ate the sausage up."

We would pour Ginger a dish of milk with bread in it and in two gulps, the food was gone, and Ginger's stomach stuck out further than ever while he wagged his tail and looked for more. Ginger slipped apologetically into the house, and we told him he could stay under an incubator. Two incubators brooded eggs in the living room, so he had a choice. If anyone said, "Get under the incubator, Ginger," Ginger dived under one of them and lay scrunched down like a coyote pack was on his tail and peeked out at us.

Harney Whitmore and Dolly showed up the first week in March.They had headed for South Dakota, and Harney's car broke down halfway here. They left the car and hitch-hiked the rest of the way. Ida Vollmer came out to visit and see Harney. We traded Ida out of her two-year-old gelding and named him Tuffy.

Harney wanted to go hunting so he and Lee saddled Darkie and Laddie, took their shot guns and went out to see if they could find any grouse. They came home without any birds and shouted for someone to take their guns. I went out, and they each handed me a shotgun. I went into the house, shut the kitchen door and set the guns in the corner behind the door.

"Boom!" a blast went past my face so close I could feel the wind of its passing. The shot tore a hole in the ceiling. I was too stunned to say a word. I stood, half deaf and in shock.

"Tim," Dolly said in a whisper, "are you okay?" By then, I wasn't in shock anymore. I was angry.

"Yeah, I'm okay." I jerked the door open. Lee and Harney sat their horses, looking scared. I was steamed up enough to blow my cork. "Don't you know enough to unload your gun, Harney?" I asked. I felt like pulling him off the horse and kicking the bejab bers out of him.

"It wasn't my gun," Harney said. "I unloaded mine."

I looked at Lee and shook my head. "I didn't think you were that stupid."

"And I suppose you thought I was," Harney said, looking injured.

Harney loved to make Ginger dive under the incubator. Ginger knew he belonged under the incubator when he was in the house, but Harney lured him out. When Ginger slipped shyly out from under his sanctuary and sidled toward Harney's chair, Harney roared, "Get under the incubator, Ginger." Poor Ginger turned tail and dived while Harney roared with laughter. Harney and Dolly stayed a week, long enough for Harney and Ida to have a fight and decide to go their separate ways.

We disked and harrowed the thirty-acre field west of our house and planted barley with Dad's endgate seeder. He gave us the seeder, sold us a sixteen foot disk for $10.00 and gave us his lister. I paid him $2.00 and never found the other $8.00 until he didn't want it anymore. He also gave us his corn cultivator. He didn't need horse machinery anymore now that he was using tractors. Uncle Charley gave us a wagon and his five foot mower. We built a small hayrack on a wagon Uncle Alvin gave us. We were set for farming, except we needed more draft horses.

I was still rising at four o'clock to go to work at the cafe. I found time on Sunday to take a hog to Dad's place and trade it to Mom for a horse, a stupid trade. She beat me badly. In February, a fire burned out the top floor of Rapp's cafe where they lived. The fire didn't harm the first floor where the cafe was so they kept on feeding the public.

We were feeling the first effects of war. The Government rationed sugar and tires, then added meat, coffee and gasoline. We hadn't bought tires for our Model A when we had a chance. Now it was too late. The Government office in Omaha, Nebraska was making emergency seed loans to farmers in South Dakota, but in order to get a loan, the farmer had to agree to plant a garden. They were called Victory Gardens. Mom happily planted a huge garden with the reluctant help of Buddy and Mickey. The Government assured farmers that an inspector would be around to see that farmers were weeding and tending their gardens.

During the first part of March a bunch of Haakon County boys , among them my brother Hank, were called into the Army. We all went to a big party for them at The Senechel Hotel in Philip. We trooped to the depot to see them off as they boarded a Chicago and Northwestern passenger car and headed for Fort Leavenworth, Kansas. The passenger trains those days were full of young men going to army camps or naval training stations or soldiers coming home on furlough or going back from a last visit home before going overseas. Herb didn't go. He decided he would rather fly over Germany than walk it carrying a rifle, so he joined the Air Force. He had several months to wait for induction.

Lee and I discovered the joy of horse sales when we rode to a sale in Belvidere twenty miles away. We saddled Buck and Darkie and rode southwest to the Nowlin road and then south to Belvidere. By the Highland Center school where I had gone to first grade, we found a horse caught in a barbed wire fence. He stood patiently as we lifted his front foot out of the wire. We rode on to Belvidere to Nick Weis's sales barn.

We bought a couple of two-year- olds from the Krogman ranch for $15.00 each. We had no idea we could buy horses so cheaply. We drove them home to Bad River. One was a lovely chestnut filly of Quarter Horse stock, although I hadn't heard of Quarter Horses yet. The breed was new to South Dakota.

We halter broke her and took her to the Calhoun place to ride her because the corrals were better there. I sacked her out, saddled her and mounted. Lee rode Darkie around in the big corral, and she followed. She didn't offer to buck so Lee opened the gate. We rode out of the corral to the wide open prairie. The filly saw all that space and bolted. She ran north, with me pulling back on the hackamore reins, hoping she would tire and stop. Lee galloped behind on Darkie. She didn't have to hit this bronc to make her run. We needed to figure out how to stop her. She ran a mile north, came to a fence, turned and ran another half mile. She slowed down, blowing hard and finally walked home beside Darkie. She decided she was broke and didn't give me any more trouble. I wasn't sure which was worse, having a horse buck or run away. I didn't like either. There had to be a better way.

We were getting too many horses for Uncle Alvin's winter pasture, so we needed more land. Alice and Claude Harren were running sheep on the Owen Lohan place about four miles north of our Mitchell Creek place. They had purchased three quarters of Stanley County land for fifty cents an acre. Alice said a section northwest of their land was for sale. "Why don't you buy it?"

Sounded like a good idea. We bid fifty cents an acre on 640 acres and waited three weeks while the land was advertised. We would pay 20% down and have five years to pay the balance. I was still working at the cafe when Lee went to Fort Pierre to finalize the purchase.

To her surprise, she had competition. Ernest Nemec was sitting on a bench, waiting for the bidding to begin. He raised the bid to .55 cents. Lee said .60 cents. Earnest sat a long time, then said .65 cents. Nickel by nickel, six hundred and forty acres was going. Lee ran out of nickels, so Ernest got the land.

Next we contacted The Federal Land Bank in Philip and bought a 320 acre farm in the Grindstone vicinity northwest of Philip. The farm had a two-story white house, decent outbuildings and a family living there. We were getting set to move into our new farm when the man who lived there showed up at our kitchen door.

We invited him in, and he sat in the living room and explained that he didn't want to move. He wanted to buy his farm and stay there with his family. We hadn't thought about that farm in human terms before. The farm had been for sale, so we bought it. He offered to give us our down payment plus $40.00 if we would turn the contract back over to him. We couldn't tell the man to load up his family and leave so we sold him the contract. We needed some place to go again, preferably a place with acres of good grass and a river.

We found the ideal place in *The Pioneer Review*. John Forsell wanted to rent his 1,200 acres on the North Fork of Bad River for $200.00 per year. A white two-story house sat on a knoll on the north side of the river. We'd have the river to fight with again, but the farmstead had a large red barn with haymow, cow stanchions and two horse stalls. (Any horse in its right mind would rather be outside running around in the corral, than tied to a manger in the barn. It's people that tie them in the barn.) North of the barn was a thousand bushel steel grain bin. A round corral and set of large corrals flanked the barn. The snug, white chicken house would keep our motley crew of hens and roosters warm and dry. A small door let the chickens march out without leaving the big door open. I had never lived in such luxury. We had $200, so we rented the place.

We also got a 320 acre pasture south of the river that we didn't have to pay for. The only plowed ground was an eighty acre field west of the house. The school section pasture a mile north had a large dam. We had a well with good drinking water below the house. We were set. We had more pasture than we could use. Too bad we didn't have brains to match our enthusiasm. North of the barn was a woven wire hog pen that wasn't exactly hog tight. We weren't worried. We were going to keep our hog feeders full and let our hogs roam free like Uncle Alvin did. Uncle Alvin said, "A hog that's got plenty to eat at home won't wander far." Famous last words.

We headed back the next morning. The rain that fell during the night had turned to ice on Highway 14. I was driving. I ran off the first curve we came to. I turned, and the Model A kept going straight ahead, off the road and onto the grass. After running off the road four times, the Model A dived through a barbed wire fence. The wire punctured the radiator, and the water ran out. We caught a ride to Midland with a more prudent driver.

We heard Uncle Alvin come in early one morning. We were used to him coming home at all hours. He was courting Essie Curtis so he might be visiting her, or he might be helping to close Burkhart's Bar. This time it was the later. A few minutes after Uncle Alvin came home, someone tried to pound the kitchen door in. We dressed and went to the door.

Curt Anderson, Tom Stalley and Tuffy Harry stood outside. "Got my car stuck," Tuffy said. "I need a pull."

Tom and Curt started laughing. "Bertelson told Tuffy not to drive in the mudhole," Curt said.

"Yeah," Tom said. "He told Tuff to go around the mud, but Tuff thought Alvin was too drunk to know what he was talking about and barreled right into it. He's stuck tight." Tom's clothes were wet.

"How did Tom get all wet," Lee asked. "The river isn't even running."

"Curt pushed me in," Tom said. Tom and Curt had walked too close to the ten foot cut bank above a four foot deep pool. Curt shoved Tom, and Tom had gone over the bank, landing in the ice cold pool. He was as sober as an owl sitting in a cottonwood tree, and a whole lot wiser.

Lee made coffee. Uncle Alvin smelled the brew and came out of his bedroom to have a cup. "How about starting your tractor and pulling me out of that mudhole," Tuffy said.

Uncle Alvin laughed. "Any damn fool that would drive into a mudhole ought to stay there."

While they were drinking coffee and arguing about pulling Tuffy's car out of the mud, Lee and I showed Curt and Tom our livestock. They thought Laddie was a grand horse. Later I sold Curt a couple of colts that he thought would make fine saddle horses, but he didn't keep either of them long enough to find out.

We talked about the war, and how many guys were gone. Brother Hank was training in Fort Warren. Curt's cousin, Vern Anderson, was in the Marines somewhere in the South Pacific. Curt said he tried to enlist in the Marines, but they didn't want him. People had said Hank wouldn't have to go because he had a short trigger finger, but the Government decided he could use one of the others and took him anyway.

Curt said he was going to Oregon and work. Several people from Midland had gone to Oregon: Ramona and John Gabriel, Pat and Lyle Stinson and the Jack Oviatt family. Tom said he was going to enlist in the Navy in the Sea Bees. At least in the Navy, a guy got good food and a dry place to sleep, unless the ship sank.

Mike and Bob Schofield went into the Army at the same time Hank did. Bob hoped to get in the cavalry so he told the interviewing officer that he had been raised on a ranch and had ridden horses all his life. "Is that so," the officer said. "Were there any pigeons on your father's ranch?"

Bob said, "Yeah, I guess so."

"Good," the officer said. "I'll put you in charge of carrier pigeons."

The March weather was warm and balmy when Lee and I began our move to our new ranch. I saddled Laddie on the frosty morning of March 18, 1942 and headed the horse herd west up Highway 14 toward Philip. The day was bright and lovely. One could almost smell the green grass starting to grow. We left Flash and Fly to pull the hayrack and wagon to our new place. Fly was tied to the manger in the barn. The manger was full of hay, and we were coming back the next day. Uncle Alvin was farming on the Calhoun place. The sun was barely up when I started the twenty head of horses up the road with Lee following in the pickup.

The horses moved at a steady trot up the road ditch. Highway 14 went past where the Sales Barn is now, down the hill and straight through Philip. About eleven a.m. I drove the horses through Philip's business district, between The First National Bank and The Senechal Hotel, on past Dorothy Brothers Garage and west a mile, then north up a dirt grade.

We passed the Jones school where Dottie Jensen taught. Dottie lived with her Grandma and Grandpa Jensen and her Uncle Carl Jensen on a farm a mile down the river from our new place. We went past the Bob Jones ranch and the Sorenson farm, which was a half mile downriver from ours. Maurice Sorenson operated the farm with his mother. His younger sisters, Letitia and Doris, were still home. His older sister, Eleanore, lived in Rapid City.

I was happy to shut the gate behind me and watch the horses spread out to graze. Thirty-six miles is a long way on horseback if you don't even stop to eat. I rode across the river, hung my saddle in that beautiful red barn and tied Laddie to the manger. He was happy to stick his nose in a manger full of hay.

We were met by a mother cat with four kittens when we put our furniture in the house. Tabby had crawled through a loose screen on the screen door and taken up residence in a corner, under a shelf. Back arched and tail fluffed, she had already informed Ginger that he couldn't enter her domain.

We went to bed, intending to get an early start the next morning so we could move our pigs, cows, chickens, turkeys, ducks and geese to their new home. We awoke to a howling blizzard. A foot of snow already covered the ground. The wind howled and moaned around the eaves and kept the visibility near zero while we stewed and fretted, prisoners of the storm. The wind let up occasionally, and we could see horses grazing across the flat west of the house. They grazed south with the wind for a quarter of a mile, then ran back, turned south and grazed with the wind to their backs again. We worried about Fly tied to the manger, needing food and water. Would she survive?

When the wind died three days later, the snowdrifts were too deep for us to go anywhere. We waited two more days while the sun began to thaw the drifts. The snow had blown off the ridges, but enormous drifts lay on the south side of every hill. The county didn't have enough snow plows to open roads. We had to get out and let Fly out of the barn.

On the fifth day, I shoved the Model A off the hill, and we headed for the Bertelson ranch. We got across the river all right and up the hill to the graded road. The road had blown clear until we turned south. We passed the school house and came to a huge drift that reached nearly to the foot of the hill. We got out and inspected it. The drift was as hard as a board; the snow at least ten feet deep. "Maybe we can run over it," Lee said.

I shrugged. "Maybe." We had to get Fly out of the barn.

We got in the car. Lee backed up for a good run at the snow bank. She revved the motor, put it in second and raced up to about forty miles an hour. The Model A was all but flying when we hit that drift. If the car broke through, she'd be there till the snow melted. The Model A skimmed over the snow, wheels barely touching, and we were down the hill and headed up the next one. From there to Philip, the road was mostly clear. When our neighbors saw the Model A tracks going down that gigantic snow bank, heads were shaking in amazement.

Uncle Alvin was still up north. No one was at the Bertelson ranch. Cautiously we approached the barn. We were greeted by an eager nicker as we opened the door. Fly stomped her feet. She had eaten every spear of hay, and she was perishing for a drink of water. I turned her loose, and she galloped to the river.

We spent the next two days getting our poultry, cows and hogs moved. Fred Holden hauled the cattle and hogs. We set the incubators up in the living room. I drove Flash and Fly, bringing the wagons and machinery, going down Main Street again.

The chickens were happy with their new home. The turkey gobblers strutted around like they owned the farmyard. The ducks and geese waddled to the river to check the water. The sows rooted happily while the cows inspected the pasture, and the sheep promptly got lost. We had a billy goat and a couple of nanny goats, because Alice Harren told us we could raise a bunch of bum lambs on goat milk. The goats didn't get lost, but Alice forgot to tell us that a nanny goat has two or three kids, and, if you want milk for lambs, you have to knock the kids in the head. That, we could not do.

Ginger was also inspecting the farm.

Timmie Martin and horses on Calhoun place when Darkie was young. Time is early spring. Horses, Darkie, Whitefoot and her colt called Warrior.

Lee Schroader and Alvin Bertelson on his horses. He called them simply "The Big Brown Horse" and "The Black Horse".

CHAPTER 9
Ranching On The North Fork

Ginger viewed the chicken house with happy anticipation. That white house was full of hens; hens laid eggs, and Ginger loved eggs. He ate them shells and all. Nothing we tried dulled his appetite. We gave him an egg laced with red pepper. Ginger liked his eggs hot. He discovered the little door that the hens came out of. The little door was just right for him to enter.

Ginger sauntered up the ramp and stuck his head through the door. He ran head first into an angry hen who was just coming out. She flew at him, clawing and pecking. Ginger turned tail and fled, howling, to the barn.

Lloyd was right about Ginger's nose. He could trail anything. He trailed the Model A when we went to town. We'd hear his deep, bell like tones as he loped, nose to the ground after the car, baying with every jump. After a half mile, he'd give up and go home. Ginger trailed the turkey hens to their nests and stole the eggs. If we heard Ginger baying in the early morning, we knew he was on the trail of a turkey hen. We had to leap out of bed and catch him before he found the nest.

I took Ginger with me after the milk cows at eventide. He could find the milk cows no matter how thick the woods. He'd get on the trail, yelping until he ran into the cows. That's when his help petered out. He never learned how to chase a cow. I would start the herd toward the barn, and Ginger would tear after a cow, nipping her nose instead of her heels. The confused cow spun like a top, not knowing which way to go. Ginger was a detriment to the farm, but Lee still had hopes of hunting coons come fall.

Our place had a good three wire fence around the outside, and around the north pasture, but most of the cross fences were falling down. At first, we tried to repair them, but soon fence fixing seemed like a useless task, so we left the fences where they were. We had plenty of other things to do. Our cows had to be milked twice each day if we wanted to get cream to sell so we could buy groceries. Our incubators hatched baby chickens and baby turkeys. We hid a few babies under setting hens, and the mother hens happily adopted them and took over their raising and education. They led their broods around to scratch in the dirt and catch bugs, sleeping in their tiny houses at night.

When one of the gobblers got sick, Lee said he had blackhead, a usually fatal turkey disease. "We'll have to drench him," she said. She fixed the medicine and prepared to pour it down the big bird's gullet while I held him still. "Did you ever drench a turkey before?" I asked as the poor, sick gobbler struggled to get away." "Lot's of times," Lee said, "and they always died." This old bird didn't spoil her record. He died, too.

The first neighbor to visit was George Oldenberg. The Oldenbergs, George, Phyllis, Marie and Gladys lived a half mile up the river. Marie and Gladys weren't in school yet. When George came, Lee was down in the creek, getting some wood for the cookstove. I was working on a writing lesson. George visited a bit and said, "Well, I'll go down in the creek and look for a man.

I didn't tell him any different. He was surprised when he found a red-haired woman chopping wood. The Oldenbergs became dear friends and as good a neighbors as we ever had. We've kept track of each other for over fifty years. George helped us fix the Model A when it got balky, gave us advice when we needed it and told us wild stories when he felt like it. George sported a gray mustache at a time when mustaches were mighty scarce. Phyllis had dark hair, brown eyes and a lovely smile. She always invited us in for dinner or supper or cookies if we got near her front door.

George was fond of saying, "I wouldn't take a million dollars for my girls, and I wouldn't give a million dollars for another one." However, three more babies came to bless his humble home, Connie, Grace and Gary, and he was just as proud of them.

The little Oldenberg girls had a black bitch about Ginger's size. When she gave birth to a nest of puppies, Marie said, "These are Ginger's babies, too." She showed us the nest of wiggling puppies. They were plainly Ginger's children. Three looked exactly like him. The fourth was black like the mama. George suggested that we take half the pups because the father should bear some responsibility, but we declined. I could see three more Gingers running around, sniffing for eggs.

George told us they traded at Copp's Market, a grocery store around the corner from the old First National Bank. The bank was now on the corner, a block north. George told us that we could trade our eggs for groceries at Copps, but to watch out for old Mr. Copp because he liked to pinch ladies. George said we could sell cream at Pohle's Cream Station which was about where Corky's Super Valu is now. We sold our cream to Pohle and traded our eggs for groceries at Copp's Market, but Mr. Copp didn't pinch us.

The next year, Copp's Market closed, and they moved to Montana. We had discovered the joy of charge accounts. Most farmers and ranchers charged groceries and paid for them in the fall at market time. We owed Copp's Market $4.49 when they left. I ran into young Mr. Copp when he came back to Philip. I said, "Here's the $4.49 we owe you." He looked surprised and shoved the money into his pocket.

Verna Lammon told me she never charged groceries because "that's just like paying for a dead horse." She had a good point, but some people eat dead horses on purpose or by accident.

Curt Anderson said he and Mike and Martin Schofield had ridden all day, and, about dark, they arrived at Bob Schofield's house. Bob wasn't home, but they were hungry as wolves that hadn't made a kill for a week. They looked around for food and Martin found a quarter of beef hanging in the cold back room. He sliced off three generous steaks and fried them for supper. They were relaxing, full and satisfied, when Bob came home.

They told Bob they'd had supper, some fine steaks off his quarter of beef. Bob laughed. "That's not beef. That's a quarter off an old dead horse, I've been feeding to my dogs." Three cowboys nearly lost their supper.

Bill Daly soon found out that we had moved to the North Fork. He came out to trade us worthless horses for things of value like hogs and calves. He traded us four horses that he got from Herman Stahl that were wilder than mountain goats and a hundred times bigger. Earl Morgan hauled them to our corral and unloaded the brutes.

Earl Morgan invited us to help move a herd of horses from his place on The Government Range south of Philip to a section he had rented east of Philip across the road from the Paul Roseth ranch on Bad River. Earl was going to drive his herd of about thirty horses across the country some thirty miles to his new pasture.

I arose with the sun to milk the cows before we left. I never minded rising early, even in winter. I liked to hear the birds greet the dawn with their sleepy morning songs and watch the sun rise in all its splendor. In the winter, stars were so bright and so close, I imagined I could reach up and grab one.

We hurried to separate the milk and feed our bum lambs. We'd tried to get a bunch of bum lambs to raise, but only got about a dozen. We bought them for a dollar each from Merle Temple who ranched west of Cottonwood. Earl came to get us. We put our four smallest bums in a root cellar dug into a hill northeast of the house so they wouldn't get lost. We loaded the chestnut mare and Laddie in his truck and headed for his place. Earl and his wife lived in the only cave house I ever saw that had people living in it. Mrs. Morgan was a dark haired, French lady, wearing bib overalls. Her house was as clean as a house with sifting dirt walls could be. The floor was hard packed as a slab of concrete. She swept it every day, which was more that we did our lovely wooden house.

Mrs. Morgan cooked a fine dinner with potatoes, gravy and canned beef, and we were hungry. After dinner we were on our way, driving Earl's horses twenty miles over hill and dale. By the time we arrived at his place, the sun had set, and stars were twinkling overhead.

Earl's new house was a board shack about fourteen feet square, sitting on a small knoll above a creek. The boards ran up and down with battens over the cracks. No wall board graced the walls. No tar paper helped hold out the wind. Mrs. Morgan moved from her cave into the board shack. Her cave was cool in summer and warm in winter. This abode promised to be neither, but I never heard her complain. She never went anywhere, not even to town for groceries. She stayed home and waited for Earl to come home from his trucking jobs, usually with more horses for her to care for.

When we got home, we milked the cows that were waiting by the corral gate. We filled our lamb bottles and ran to feed the hungry babies. When I opened the cellar door, only two lambs rushed out baaing for milk. The other two tiny lambs were dead. We didn't get paid for wrangling horses all day, and we lost two lambs to boot. Not a profitable day. It didn't help to have Bill Daly say, "If you ate meat at Earl Morgan's house, it was horse meat." I felt like a cannibal.

Nels Carstensen stopped by and saw the dead lambs. "What's the matter with your lambs?" he asked. "Did they quit eating?" Nels gently chided us when we did something stupid, which was rather often. Mrs. Nels chided us, too, but not so gently.

When I tied Darkie to their corral fence and she slipped her bridle and headed for home, Mrs. Nels said, "Anybody that doesn't have sense enough to put their horse in the corral deserves to walk home." I walked a mile to the closest gate where Darkie waited.

The snow melted, cascading down the river. We planted twenty acres of wheat with the endgate seeder and had sixty acres of corn to plant. Already the spring wind whispered through grass thick and green. Colts kicked and danced across the valley. In Jensen's pasture, we could see Hereford calves frolicking on the hillsides. Our calves were locked in a pen, because we milked the mothers.

We needed four horses to pull the lister and plant corn, but the only broke team we had were Flash and Fly. We tied Mom's bay mares to a log and let them halter break themselves. They made a fine team, trying to do everything right. We tied each mare in turn to Flash's hame and hitched the team to the stoneboat. Flash wouldn't run away, and she got angry when a bronc panicked and tried to bolt. The bronc couldn't run, but being hitched to the rattling wagon the first time nearly scared the hooves off her.

We asked Bill Daly how to teach a bronc not to run away. "Put a'W' on," he said. "A horse can't run with a 'W' on. You can knock her down."

To make a "W", we tied a thirty foot lariat to the bronc's collar, ran the rope through a ring on the bronc's foot, back up through a ring on the center of the collar, down through a ring on the other foot and back to a ring on the other side of the collar. Lee drove the team while I held the lariat end. When the bronc started to run, I pulled the rope and knocked her to her knees. Her teeth hit the ground. A few times of having her front feet jerked from under her, and the bronc acted like she loved to pull the wagon or anything else.

The lister is a great piece of machinery to break horses on. Listing corn is hard work. All day up and down the rows, pulling the lister, throwing the black earth to each side, and the team was happy to stand in the barn and eat hay. I was ready to go to the house and eat supper, then back to the barn to milk cows. After chores, I brought the anvil, a piece of railroad track, to the house, took hammer, punch and copper rivets and mended harness.

I carried baling wire to the field to make emergency repairs, but at night the straps were fixed right.

Uncle Charley's harness was old and dry. Horses kicked at flies, caught a hoof in the harness and "snap!" Broken strap. Sometimes they even broke tugs. We'd have to take the tug to Joe Heidler's Harness Shop and get it fixed. We looked at new harness in the farm catalog and wished.

By the time we had planted sixty acres of corn, Mom's team was working like old timers.We broke another team that summer. We bought a matched pair of two-year-old geldings at the McGrath sale. They were halter broke and gentle as a pair of St. Bernard pups. They promised to tip the scales at close to a ton each when they got their growth. They were expensive. We paid thirty dollars each for them.

When I decided they were a team, I hitched them to the wagon and went to sow crested wheat grass. The Government paid farmers to seed crested wheat grass on farm ground. When I threw the seeder in gear, the gears howled. The seeder blades whirred, and those docile horses went wild. They tore down the field in full flight. I bellowed, "Whoa!" and hauled back on the lines while trying to keep my balance in the wildly bouncing wagon. Crested wheat grass spread out the back. The horses raced toward the river. The trees closed fast. I hauled back hard, and the team slowed to a trot. I turned them before they rammed a cottonwood tree and turned the wagon into kindling.

We had a couple of two-year-olds to break to ride, too. We went to the Koehler farm sale to see how the horses sold. Koehlers lived in the large, white house across Highway 14 from the Powell turnoff. They were moving to Washington to see if it was better than South Dakota, but I guess it wasn't because they came back.

A bay and white paint filly caught our eyes. She had one enlarged hock from a wire cut, but she wasn't lame, so we bought her. We took out our last twenty dollar bill and debated about spending our last dollar on a horse, but decided somebody would give us food before we starved. We bid our last dollar and owned our first pinto.

John Cowan, an old fellow living three miles north of our place, offered to lead her home for us. He said he would have bought her, if she hadn't had a bad hock. John didn't own a car. He drove his team everywhere. He drove down the wagon trail past our house when he went to Philip. We were anxious to get our saddles on the paint and Tuffy.

In April, our sows started to pig. We made pens in the barn so each sow would have a comfortable place to bring forth her litter. The sows not ready to pig ranged outside and ate grain from troughs near the granary. One day, a red sow showed up sick. She had found some tender cockle burr plants and gobbled them down. She came home and died.

Most of the sows pigged normally and loved their cute, squealing babies, but a spotted sow hated hers. As fast as a piglet was born, she ate it. I sat behind her while she finished pigging so I could grab the baby before she did. I stayed with the sow while Lee made supper. She cooked a pot of bacon, corn and potato chowder. She ate and left the kettle on the back of the range, bubbling away while she came to the barn to relieve me.

I hurried to the house, hungry as a coyote pup. Lee made delicious chowder. I dipped a bowl and sat down to enjoy it. I took a spoonful and nearly choked. The chowder tasted horrible. I told Lee I had never tasted anything so disgusting. She looked mystified. "It tasted all right when I ate," she said. She took a spoonful and nearly gagged. "It's horrible, all right," she said.

We discovered that when she took the lid off the kettle to get her stew, she set the lid on a bar of soap. When she picked the lid up, the soap stuck to it and dropped into the chowder. I ate peanut butter and bread. We saved most of the little pigs from their cannibalistic mother. She later decided she loved them.

When our sows were all pigged out, we had about seventy porkers running around getting fat. Our turkeys and chickens were growing fast as they followed their mothers around the barn yard. The hens showed their babies how to catch bugs and grasshoppers.

A hen with little ones is absolutely fearless. She'll fly in the face of the largest hog, cow or horse. The hens put the run on Ginger early. He found out their claws and beaks were sharp. He walked a wide circle around them. As for the hens, dogs like Ginger were hardly worth ruffling a feather for. Geese were even worse. An angry gander would send Ginger screeching for shelter in a cloud of dust. Our farm was alive with babies of one kind or another, pigs, colts, calves, and poultry.

On the seventh of May, a drizzle began to fall. I put Darkie in the hog pen because she was due to foal, and the pen was empty. She rubbed the gate open in the night and headed for the shelter of the woods along the river. The rain turned to snow. By morning, the ground was buried. I slogged through the deep, white powder looking for Darkie. I found her beside the river bank. The river was running four feet deep. Her foal had fallen over the bank and drowned.

With 1942, the long dry spell was completely broken. Heavy rains fell in May. Bad River roared by out of its banks and washed out the Bad River bridge east of Midland, causing the bridge to collapse into the river. Mitchell Creek flooded and took out the bridge east of the Midland stockyards.

Herb got a job building dams for Heinie Koch while awaiting induction into the Air Force. He would be a cat skinner and move dirt with a big scraper. He was set to make more money than he ever had before, but he didn't build a single dam. So much rain fell in May and June that the cats sat and rusted. He went to Fort Meade to be inducted into the Army Air Force in June. Shortly thereafter, he left by train for Texas.

Lee and I bought two Geurnsey heifers, planning to have more good milkers. When we worked stock, Nels, Jack and Lucille Carstensen helped us. Jack and Lucille and their small children, Chuck and Doris lived a half mile upriver from Oldenbergs. Nels and Ethel Carstensen were Jack's parents and lived a half a mile further up the river where Nels had homesteaded. They were wonderful neighbors.

The Les Watson family lived a mile south of our place in the breaks between the North and South Forks of Bad River. About a mile further south, the Walker homestead stood on a windy flat. Nestled against the South Fork was the Claude Ramsey ranch headquarters. We got to know everybody for miles around in the years we lived on the North Fork.

Nels and Jack came down and helped dehorn our new heifers. Nels liked to do his work by the signs of the zodiac. He told us when to dock lambs so they wouldn't bleed. He must have been right because it worked, except on one of the heifers. The sign was just changing, and she bled to death. Nels helped us butcher the heifer, and we had to hurry and can the meat before it spoiled. There were no freezers.

When school was out, we went to the school picnic at Ramseys. Mrs. Ramsey said we could bring pork and beans. I wondered if she thought we couldn't cook. Pork and beans was fine with us. We could buy a large can for fifteen cents. We didn't even have to cook them. We just opened the can and poured the beans into a large bowl. Dottie Jensen rode over one day with her small dog trotting beside her horse. The dog ran through the hole in the screen door into the entryway. Back arched and tail fluffed to magnificent proportions, the mother cat met him, a spitting fury. She clawed his face. He howled and turned tail. He bolted through the hole in the screen door. The mother cat streaked after him. She leaped on his back and rode him down the hill. He yipped with every jump. Halfway down, he rolled. The cat jumped off. He scrambled to his feet, and she jumped on his back again. She rode him to the barn, jumped off and marched back to the house.

We asked Dottie to haze for us so we could ride our broncs. She agreed. Lee saddled Tuffy and I saddled Redwing, the paint filly. Lee handed Dottie a strap. "If one of the horses starts to buck, whack his rump with this strap." Dottie took the strap, and we headed east across the meadow. Dottie rode between us, keeping a wary eye on both broncs.

We kicked our horses into a trot. Redwing ducked her head and pitched. Tuffy looked at Redwing, bowed his neck and bucked in the opposite direction. Dottie sat on her horse, watching the rodeo. When we got our horses under control, Lee asked, "Why didn't you pop the horses on the rump, Dottie?"

"They were both bucking," Dottie said, "I didn't know which one to hit."

They broke out gentle. Tuffy was Lee's horse, and a first rate cow horse. He could, as Mom said, "turn on a dime and leave some change." He never grew over fourteen hands, small but mighty. Lee said she could do anything with a little horse that anyone could do with a big one and do it better. Tuffy proved her right many times.

Flowers grew and bloomed in the green grass that carpeted our once barren landscape. American soldiers were going to England and Africa and the South Pacific in ever increasing numbers. Sonny O'Neal from Philip was the first American soldier to set foot on British soil in World War II. We were singing the songs of war: *The White Cliffs Of Dover, Praise The Lord And Pass The Ammunition,* and *When The Swallows Come Back To Capistrano.* Philip still had dances in their auditorium where Ace Hardware is now. In June, Lawrence Welk's Orchestra played for a Saturday night dance there.

Bill Daly took us to meet his Aunt Lena King who lived in a large, square house on what was called Top Bar. Wearing bib overalls, a man's shirt and a cap with ear flaps, she looked like a little, old man. She made us welcome and invited us in for dinner. We walked to the house past a clothes line with cat hides hanging on it. The bed in her living room was covered with cow hides instead of blankets. She fixed a delicious dinner with some of her famous biscuits and gravy.

I traded her a baby goat for a worn Indian blanket. I had always wanted one. She showed us a clock with a wooden base covered with red and green velvet decorated in gold braid. A bull horn protruded from each side and cow hooves graced the stand. A regal, bronze Durham bull marched across the top. The clock peered out from a gilded, lead sunflower. I had to have that clock.

Mrs. King said, "An old man at the stockyards in Sioux City made that clock. It doesn't run anymore." I offered to trade her a white billy goat, and we made the swap. I bought a new time piece and replaced the old one. Today, my daughter, Deanna, has the eighty-year-old clock on her mantle.

We drove to the pasture to look at Mrs. King's herd of around fifty horses. Tom Stalley told us that Mrs. King liked to trade horses. He didn't tell us that she was much too shrewd for us. We got out of the pickup to inspect the herd of many sizes and colors.

I picked out a small gray and said, "I like that little gray. Is he sound?" Stupid question number one.

"He's all right," Mrs. King said, and moved away to point out a horse to Lee.

"You don't want that horse," Bill said. "He has thoropins."

"What are thoropins?"

"See those little bumps like marbles on each side of his hocks. Those are thoropins." I saw them. Lesson number one.

"But she said he was sound," I said.

"No, she didn't. She said he was all right." Lesson number two.

My eye was next attracted to a trim, black and white paint mare. We made a deal; Mrs. King was richer, and we had a paint mare we didn't need. Mrs. King pointed out a small, roan gelding she wanted broke to ride. She also had a black and a roan she wanted broke to harness. We foolishly took three horses to break that were wild as antelope.

We wondered how we were going to get our wild bunch home. Bill said, "Tie one horse to the other's tail. They can't get away from you because they'll have to run in the same direction. By the time you get home the trailing horse will be halter broke." Another wild west trick, and it worked, kind of. We saddled Darkie and Laddie and went after the horses. We tied the big roan to the black's tail. I would never do that again. It was brutal.

Mrs. King said, "You could leave the paint mare here till she gets some grass in her belly and is stronger." We didn't want to come back after her. We tied her to the little roan's tail and headed southwest. The little roan and the paint mare ran west. The other two headed south. I galloped after them. Lee pursued the other pair, and we parted company. I kept my horses headed mostly south until I came to Bernard O'Connell's place about sundown. I had no idea where Lee was.

Bernard and his mother lived about eight miles north of our place, so I stayed the night. Bernard asked if I had any saddlehorses for sale. I sold him a bay three-year-old named Warrior. Warrior was Darkie's brother. Bernard loved his horse.

Lee ran into the Clement's sheep camp a few miles west of O'Connells, after dark. A rain storm had come up, and the horses ran up to the sheep wagon and stopped. She hollered until old Bill Harry opened the door. He was dressed for bed in his long handled underwear. He held his lantern high and peered through the darkness at her. She asked where she could find the main ranch.

"No need to go there, son," he said. "Just light and come in. You can sleep with me."

She said she believed she'd go over to the main ranch. He shook his head and told her where the main ranch was. She stayed there the night, and we got home about the same time. We tied the black and the little roan to the log to halter break them. The poor black's tail had been nearly jerked off by the big roan. He got even. He didn't want to go into the black hole beyond the barn door, so I tied him to my saddle horn and tried to drag him through it. He laid back and pulled the horn out of my Duhamel saddle. Lee fastened the horn back, but I never tied onto anything with it again.

Mrs. King was right about the paint mare. The trip was too much for her. She lived about a week. She hadn't had hay all winter, so she died, gobbling green hay.

I started riding the little roan. He didn't buck, but he bolted every time he got scared. Bill Daly had some old cowboy advice. "Twist his head around to your foot. A horse can't run or buck with his head sideways."

The next time Roany bolted, I jerked his head around to my left foot and nearly threw him on his head. Now I knew how the stunt men threw horses in the movies.

Mrs. King's black horse broke easily, but the roan was suspicious, high strung and unpredictable. I knocked him on his head a few times, and he learned not to run away, but he didn't like us. He was always tight on the bit. I hitched him to the mower with Flash, and they made the mower hum. When I broke a pitman stick or sickle bar, Lee took it to George Owen's Blacksmith Shop for repairs. We had to pitch hay onto the rack and pitch it off until the haymow was full. Two loads a day was the limit.Nels Carstensen taught me to start haying in June while grass is still lush and green. I had bought a load of hay from him when we first arrived. We pitched green hay from his stack. I had never seen green hay before.

"You have to cut hay early while it's tender and green," Nels said. "Then it will stay green."

Dad and Uncle Walt and most farmers mowed late. In 1942, the wheat grass grew taller than my saddle stirrups. Late hay was green, but rank. Hay makers from Nebraska came to the Midland area to cut and bale hay to haul back to Fort Robinson for the cavalry horses. They said western South Dakota hay was the best horse hay in the world. They taught the ranchers how to make hay.

The first week in June, we went to Midland to an Open House for Aunt Tina and Uncle Charley to help them celebrate their 50th wedding anniversary. They had lived in the Midland area for thirty-five of those years. The day was sunny. The crowd of relatives and friends spilled into the yard. The Midland Mail said, "All of Midland was there." The crowd was huge. I met relatives I didn't know I had. I saw my mother walk without crutches for the first time in three years. She proved Dr. Riggs wrong. She never used them again.

Also in June, my schoolmate from Liberty, Verlyn Hagan, married Esther Peterson. Petersons were homesteaders who lived a bit over a mile up Mitchell Creek from our little rancho. Esther's mother and father had been on Mitchell Creek since pioneer days. John Peterson came to America from Denmark, landing in Pierre in 1890. He helped drive a herd of cattle from Pierre to the Midland area and never left.

Essie's Uncle Ham McCready died in February, and, in September, Aunt Tina and Uncle Charley moved into into her small house two blocks north of Main Street in Midland.

The summer of 1942 changed our world. The long years of drought were over. Every farmer and rancher wore a smile from ear to ear. The grass stayed green all summer. We slogged through mud,watched the river run, and loved it.

Bum lambs.

Cadet Herb Martin at Air Force Training School.

The team we bought at the McGrath sale and broke to work that summer.

CHAPTER 10
The Black Appaloosa

Our corn and wheat grew beautiful and tall with heavy wheat heads and corn ears hanging down. The barley crop on our Midland farm looked like a bumper crop coming on. The summer of 1942 was one of pouring rain and violent thunderstorms.

A man and wife were driving home from the hayfield with team and hayrack. Lightning flashed and hit the hayrack. The bolt killed the farmer and one horse. His wife and the other horse were unharmed.

Fifteen-year-old Harvey Ericson was riding north of Powell when a storm caught him. He was riding in Curt Anderson's new Porter saddle. Lightning hit Harvey killing him and the horse and tearing the saddle to shreds.

So much rain fell that Bad River raged out of its banks about once a week. Bad River flooded Midland, then Mitchell Creek roared down half a mile wide and flooded Main Street so deep that Hazel Petoske rowed a boat up the street right between the flooded hotels, restaurants, stores and post office.

Bill Daly showed up one day with a lovely Thoroughbred mare riding in the box of his pickup. She was solid bay, and the best looking saddle mare I had ever seen. This time Bill didn't want to trade. He wanted money, fifty dollars, for his bay mare. We said we didn't have fifty dollars, but, if he wanted to wait until fall when we sold hogs, we would buy her.

Bill didn't want to wait. "Go down to the bank," he said. "Lovald will loan you the money." We hadn't thought of that. Banks are full of money. Mr. Lovald was happy to loan us fifty dollars, although he frowned on using the money to buy horses. As long as we had cows and hogs to cover the loan, he let us have money. We had learned the joy of borrowing. The joy of paying it back, plus eight percent interest would come later.

Bill said the mare's name was Sugar. She was five years old and broke gentle. A matter of opinion, I found. I threw my saddle on Sugar and mounted. She moved as easily as if she walked on eggs. I had never ridden a horse like her. We should have stopped there, but we had large dreams. We wanted twenty-five saddle type mares, twenty-five draft type and a hundred cows. The horses were our first priority. We set about collecting horses, and they were easy collectables. We should have collected cows.

A couple of days later, I saddled Sugar, took my hammer and rode down the creek to fix fence. I tied Sugar to a post while I worked. A blustery wind blew, ruffling Sugar's mane and her disposition. A couple of hours later, I mounted to go to dinner. Sugar squealed and leaped into the air. I dropped my hammer, grabbed the saddle horn and hung on. When she had the kinks out of her back, I got off, found my hammer, mounted and rode to the barn. Sugar taught me that all broke horses aren't like Darkie. I learned to keep Sugar's head up till she got the hump out of her back and never to kick her into a lope until she was warmed up.

Fall slipped in with gold and orange. The wind whispered through grass still lush and tall, and Bill Daly showed up with more horses to sell. "I got a good horse in the stockyards. Come down and look at him."

Of course, we dropped what we were doing and went to look at his horse. Henry Brady was there, too, with horses to trade. Bill introduced us. He looked at me as I sat on the corral fence, looking at the horses. "I knowed her when she was sucking her ma," he said. I was so embarrassed I nearly fell off the fence.

Bill's horse was a two-year-old black Appaloosa with a trim build, a few wisps of mane and a tail without much more hair than a mouse's tail. His mean eyes regarded us with suspicion and malice. I wasn't worried. I didn't figure there was a two year old born that I couldn't ride.

We dealt for Bill's Appaloosa. He hauled the wild eyed colt to our corral and unloaded. I couldn't wait to get my saddle on him. I thought I could ride about anything with four legs and hair if I locked my spurs in and took a choke hold on the saddle horn. At least in the round corral, I could. I was about to embark on an adventure I would never forget.

We were learning more about how to break horses the easy way. We buckled Lee's chaps to the saddle pommel and let Appy buck and tear around the corral until he was through stirring up the dust. I mounted and rode him around the corral. He didn't offer to buck. He walked and trotted like he'd been ridden all his life.

Lee got on Darkie and snubbed Appy to the saddle horn with about two feet of rope like Bill Daly said to do. It worked much better than hazing with a strap. I mounted and we headed west. "Let's ride over to Oldenbergs," Lee said. I agreed. I would trust Lee and Darkie to snub for me anytime. Darkie knew exactly what she was doing. If the bronc crowded too close, she raised a hind leg and whacked his chest. That startled the bronc out of whatever devilment was running through his pointy, little head.

Riding at a walk, we skirted the corn field. About halfway there, Lee decided to give Appy a little more rope. She let him out on about four feet of rope and kicked Darkie into a trot. Appy trotted beside Darkie for a short distance, then threw his head up. The pointed bone between his ears slammed against my left eye, splitting the eyebrow. He ducked his head and began to buck.

Lee jerked him off balance and took up the slack in the rope. Blood ran down my face. Appy couldn't get his head down so he quit bucking. We rode to Oldenbergs and went into the house. Phyllis gave me water to wash the blood off my face.

The little girls were impressed with my battle scars. Gladys, who was four, ran around saying, "Timmie got bucked off, Timmie got bucked off," to my annoyance. I explained that I hadn't fallen off, but she didn't believe me.

Warren Walker rode by looking for cattle that had strayed. I said, "How about taking a ride on my appaloosa, Warren?" I showed him Appy standing in the corral, looking malevolent. "Ride Appy and I'll help you look for your cows."

He said, "Sure," and transferred his saddle to Appy. Appy stood perfectly still and watched Warren out of the corner of one wicked eye. Warren swung aboard. I held my breath. Nothing happened.

I mounted Darkie, and we headed for Jensen's pasture to search for his strays.We kicked our horses into a trot, then a lope. Appy traveled right along. We rode for miles. Appy trotted and loped over hill and dale like he'd been ridden for ten years. We didn't find any strays, and we went home without mishap.

"He's a pretty good horse," Warren said as he took his saddle off Appy and put it on his own horse.

I figured if Appy wouldn't buck with Warren, he wouldn't buck with me. Just to be sure, I tied his left hind foot up in a scotch hobble so he could barely walk on it, like Uncle Alvin said. Against my better judgement. I mounted.

Walking like a frozen-toed rooster, Appy gimped around to the north side of the barn. Then before I could even get set good, he exploded like a keg of dynamite. I grabbed the saddle horn and clamped my right hand on in a choke hold. Appy went high and hit the ground hard. On the second jump, he launched me like a missile. I lit rolling and got up wondering how he did that.

I looked at my bleeding hand. The naked saddle horn had split my palm from the thumb to the little finger. I looked at Appy. His gimped up foot now rested firmly on the ground. He stared at me, and his look said, "I'm too smart to buck with somebody I can't throw, but don't think you can ride me, stupid."

I never got on that brute again. Like the cowboy in "The Strawberry Roan", I had learned, "There are horses that I cannot ride. There are some of them living, they haven't all died."

I traded Appy back to Bill Daly. He traded the wiley bronc to his brother, Maurice. Appy threw Maurice and broke his arm. I don't know what happened to Appy next, and I don't care.

In August, Lee went to Midland and hired Fred Holden to combine our barley and haul it to the North Fork. One of our neighbors ground the barley, and we stored it in the granary. We had ample feed for our hungry hogs. George Oldenberg cut our wheat with his binder, and we stacked it at the south side of the field. The Reynick brothers threshed the wheat. Between the wheat and the hogs, we got enough money to pay Forsell $200.00 for the next year's rent. We let the cattle and hogs harvest the corn ears that hung down, heavy and yellow.

George's cows liked to help harvest the corn. I ran them out of the field and back to Oldenbergs. "I got a couple of fence crawlers," George said. "I'll fix them so they can't get through."

He nailed some lx4's into picture frames and hung them around the fence crawler's necks. The cows reached and fell through the fence, dragging a hundred feet with them. The whole twenty head marched along, heading for our cornfield.

I caught George's cows nibbling corn one afternoon and ran them home and locked them in his corral. George and Phyllis came home from town after dark. They were happy to find their cows in the pen waiting to be milked. My temper cooled down when Phyllis thanked me for putting their milk cows in the pen so they didn't have to look for them in the dark.

Our pigs got even with George. They went right past our corn field and found his canefield west of his house. I got up early one morning and there was nary a pig in sight. I poured ground barley into the troughs and took my best hog calling stance. "Sooey, sooey, sooey, here piggies." I called in a voice that should have reached at least half a mile. No hogs came running.

I saddled Darkie and headed for Oldenbergs with Ginger trotting beside the horse. Ginger was good for one thing--chasing hogs. He loved to tear after pigs, yodeling at the top of his voice. We found the pigs, all seventy of them, busily tearing George's cane shocks apart. The cane shocks were scattered like tiny tipis across a forty acre field. Our hogs were trying to destroy the entire village.

Darkie galloped around the field with me yelling like a Lakota warrior and Ginger baying retreat, loud and clear. The hogs stampeded out of the field and bolted for home. One red sow ran under a shock and carried it halfway across the field before she lost it. Phyllis came out on the porch and yelled as she watched the pigs tear past. The thundering herd raced past the barn. They tumbled and slid down the high shale bank.

By the time I rode to the gate and back to the river, the hogs had disappeared. Not a hog was in sight. I couldn't hear a sound. The pigs were hiding in the weeds and brush that grew as high as a horse's back, weeds and brush so thick I couldn't see five feet into it. The hogs were in there, standing as still as a marble statues and just as silent.

Ginger put his nose to the ground on a pig trail and ran, baying, down the river. I could hear his bell like tones ring out every time he hit the ground until, suddenly, he ran head first into the rear end of a pig. With a startled "Whoof!", the pig tore headlong for home. Ginger didn't miss a pig. He took the pigs home whoofing and squealing, where they crowded around the feed troughs and gobbled barley.

Mom came to visit us as did Aunt Tina and Uncle Charley. Mickey came and stayed a couple of weeks and so did Buddy. We took Mickey to Rapid City, catching a ride, and went to the Sales Barn where we bought a huge gelding, as though we needed any more horses. We stayed overnight in Rapid City. Nobody made the trip in one day. About the only places to stay were The Harney Hotel and The Alex Johnson which were always full. We usually had to spend the night in the lobby of one or the other. The lobbies were always full of soldiers also looking for a place to stay. If one was lucky one got one of the over-stuffed chairs.

The sidewalks were crowded with soldiers. Mickey had never seen soldiers before. She stared so hard at men in uniform that she almost walked off the sidewalk. We teased her about walking with one foot in the gutter to get away. One soldier walked up to the cute twelve-year-old and asked for a date. Mickey hid between me and Lee, and he went down the street grinning.

That fall our pump quit. The livestock could drink from the dam or river, but we drank from the well. George said, "The leather is probably wore out." He said we'd have to pull the pump to put in a new leather. Carl Jensen helped us. We put a couple of 2x6 planks across the hole while we fixed it. Some inquisitive pigs came snooping and pushed the planks into the well. We looked at the boards floating on the dark water, thirty feet below and wondered how we were going to get them out.

"I'll go down and get them," Lee said. I looked at her like she was crazy. Money wouldn't have got me down in that well. "There's nothing to it," she said. "I can brace against the sides of the well and go right down. I'll grab the boards and bring them up."

I still thought she was crazy, but Lee wasn't afraid of much except rattlesnakes, and I hardly gave them a thought. She tied a hay rope around her waist and climbed into the well. Bracing her back against one wall and her feet against the other, she inched her way down about twenty feet. She said the air was bad. I peered into the well. "You better come back up and leave those darn boards."

She climbed slowly, a foot at a time while I took up the rope. Halfway up, she stopped to rest. I was worried. I couldn't pull her out. She had to climb out. She began climbing again, andwhen her head finally came out of the hole. I grabbed her belt and tipped her out where she gulped good, fresh air.

By the next morning, I had thought of a way to get the boards. I fastened a pitch fork to my lariat and dropped the fork into the well. The fork plummeted down and plunked into a plank. I pulled the plank out and speared the other one. Carl helped us put the pump back, and we had water again.

Aunt Tina and Uncle Charley came to visit in October. The river was down so they could drive across. Aunt Tina told us that Uncle

Alvin had married Ethlyn Curtis. They were married in the Catholic Rectory by Father Sweeney. After a honeymoon in The Black Hills, they were at home on the Bertelson ranch.

The Midland Mail said, "Mr. Bertelson is a prosperous rancher living south of town." Actually, he lived west of town and prosperity was in the pen of the writer. He had bought his ranch back from The Federal Land Bank and built his cow herd to over a hundred good Hereford cows. He owned a Ford sedan that was only a few years old and was the proud owner of a new Farmall M tractor. He was doing well.

Buddy and Mickey started high school in Midland in September. Dora Waitman, their teacher at Liberty, had advanced Mickey to eighth grade so, at twelve-years-old, Mickey was a freshman at Midland High. She stayed with Aunt Amanda and Uncle Walt. Buddy rode a horse to school from Bertelsons.

Bill Daly came out with a Percheron mare that he wanted to deal us. She was a beauty. He wanted $50 for her. We didn't have $50 but, since we were acquainted with the wonderful world of high and low finance, we went to Mr. Lovald at The First National Bank and borrowed it. Mr. Lovald loaned us money and gave us good advice which we foolishly ignored. Big Bertha, as we named her, was worth every penny.

Lee got sick that fall. She had been stricken with rhuematic fever when she was about seven. Now, sixteen years later, her heart started jumping and bouncing like a caged bird trying to escape. I wrote to her parents, and Frank immediately drove out to get her. He brought Dolly and Fern Hefte, the lady we picked tomatoes for, with him. Fern wanted to see our place, and Dolly stayed to help me.

Mickey on a colt, wearing Lee's chaps and being a cowgirl.

Buddy Martin and Cloudy, a horse he broke, standing in front of Dad's barn.

CHAPTER 11
Winter Comes To The North Fork

The doctor put Lee in bed at her parent's house for six weeks. She was not to get up for any reason. It was probably the most boring six weeks of her life.

Dolly and I hauled tons of hay. We rose early, milked the cows, fed the hogs, hitched the team to the haywagon and bounced merrily to the field. We pitched hay on the rack, then rested on the load as the team trotted home. I pitched the hay into the mow, and Dolly pitched it back. Forsell had hired Ernie Cooper to extend the haymow all the way to the ground. That haymow held a pile of hay, and we handled it all at least three times. Dolly wasn't used to such heavy work, but she labored in the hot haymow, pitching fork after fork full of hay back to make room for more.

Ernie had worked on the barn during the summer. He was on a ladder about twenty feet in the air when I was cleaning the barn. A colt ventured in. I shooed the colt. He bolted out the door, hitting the door frame a healthy pop. The jolt knocked Ernie's ladder about a foot away from the wall. The ladder teetered, then bounced against the barn wall. Ernie never said a word, but his tan lightened up several degrees.

When the mow was filled, we rolled the rest of the hay into a stack south of the barn, a much easier task. We were both happy when the haying was finished. It was cause for celebration. We went to The Gem Theater in Philip to see *Gone With The Wind.*

We watched the North and South killing each other for two hours, then, had a half hour intermission. People who could afford it went to a cafe for lunch. The crowd returned for another two hours of the longest movie I had ever seen. The best thing that came out of the movie or the book, for me, was when Scarlett's father told her, "Hang onto the land, it's the only thing that lasts."

Dolly boarded the train and went home when Lee was through with her bed rest, and I was alone for a few days. I had a couple of Stahl horses and Flash tied in the barn, feeding them hay like an Iowa farmer when I should have left them in the pasture to run off steam and mow their own hay. I was driving each of them on the stoneboat with Flash. One wasn't so wild, but the other was big and tough and wild as a buffalo bull.

I had been tying my bronc to a post in the round corral and squeezing him close to the fence with a rope to harness him, but one morning, I decided he should be harnessed in the barn like a good work horse. I took the collar off the peg. "Whoa, boy." I sid-dled up and fastened the collar around his thick neck. He rolled his eyes, shivered and shrunk against the wall. I took the harness down.

He watched me, eyes wary. "Easy now." I threw the harness on his back. He jumped at me and knocked me flat. He stomped on my left leg and jerked back. The harness slid off his tail. He stood against the wall, shaking like a leaf in a high wind. Fortunately, he didn't wheel and kick. He taught me that if a horse lives to be four years old without wearing a halter you had best leave him that way. I got up and staggered out of the barn, leaving the harness where it lay. I limped to the house and nursed my wounds until milking time. I did break that beast to work, very carefully.

Lee came home on the train. She was allowed to walk around a bit, but was not supposed to ride a horse or do any work. She spent a lot of time sleeping that winter.

In early November, we needed to get our turkeys picked and delivered to market. I'd never picked a turkey before. We had about two hundred of the big birds running around the barn yard, squawking, gobbling and eating. The Reynick brothers went through, hunting, one day. They were hungry so we fed them dinner, and they spent a few hours picking turkeys. When they left, we had about a hundred naked turkeys and a hundred still running around, eating corn. Les Watson said he would help me finish the job, so we picked the rest of the birds, but it was a horrible job. I sold every turkey on the farm, and we never raised another one.

Nylon was invented. The tough fiber was used to make colorful parachutes for the Air Forces and stockings for ladies, making silk stockings obsolete. The Government lowered the draft age to eighteen. The only young men left here were agricultural deferments or 4F Charleys as guys were called who didn't pass the physical. The cream of America's young men went off to fight "The War to end all wars and make the world safe for democracy."

Lee thought we should trap skunks. Since she wasn't supposed to walk much farther than from the bed to the table, I got to run the trapline. After a couple of months, I quit. I didn't care if skunks were worth a buck a piece or maybe a buck fifty. Trapping was the wickedest way to catch an animal I had ever seen. I could stand it no longer.

January 2, 1943, Maurice Sorenson, our neighbor down the river, married Helen Franklin. The paper complained that all the good mechanics had gone to war, and no one was left to keep farm trucks and tractors operating.

Jake Weber wanted to buy 80,000 cottontails. He offered seven cents each for the little bunnies, but we didn't shoot any. At the Annual President's Ball January 30 in the City Auditorium, a nickelodeon furnished the music for the dancers. Most of the muscians had gone to war.

The middle of January, the weather was still balmy. I rode Laddie and led a team to Dad's farm to get a wagon that Uncle Alvin gave us. The sun shone on a perfect winter day. The air felt like October, not January. I tied Laddie behind the wagon and drove home.

The next morning, we awoke to a raging wooly whipper. The

wind screeched, moaned and screamed around the eaves. I looked out the window and couldn't see the barn or the trees along the creek or the North Fork. The world outside was a wall of solid white. We stayed inside the house for most of three days and listened to the wind roar past, glad our cows and hogs were in a warm barn. When the wind died, and the sun came out, our world was glittering white to the far horizon in every direction. We were almost buried in snow. I struggled through the drifts to the barn to feed the hungry livestock.

Roads were blocked. The county didn't have good snow plows to keep roads open. I borrowed a pack saddle and put it on the huge horse we bought in Rapid City. I saddled Laddie and headed for Philip, leading my pack horse. Laddie lunged through belly deep drifts for much of the eight miles. Copps Market had ten oranges for thirty-one cents so I bought a dozen. They called them victory food, and I was hungry for oranges. I loaded my groceries on my giant pack horse and went to the post office to pick up our mail. The postmaster asked if I would take mail for the neighbors on the North Fork.

I said, "Sure. Load it on." He put the mail in a gunny sack and tied the sack to the pack saddle. The sun was slipping low as I headed out of Philip. By the time I had gone a mile one of the sacks had jiggled open. Oranges dribbled to the ground. My giant horse plunked a giant hoof on every orange, squashing them into the snow. He plodded on his way, and I made it home with only two oranges. Dark was closing in, and I was cold.

We took our mail out of the sack, and, the next day, I delivered the mail sack to George Oldenberg. George took their mail and gave the sack to Jack Carstensen. The mail sack traveled up the North Fork until all the mail was delivered.

The temperature dropped to thirty below, but, by February 2, the sun warmed us up to fifty-seven degrees. All of February was warm. The snow melted and began to run into the North Fork.

The cows got into the hay yard and undermined the haystack. The stack toppled over on a couple of white pigs. A month later, I pitched some hay off the stack, and the two white pigs walked out. They waddled off to the feed trough to put some grain in their gaunt bellies.

Buddy and Mickey were on the honor roll at Midland High School. Julian was transferred to the Ellsworth Air Base near Rapid City and changed her name to Judy. She married Master Sergeant John Sanford. They set up housekeeping in an apartment in Rapid City. Fighters and bombers flew over day and night. I counted ninety-six B-17 bombers in formation one day. Whenever we went into a cafe, someone put a nickel in the nickelodeon, and the songs of war poured forth.

Spring was coming to the North Fork. Water ran down the river, and we looked for new babies to come to barnyard and prairie.

Timmie and Buddy Martin carrying hog feed on North Fork Farm. The bags of feed are not as heavy as they look.

Mickey playing with a foal at Forsell place on North Fork.

Hank Martin in his dress uniform about ready to go overseas.

Lt. Herbert Martin in Italy during WWII.

Hank Martin and army trucks when he was in Basic Training, about 1942.

CHAPTER 12
Spring Comes Again

In March, Oldenbergs moved from the Babcock place to a farm near Cottonwood, belonging to George's brother, Shorty. We missed them. Warren Walker moved onto the Babcock place. Our five cows had calves. Colts romped in the pasture. All kinds of new babies played around the farm. We had chicks, goslings and cute baby ducks, but not turkeys.

Lee hired Earl Morgan to haul a load of draft horses to Iowa even though Frank said the market was poor. She climbed in the truck and went along. She immediately sold the Stahl horses to a farmer friend. The farmer was big and tougher than the horses, and they learned to work on his farm. Frank dealt the other teams off during the summer, but we didn't make much money on them. Frank didn't charge us any pasture, or it would have been worse.

He gave Lee an enormous Belgian stallion that she brought home with her. I had never seen a horse so huge. He almost shook the ground when he trotted, and she needed him like she needed another hole in her head. Bill Daly said, "That is some horse. You'd better get some oats in him, or he'll die." We didn't have oats or money to buy them. The change was too much for the old horse. He only lived about two weeks on good South Dakota hay.

The Lawrence Welk Orchestra played for a dance in the Philip City Auditorium in June. We went to dance, although with so many men gone to war, dance partners were scarce. Many people just came to listen to this band that was destined to become nationally famous.

We thought we needed some more Thoroughbred mares so we hired Earl Morgan to take us to Hans Fogh's ranch in the northwest corner of South Dakota near Buffalo. He raised remount horses for the US Cavalry. Annie Stalley went with us. We bought three aged sorrel mares to foal the next spring. The mares weren't even halter broke. Annie bought a half Shetland, half thoroughbred gelding. Her small gray was a fine saddle horse.

When Curt Anderson saw Annie's horse, he wanted him. "How'll you trade horses, Annie?" he asked.

Annie looked his horse over. "Just like you didn't have one," she said. That set Curt back on his heels, and Annie kept her horse.

We unloaded our mares at home. They found an open gate and headed up the road toward Buffalo. Cliff Brown sent word that he had our mares locked in a pasture. I rode ten miles northwest after them. Cliff's mother gave me dinner, and I chased them home.

One stormy June day, two tornadoes ripped through, leaving a trail of destruction. One went south of us, picked up the Watson house and set it down a few feet away. The large house was smashed down so the top story sat on the ground. Forunately, no one was home.

The other tornado swept through about ten miles north of our place. Charles Brown, his wife and baby daughter and a neighbor and his wife took refuge in the basement. The wind blew the house away. Rain poured down and hail pounded them. The men found a door and held it over the women and baby while hailstones beat their hands black and blue. When the storm was over they took the baby, now blue with cold, to Dr. Schultz. The baby recovered, but Mr. McGrath was not so fortunate. He was killed when a funnel cloud whirled his car high in the air, then dropped it.

By July hay was lush and still bright green. I cut a large land of hay in the north pasture, driving Flash and Mrs. King's ornery roan. Then I hitched the roan with Mom's high spirited bay mare to the hay rake and went to the field to rake some fast hay. I don't know why I did such a foolish thing.

The sun bore down. The horse flys were vicious. (No spray then.) I headed the team around the field. The thick hay rolled into windrows. The bay mare kicked constantly at the flies that stung her belly. Her left hind foot came down on the wrong side of the tongue. Frightened, she kicked and tried to run. The roan panicked. Instead of baling backward off the seat, I tried to stop the team. The tongue broke with a loud snap. The sharp end jammed into the ground, catapulting me into the air. I lit behind the roan, between his hind feet and the single tree.

"I'm dead," I thought as his hind foot lashed out to deal me a grazing blow on the left side of my head. I remembered no more as I rolled along, caught in the rake teeth.

I regained consciousness standing behind the rake. The horses, still hitched to each other, but not to the rake, faced the machine. My left arm was bleeding where a rake tooth had gone through the flesh, dragging me behind it until the tooth ripped free, leaving a two inch gash in my upper arm. My gaurdian angel must have been holding the lines. The horses stood quietly. They were still waiting patiently when Lee came after them hours later.

I was dazed and disoriented. I knew I needed to go home and get to a doctor. I walked east to the fence so I would be easy to find if I fainted. I walked home along the fence, and Lee took me to Dr. Schultz's office in the Senechal Hotel. Dr. Schultz gave me some unpleasant shots and then sewed up the wound before it was deadened. The nurse held my hand and encouraged me not to flinch. The only stitches of the fourteen that didn't hurt were the last three.

Dr. Schultz said, "Now go home and don't do any work for a couple of weeks."

Ole Hauge heard about my accident and came to visit me. He had homesteaded north of Powell in pioneer days.

Mrs. King hired me to break her horses. I broke one to ride and two to drive, kept them for a year, and she paid me $15.00. Dr. Schultz charged me $10.00. I went back to haying too soon and stretched the stitches in my arm so the scar was half an inch wide instead of a thin line.

Warren offered to help me haul hay, if I would help him mow. I hitched Flash and the bay mare to the mower and drove to the hay-field west of his house. The team headed around the field.
Hay fell before the humming sickle. My little five footer was a hay cutting whizzer. Warren's six footer kept breaking down. When I came up behind him, he stopped me to help fix his mower. Nels Carstensen said, "You'd get a lot of hay mowed, if Warren didn't keep stopping you to help him fix his mower."

Warren pitched hay much faster than I could. His hay rack was wider and longer than mine, but he'd fill his rack, then help me fill mine. When I thought I had a load, Warren said, "It'll hold more than that." He'd jump to get the last forks full of hay on the load. Warren was the only person I ever saw lope his team to the field. His hay nearly bounced off the rack.

We filled the barn with hay and built a stack south of the barn. We were ready for winter again. South Dakota hay was moving. Sheldon Reese shipped thirteen carloads of baled hay out of Midland. All the moisture meant good wheat crops. Farmers were making money again, but harvest help was short. Philip business men mobilized to go out and shock grain after the stores closed each day. They left Dorothy Brothers Garage,near sundown in a truck between six and seven o'clock, and headed for the grain fields.

Brother Herb was promoted to First Lieutenant and given a B-24 and crew. He flew his four engine bomber to Florida, then to South America. The next hop landed him in Africa. From there, he flew to Italy and flew bombing raids over Germany. He ran into Major Orville Bentley, also from Midland, in Italy.

Most of the young men I had gone to school with were in the Service. T/3 Henry Martin, my second brother, commanded a landing barge in the Pacific Theater. He piloted the clumsy craft, hauling soldiers from ship to shore often in waves twelve feet high while bombs and mortar shells roiled the water and shook the small islands like a massive earthquake.

Bernard Burns was in the Aleutian Islands. Corporal Glen Crawford was in France. Sergeant Norman Blucher flew crew on a bomber out of England. He wrote a letter to his father, A.W. Blucher, saying, "Don't worry about us, Dad. We don't worry."

Sergeant Thurman Rank was sent to Australia. Seaman 1/C Glen Muirhead was a master cook on a Navy ship. Sergeant Clarence Petoske was sent to France. Paul Sandbo was an Army cook. Lieutenant James Nelson flew a B-24 bomber. Kenneth Anderson went to England and was in the Air Force ground crew. Tom Stalley was in the Navy Sea Bees. He married Betty Seidler while home on leave. PFC Curt Anderson was in the Army infantry in the European Theater. Ensigns Lloyd and Kenneth Olson served in the Navy. Vern "Pete" Anderson was in the Army in the South Pacific. Robert, Mike and Martin Schofield were in the Army as was Edward Seidler. Zane, Charl and Edison Zeiman served in the Navy in the South Pacific. Robert Sturdevant was in the Navy. Corporal David Muirhead and Charles Anderson were in the Army, also my neighbor from grade school days Corporal Thomas Roberts. Lieutenant Charles Oberembt flew a B-24 bomber; Lieutenant Gordon Calhoon flew a Navy fighter. Willard Burns was in the Army. Scott Lovald left the halls of Augustana College and donned an Army uniform.

Young men were, as my mother would day, scarcer than hens teeth. I wrote dozens of letters to boys in the service. I wrote to Herb and Hank, Mike, Willie, until he got married, Pere, Curt, and Ike. I got letters with some of the words blotted out by the sensor, and all with the word FREE written on the place where the stamp was supposed to be. I was doing what Colonel Beckwith urged people to do; write to the soldiers. Mom wrote to many young men that she knew, some neighbors and some former pupils. The boys were always happy to get letters from home to brighten the lonely hard world they lived in.

The war was hitting home. Pete Anderson died at Guadalcanal. Lieutenant Gordon Calhoun was killed when his plane ditched in the ocean. Lieutenant Ben Owens died in Italy. Dean and Stanley Martin from the Ottumwa country were killed in battle. In September, Italy surrendered to General Eisenhower.

We borrowed gas from a neighbor to get home at Christmas.We sometimes used our gas ration stamps before we got new ones. The weather was still all right by New Years, but we still didn't have gas stamps so we stayed home. When January came, the snow piled high again all over western South Dakota. We were blocked in, but we had plenty of hay, we thought.

The end of February approached, and we were still blocked in. Range horses were getting thin. They had to work hard and long, pawing snow away to find the grass. We ran low on hay for our cattle and food for ourselves. The only way we could get to Philip for groceries was on horseback, and eight miles is a long way through deep drifts. Days were short and cold. Warren rode to Philip and brought our mail. We literally didn't have anything left to eat except navy beans. We wished for a bobsled because the snow was too deep for a wagon.

We ran out of chicken feed and borrowed some from a neighbor. John Cowan walked three miles down from his place to borrow chicken feed, but we didn't have any to spare. He walked back home. The next day, he walked eleven miles to Philip and carried supplies home. He said he sank knee deep in snow some places, but most of the time he walked on top. Mom and Dad had cousin Madge's kids, Trudy and Jackie, and were having a hard time getting them to Liberty School.

We heard that a cat and dozer was going to open the road past Carstensens. We were happy to hear the cat roar as it pushed through the snow drifts, opening the road a half a mile west. The next day, I drove the Model A across the prairie, dodging drifts, to the road. Warren caught a ride to Philip. When we got our groceries loaded, Warren said, "I'll buy you a piece of pie."

I said, "Okay." We went into the B&M and slid into a booth. I would only have spared a nickel for a candy bar. The pie cost fifteen cents and was delicious. Warren reached into his pocket and looked foolish. "I don't have any money," he said, so I paid for the pie.

A couple of days later, Jack Carstensen said, "Heard you had lunch with Warren." I agreed that I had. No use trying to keep anything from the neighbors. "Who paid for it?"he asked.

I admitted that I had. Jack and Lucille laughed like crazy. Warren's intentions were good. He just ran out of money like we all did, only I always knew to the last nickel how much money was in my pocket.

The neighbors kidded me for loaning Warren the Model A to go to town, but loaning vehicles was a two way street. Our Ford was broke down so Warren loaned us his made over Buick pickup to go to Midland for Thanksgiving dinner. On the way home, a rod went out eight miles west of Midland, and that was the end of Warren's Buick.

When the snow began to melt and send water cascading down the North Fork, Lee decided she wanted to move back to our Mitchell Creek rancho. I don't know why anybody would want to leave our lovely house and red barn on the North Fork and acres of grass to go back to a tiny shack where you could chase a mouse through the walls, and you only had a piddling hundred and sixty acres of Mitchell Creek breaks, but she did.

She wanted to plant her feet solidly on her own soil. She said we could buy three quarters from Claude and Alice Harren three miles north of our place. With the county land under fence there and our farm, we'd have over a thousand acres, less than we had at the North Fork but handy. We bought the Harren land and prepared to move.

We loaded our furniture on the pickup. Our road to Philip was too muddy for travel so we headed across Warren's pasture to the other road. We got stuck and unloaded half of our furniture on the prairie. When we returned several days later, we found that someone had stolen the antique Maple table that Mom had loaned to us. She was upset. So were we, but it was gone.

Earl Morgan hauled our cows. The only time I ever hitch-hiked with a horse was when Earl pulled up beside me in his truck as I rode up Highway 14, leading a bronc. Earl backed into the ditch. The horses jumped into the truck, and we rode to Philip instead.

We didn't have Ginger anymore. I gave him to Morris Sorenson so he could hunt coons like he was supposed to. Lee was disgusted, but I was happy to see the last of the egg eating little thief. We crated our poultry and moved everything but the horses. Once more I saddled up. I drove the horses down Philip's Main Street again, this time going east as people stood on the sidewalks watching. They saw us come and they saw us go. We rested overnight at Bertelsons and went on to the homestead the next day.

I left Whitefoot, her bay filly and a weak colt on the flat by the river. Whitefoot, full of years and weak in body and spirit, lay down in the meadow and died. She took with her a large chunk of my childhood. Her colt, foolishly, slid down a muddy river bank to get a drink and couldn't get out. The other colt followed, and both were lost to the river. We brought our wagons, disk, mowers and hay rack back to Mitchell Creek. The rest we left on the North Fork. I didn't care if I never planted corn again.

Sergeant John Sanford was transferred to McCook Air Base in Nebraska, so he and Judy moved there. John never went overseas. He spent the rest of the war in McCook. John Lee, their son, was born there in 1944.

Herb was promoted to Captain and squadron leader. He flew fifty-two missions over Germany, twice returning with two motors shot out. They called it "returning on a wing and a prayer." Our neighbor, Glen Crawford, somewhere in France, said he sometimes had to take a bath in his helmet. The Allied Forces had stormed the beaches of France and were heading for Germany to challenge Hitler in his den.

Buddy was riding the new bay mare that Uncle Alvin bought for Essie to school. The bay mare bucked Essie off. Uncle Alvin asked me to ride her for a while, but she didn't buck with me.

Essie tried her best to help Uncle Alvin with the farm work. When he got his M Tractor stuck in the mud, she pushed on a big hind wheel as he tried to back out of the mudhole. The wheel suddenly spun and threw Essie over the top into the mud behind the tractor.

When we got to Mitchell Creek, we turned the horses and cattle into a pasture that was almost knee deep in grass. We swept the house, arranged our meager furniture and built a fire to chase away the chill March air. Then we walked to Steiens to visit Aunt Amanda and Uncle Walt.

Uncle Walt had a new dog. Mac was black with a white chest, white feet, a stub tail and curly hair. He was a handsome dog. "He's half Australian sheep dog," Uncle Walt said. "You can have him."

Wagging his short tail, Mac went home with us. He lived with us for many years and was the best dog I ever had. He had natural cow sense. When I rode through the cow herd, if I told Mac to stay, he lay quietly in the grass, while I checked cattle and came running when I called him. He never bothered anyone unless they touched either of us. Then Mac was right there, a growl in his throat and teeth bared.

We were on our "homestead" again. We had eight cows and six yearlings eating grass. Horses were scattered over the hills. We turned our ducks and geese loose and put the chickens in the small chicken house. The cows hadn't calved yet so we weren't milking. We had sold our hogs. We traded Laddie off because we wanted a Thoroughbred stallion. The sheep were gone, so we didn't have many chores.

Early one morning, a coyote peeked over the hill at the chickens scratching in the dirt. He slipped closer and closer to the unsuspecting hens. With a rush, he nabbed a white hen and streaked for the hills. Lee ran out wih the .22 rifle and shot at the fleeing coyote. He dropped the hen, and the hen ran home.

Buddy was fifteen-years-old and beginning to feel like a bronc buster. He got a colt in and asked Mickey to haze for him, while he rode his bronc. He saddled his horse and Freckles, now old and lazier than she had been. They mounted Freckles, and led Buddy's bronc a half mile east to a field Dad had just plowed. Buddy figured the soft dirt would be a perfect place to take a ride. The bronc's feet would sink into the dirt like he was walking on feathers. He wouldn't be able to buck hard or run fast.

Buddy had been listening to Uncle Alvin's horse breaking tales. Like the cowboys of the old west, he slipped a blind fold on his horse and climbed aboard. He jerked the blind fold off. The horse bolted. He stampeded out of the field and onto the trail, hooves pounding against the ground as he tore for the home corral. A half mile behind, Freckles loped slowly. Disgusted, Buddy watched the old mare lope down the trail and into the corral. He cussed Mickey, but it wasn't her fault. Freckles wouldn't have moved faster if her tail had been on fire.

Buddy brought a bronc down to Uncle Walt's place and asked me to haze for him. We saddled up and led our horses to the rise west of the house. We could head up the hill and have the whole outdoors to ride in. Uncle Walt came to watch the fun. We mounted. I sat on Darkie, my rope ready to whack his bronc on the rump, if he bucked. Buddy kicked his horse, but the bugger was rooted to the ground. He grunted every time Buddy socked spurs into his ribs, but he wouldn't moved off the spot. I tried to ease him into a walk.

Uncle Walt let out a bellow like a wounded buffalo bull and threw his hat. The hat hit the bronc's rear end, and he took off like a scared rabbit. Darkie shot after him. We raced over the prairie, leaving Uncle Walt, the old time cowboy, laughing like a maniac behind us.

Aunt Amanda, at sixty, was out of saddle horses. All of the Steien horses had gone to happier pastures. She wanted a gentle horse to ride. Buddy told her he had a gentle horse she could ride. He brought the horse down for her, but he forgot to mention that the pony was balky. Aunt Amanda saddled up and rode out to find her cows.

The horse moved right along for a mile, then stopped, stock still. Aunt Amanda kicked him. He wouldn't budge. She whipped his rump with the reins and beat a tattoo against his ribs. He stood glued to the ground.

Thoroughly disgusted and madder than a rattlesnake in August, Aunt Amanda walked home, leading the horse. She was slow to anger and soft spoken, but by the time she got home with her mule-headed horse, she was steaming. She told Buddy what she thought of his horse, and what he could do with the beast. She wanted nothing more to do with this imitation of a saddle horse.

Uncle Walt bought a gentle black mare from Carl Nordstrom for her. Carl had sold his ranch and bought a shoe and harness shop in Midland. We bought bridles, cinches and latigoes from Carl and took him horse equipment to repair.

We wandered over to Steiens one afternoon, thinking about the ice cream Aunt Amanda froze in her new kerosene refrigerator. Jack and Luella Rank were visiting there. Jack said he needed someone to live on his ranch and care for his herd of 250 sheep. He and Luella had moved to Midland. Old Mr. Halvorson cared for the sheep, but he didn't want to be a sheepman any longer. Jack said he would give us half of the lambs and half of the wool, and we could use his 2000 acres of grass.

I didn't want to herd sheep. Uncle Walt advised us not to take the deal, but Lee had wool over her eyes. She saw a chance to get into the sheep business, in a big way, a business I had no desire to indulge in again on any scale. Uncle Walt and I lost. We moved to the Rank place, lock, stock and chickens. Lee was about to herd sheep and regret it. Mac didn't mind. He was a born sheep dog.

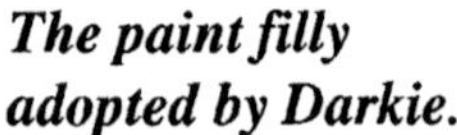

The paint filly adopted by Darkie.

Cpt. Herbert Martin in Casa Blanca Morrocco when he was flying transport during WWII.

Mickey with Cousin Jackie Heibner.

CHAPTER 13
Sheep, Coyotes and Eagles

The Rank ranch had a sprawling barn made from poles, wire, dirt, hay and assorted things. Harnesses hung on the walls, and pigeons nested everywhere. Hanging from a rope, was a bronc saddle without fenders, the best bronc saddle I ever rode. A small house stood across the draw west of the barn with a large dam full of water in the draw. The house had kitchen, living room and two bedrooms downstairs. Upstairs, through a trapdoor, was another bedroom.

The road to Deep Creek Lutheran Church ran past a quarter of a mile west. Hilmoes lived a half mile south. Newbys lived a mile north and Pete Fosheims and Percy Hands lived a couple of miles east. Neighbors weren't thick in the Moenville country. We were thirty miles north of Midland and about fifteen miles northwest of Hayes.

A bunch of foals played in the east pasture. Darkie had a lovely bay filly. We had acquired a club footed bay and white paint mare that gave birth to a beautiful bay and white paint filly. Our foals showed a lot of quality, many from a half Thoroughbred half American Saddle stud, we were keeping for Bill Daly. One of the Fogh mares dropped a handsome chestnut foal. A large gelding, belonging to Newbys, got into our pasture and killed it. I saw the big brute grab the newborn buckskin foal by the neck and throw it ten feet in the air.

I leaped on a horse and chased the monster south into a pasture that had no livestock in it. I shut the gate and left him there. The other two Fogh mares didn't foal. We should have let Hans keep his horses. They never gave us a living foal.

A pair of eagles floated above the farmstead, keeping close watch on our poultry. One eagle swooped down and grabbed a goose that strayed too far from home. The eagle flew north, the goose dangling from his talons. Lee dashed out of the house with .22 rifle and shot at the eagle. The big bird dropped the goose. The goose floated to earth and ran, short legs churning, to the dam.

Lee's dad said she could rent a forty acre field adjoining his farm. Frank had purchased his father's farm from his brothers, Roy and Dewey, in 1944 after Lee's Grandpa Schroader died. He and Ula and Buster moved there in March. Lee hitch- hiked to Iowa and planted forty acres of corn. She hitch-hiked there and back several times that summer to cultivate the corn. Lee never worried about hitch-hiking. She carried a .22 pistol in a shoulder holster, and she knew how to use it.

On one trip, she brought her cousin, Carmen Schroader, home with her. Carmen, with black hair and eyes to match her name, was about three years younger than I. I drove the Model A to Midland to get them. Since it was Saturday, we went to the show and dance, then we went to my parent's house to spend the night. A rain shower had passed by, leaving the dam grade too slick to cross. We left the car on the east end and walked to the house. Halfway across the grade, Carmen slipped and fell into the dam. She lost one shoe, and so she was initiated into South Dakota ranch life. We went home the next day.

Lee had a quart of wine that Aunt Amanda gave her. Someone had given it to Aunt Amanda for Christmas, and she didn't want it. I came into the kitchen and heard Lee and Carmen giggling and plotting to get me drunk on Aunt Amanda's wine. They had popped the cork and were ready to carry out their little scheme. They forgot, I'm not a drinker. Three glasses of lovely, purple wine sat on the living room table. I don't know how many they had con sumed, but they were well on the way to getting sloshed.

I looked happy and sat down by the table. We all sipped our wine and giggled. When no one was looking, I poured my wine back in the jug. Soon they were doing more sipping than looking. The more Carmen and Lee drank, the sillier they got. I kept filling their glasses and they kept emptying them. They forgot who was getting who drunk.

When the bottle was empty, Lee decided to fix supper. She had trouble keeping the frying pan on the stove when she stirred the gravy. After supper, I tried to get them to go to bed, but neither of them was interested. Carmen wanted to go to Hayes and see if there were any people there. Lee thought that was a fine idea.

I was tired. I had worked hard all day, and now I had a pair of clowns that were bent on going to Hayes if they had to walk the whole fifteen miles over hill and valley. When I finally got them both in bed, I was ready to collapse. I was just drifting off when I heard the kitchen door slam. I caught Carmen heading across the prairie toward Hayes. I got her back in the house and Lee took off. I spent most of the night chasing after them when I should have let them go. Lee would have come to somewhere on the prairie and headed home, but Carmen was from the green hills of Minnesota, and I don't know where she would have wandered.

It was a long night. I was more tired when morning came than I'd been that night. I crawled into bed and went to sleep. Lee went to the barn to milk the cows. I was sleeping as peacefully as a baby when Carmen started shaking me and yelling. "You better go see what happened to Lee, Timmie. She's still gone."

I didn't care where she went, but Carmen wouldn't shut up. I went looking for Lee. The combination of milk and wine was too much. Lee was sick. I went back to the house and went to bed. Carmen was asleep. Lee came in with a pail full of water and dumped it on us, so we got up.

Our calves and colts were growing. The lambs were wooly little critters, bucking and jumping as they played. We put the old paint mare and her foal in a pasture by the house so the other horses couldn't bother her until the little filly got huskier. Somehow a couple of horses got in with her. They chased her into the barbed wire fence, and she got cut so badly she died. We didn't know how we were going to feed the tiny foal.

Darkie had lots of milk, so we decided to get her to take an extra baby. We foolishly put Darkie's colt in the round corral so she wouldn't drink all of the milk before evening. The colt ran around and around inside the corral in the hot sun, nickering for her mother. She got overheated and died. Darkie took her new baby and raised it.

Cousin Madge's boy, Jackie, who was nine, came to visit us. Jackie liked everything about farm life. He thought Darkie was huge, but he loved to ride her and see her rear up doing the trick we had taught her. Jackie helped me count the sheep out of the corral each morning, and sometimes he rode with me when I went to turn the sheep back if they got too far from the barn.

In June, Jack Rank sent a young man out to shear the sheep. When the shearing was finished, we helped him pack the wool into the huge wool bags. The shearer grabbed Jackie and said, "I'm going to stuff Jackie in a wool sack." He hoisted Jackie up. Jackie screamed and Mac jumped between them, growling. The shearer dropped Jackie and froze. I called Mac off, and we finished bagging the wool. We didn't get any of the money.

When Jackie decided he wanted to go back to Dad's place, I sent him to Midland with Mail Carrier Frank Dinsmore for two dozen eggs. Trudy came when Jackie left. She was older and could handle her saddle horse. As we rode Blue and Redwing down the long slope beside the graded road one day, Roy Blackmore whizzed past in his gas truck.

Trudy and Blue raced the truck. The paint mare tore down the ditch, nearly flying. Blue shook the bridle off. Trudy raced beside the truck, hanging onto the reins and the saddle horn with the bridle hanging under Blue's neck. I raced behind her unable to do anything about it. Blue turned in at our gate and thundered down the slope, across the dam grade and up to the barn. She stopped and waited for Trudy to dismount. Trudy slid off, grinning, proud of her ride.

When Lee went back to Iowa in mid-summer to cultivate the corn, Buster, now a husky sixteen-year-old, hitch-hiked back with her to help with the haying. I had mowed a quarter of hay a half mile north. Jack had a horse drawn bucker and I bucked the hay into large mounds with the clumsy contraption. A horse was hitched to each side of the bucker, and the driver rode the seat in the middle. I went down the windrow, watching hay pile on the bucker teeth when a rattlesnake bucked up and came down the teeth toward me. I rolled backward off the seat, jumped up and killed the snake.

We drove two hay wagons to the field and pitched the hay on the racks in the hot August sun. We rested, riding the loads home where we rolled the hay into a huge stack beside the barn. Buster was a big help and fun to have around. Lee got upset with us because she didn't think we took hay pitching seriously enough. We weren't supposed to waste our breath on wise cracks or play practical jokes. We were supposed to watch out for rattlesnakes and plod from hay pile to hay pile, loading racks. We did watch out for rattlersnakes, but our exuberance annoyed her. We couldn't help it.

Brother Buddy was working for a hay crew, making more money than he ever had in his life. Mickey was home, helping Mom can vegetables from the Victory Garden, watering and feeding the poultry, going after the milk cows and bossing Trudie and Jackie.

One day, Buster and Lee rode the paint mares to a dam a half mile south to catch bullheads for supper. They caught a fine string of fish and headed home. Buster rode Blue, carrying twenty-two fish that dangled from a stringer. His arm got tired. He let his load sag. A bullhead stung Blue, and she decided to unload. Buster dropped the fish and grabbed the saddle horn. With the fish on the ground, Blue quit bucking. Buster retrieved the fish and carried them carefully home. We fried the fish and ate a delicious supper.

Lee was gone a good bit of the time in June and early July, culti vating the Iowa corn. I stayed home, herded sheep and broke horses. While Lee was home, she went to a horse sale in Whitewood and came home with a bay and white paint stud that she bought from her old friend, Nellie Westerskow. Pronto was two years old, fourteen and a half hands high, and lively as a cricket. He was halter broke and had been ridden a few times in the corral. I was soon riding him on my ranch chores. He was a fine saddle horse, but inclined to be skittish.

If I mounted and forgot to ease him along till the hump came out of his back, or if something frightened him, Pronto ducked his head and unloaded. I learned to start him slow and keep track of the reins, because, if Pronto bucked, I flew through the air like a bird and landed on the ground. I never, ever stayed with Pronto when he bucked. I was riding him at full gallop, chasing horses when he stepped in a badger hole. He went end over end, and I somersaulted through the air. We both got up a bit dazed, but unhurt.

Toward fall, a pair of coyotes started feasting on sheep. If the flock got a quarter of a mile from home, the coyotes would sneak in and nab one. I rode out, one day, to turn the sheep toward home, and the coyotes had already gutted a ewe and were feasting on her innards. I chased the marauders over the hill and brought the sheep closer to home.

Those sheep were a pile of trouble. Some young bucks were romancing the ewes. Jack promised to castrate his young bucks, but he never got around to doing the job. He said they wouldn't do any harm anyway. He sold them with the lambs in the fall, and we didn't get any of that money either. We were too dumb to object.

Buddy and Mickey were Juniors in Midland High School that fall. Buddy played six man football, and Mickey was feature editor of *The Hill Top Flashes*. According to the paper, both were on the Honor Roll.

The American Army was fighting across France while the Pacific Force was slowly conquering more islands, pushing the desparate Japanese Army and Navy back toward Japan. Captain

Herbert Martin was made commanding officer of his company. T/5 Henry Martin was in New Guinea. He and other soldiers piloting landing barges received Honorable Mention from President Roosevelt.

The Commendation appeared in The Midland Mail: "They man landing craft which carry men and supplies from ship to shore in the heavily armored buffaloes, amphibious vehicles at home on the land and on the water. They went ashore in the face of a twelve foot surf at Nassau Bay in New Guinea and didn't lose a soldier despite the angry water battering away at their boats.

They were in the thick of fighting at Lae and Finechafen, two other New Guinea points and at Arawa and Cape Gloucester on New Britain. They worked and they fought to keep supplies and men moving to their proper points. At Biak they saved an American Battalion from possible destruction by braving heavy Japanese gun fire to take ammunition to the hard pressed troops."

We were ready for winter with a respectable stack of green hay piled along the north side of the barn to feed our cattle, sheep and saddle horses. We had ample good pasture to winter the range horses. Then Earl Morgan came with his tale of woe and his skinny horses.

Earl said his horses were short on grass. He made a deal with Pat Feaney to winter his horses on the Feaney pasture across the road from the Rank place. Earl asked me to help him drive his horses to their winter range which was skimpy as well. Also since we lived nearby, would we kind of look after his herd. We agreed.

I saddled a horse and rode forty miles to Earl's pasture. Earl's horses weren't just short on grass, they were starving. His pasture didn't have enough grass to feed a mouse let alone forty horses. They looked like they had been eating dirt for a month.

We headed north into a nasty, cold rain and made the Jim Heeb ranch about dark. Wanda cooked us a big supper. We stayed the night and were on our way early the next morning, arriving at the Rank place about dusk. The poor horses were so tired they could barely move. We put the strongest horses in the Feaney pasture and left about ten weak animals with our horses. Earl went merrily back to Philip and left the mess for us to deal with.

A handsome pair of appaloosa two-year-olds were the first to go down. We rigged a tripod and tried to get them on their feet, but they didn't have the will to stand. We fed them hay to no avail. Lee got her pistol and shot them.

They were only the beginning. Every few days another horse gave up. When a horse goes down, you may as well end his suffering because he's not going to get up again. A horse will beat its head on the ground until it dies. Lee said I had to take my turn with the pistol. I didn't want to do it, but I did. She was in Iowa getting the corn picked and hauled back to our Mitchell Creek ranch when a horse went down west of the house. I thought I couldn't shoot another horse. I let the poor animal beat its life away on the frozen ground, but I couldn't do that either. It will haunt me for the rest of my life. It was a miserable winter.

I got tired of my own company while Lee was in Iowa and rode south eleven miles to visit Mom and Dad on a blizzarding day. It was foolish, but the wind pushed my horse through the driving snow. The next day was bright and clear and I rode back.

Just before Christmas, Uncle Alvin and Essie hit a concrete bridge east of Philip with the Ford. They were taken to the Philip Hospital. Uncle Alvin, seriously injured, was moved to The Veteran's Hospital in Hot Springs. Essie stayed in the Philip Hospital for a few days, then went home with Mom to recuperate.

A warm spell melted most of the snow. We ran out of hay and moved our cattle, poultry and the sheep to the Mitchell Creek ranch. Mickey and her school pal, Zelma Zucarro, helped us. They ran behind the cows and sheep for miles and thought they were having fun. The cows and sheep were happy to get to the good grass on Mitchell Creek. We cared for Uncle Alvin's cattle on Bad River while he spent the winter in Hot Springs.

In January, Captain Herbert Martin came home on furlough from the Mediteranean Theater after flying bombing raids over Germany for two years. In February 1,000 American bombers raided Germany. Herb missed that one. He went to see Uncle Alvin with Mom and Dad and Essie. Uncle Alvin introduced him to his favorite nurse, Nila Barney.

In February, Herb reported to The Santa Ana Army Air Base in California and ferried bombers across the ocean. He was awarded The Distinguished Flying Cross, The Air Medal with 5 Oak Leaf Clusters, Unit Citation for the 15th Air Force with one Oak Leaf Cluster and the European Theater Ribbon with three Battle Stars. He was lucky. He came home alive and with no battle scars.

In March, I helped Earl Morgan drive what was left of his horse herd to Philip. Some kind soul started the rumor that I stole a herd of horses. I wish somebody had stolen them, so I wouldn't have had to watch them die.

The sheep were enjoying the hay, grass and corn, and the ewes were starting to lamb. Jack's little bucks had been busier than he thought. The ewes weren't ready to lamb and we weren't ready for lambs. We built pens in the barn and in the chicken house. The chickens didn't care. They roosted on the pens and stole corn from the sheep. I stayed up nights to check the flock. I was fully dressed day and night for three weeks, which wouldn't have been so bad, if the sheep had cooperated, but they didn't. I had to pull many lambs only to have the mothers refuse to own their babies. I would have hated the stupid sheep, if I hadn't felt so sorry for them.

I checked the ewes every two hours all night. When a ewe lambed, I put her in a pen, marked the ewe and lamb with the same red number and hoped they liked each other. The lambs always liked their mothers, but too many mothers didn't like their babies. I would grab the ewe and hold her so the little one could get some breakfast. After a few sessions some ewes accepted their lambs, some never did. We didn't have milk to feed the bums. Our cows were dry, waiting for calves to be born. Milk replacer hadn't been invented. Then to add more misery, many of the lambs got sore mouths and couldn't suck.

Lee went to Ole's Stockman's Exchange and asked Ole's advice. He said, "You can cure sore mouth lambs right up with iodine. Just paint the lamb's mouth. He'll heal right up." Lee bought a bottle of iodine, and we painted the mouths of a couple dozen lambs. They ran around with brown noses, but most of them died anyway.

The few healthy lambs grew fat and foxy. They ran, jumped and played. When I was in town one day, Jack Rank walked to our farm to see his sheep. He was upset. I couldn't blame him. They were a sorry outfit, but we had done everything we could for them. It was his fault the lambs were born too early, before green grass. He said he was going to take his sheep, and started to round up the little band.

Lee said, "If you are going to take the sheep, you'll have to pay $200.00. We put a lot of time and corn into those sheep."

Jack shook his head. "Nope, I'm taking my sheep. You're not getting a dime." He headed the band south.

"Put the sheep in the pen, Mac," Lee said. Mac charged around the sheep and chased them all into the pen. Jack paid the money, and Lee let him take the sheep. I came home and was glad they were gone. I never wanted to see another wooly critter grazing in my pasture. The lesson was expensive, but it took the wool off Lee's eyes.

We rode to the Rank place and brought our herd of horses home. They spread out in the good grass of the north pasture and began filling their bellies. One horse was a chestnut and white gelding that Earl Morgan gave us for looking after his horses. It was all we got for all that grief, and he died a couple of weeks later.

We helped Essie care for their cattle. The mild winter didn't take much feed, but we had to open water in the river so the cattle could drink.

In April Arline Nelson caught the bus in Midland and traveled to Camp Butner, North Carolina to marry Sergeant Clarence Petoske. The last part of the trip, she shared a seat with a tobacco chewing old lady. Busses had no air conditioning so the windows were open to let in the fresh breezes. Every now and then the old lady spit tobacco juice past Arline's nose and out the open window. She never missed.

The Allied Forces were slowly pushing Japan toward home in the South Pacific. In Europe, soldiers were drawing closer to Hitler's stronghold in Berlin. At home, we were singing, "There will be peace ever after, tomorrow when the world is free."

Sergeant Norman Blucher, radio operator and gunner on a bomber flying out of England, got his third Oak Leaf Cluster. In April he was home. Lieutenant James Nelson, pilot of a B-24 Liberator bomber, was awarded the Air Medal. Many of the boys were coming home. Herbert, Lloyd and Kenneth Olson were all home at the same time. Major Orville Bentley came home, and PFC Curtis Anderson showed up on the streets of Midland not long after.

We didn't have sheep to worry about, but our horses got distemper. Noses ran and legs swelled so tightly that sores broke out and pus ran down their legs. They were a miserable bunch. My beautiful paint filly that Darkie had adopted was the sickest. Lee went to Dr. Theberge and asked him if he knew anything we could do for the suffering filly. There were no veterinarys, but Dr. Theberge was always willing to treat our animals.

He said, "I have some new stuff that might work. It's called penicillin." Lee bought a bottle of penicillin and a syringe. She came home and shot penicillin into the filly, but the little creature died a few days later.

I dug her grave beneath a cottonwood on the bank of Mitchell Creek. It takes a big hole to bury a horse. I dug that dirt out of the hole with a fencing spade. I cried and so did Darkie. For weeks, she came daily to stand with her nose pressed to the mound of earth that covered her child, mourning for the happy filly she would not see again. The paint filly was the only horse we lost.

With the coming of green grass, new calves and colts ran in our pasture, and I got another job, herding sheep.

The barn on Rank's place.

Timmie on Pronto, who is not as small as he looks.

Timmie Martin

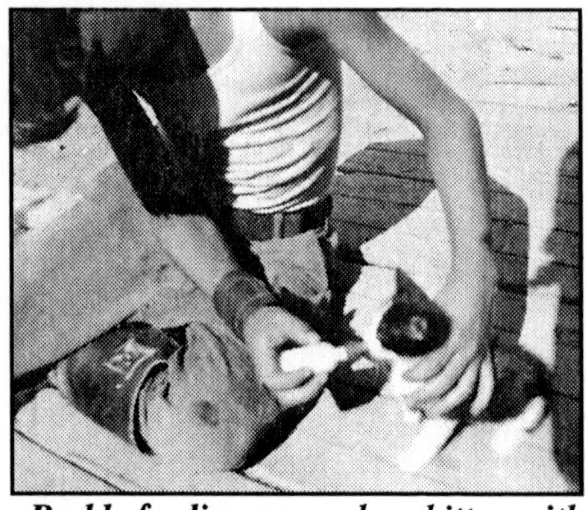

Buddy feeding an orphan kitten with Mickey's doll bottle.

Buddy on Freckles and Mickey on Star at the Martin house.

CHAPTER 14
Herding Sheep On Ash Creek

I didn't want any more to do with sheep, but when Alice Harren offered me a job herding their lambing flock, I accepted. I herded 500 ewes on the Harren ranch.

Harren's outfit was primitive. They lived on the Root homestead south of Midland right in the rough Ash Creek breaks. The house was dug into a hill side and shored up with with railroad ties. It was eight feed wide, sixteen feet long and had one bedroom and a kitchen. When people sat around in the house, they sat still and tried to keep out of each other's way.

Harrens hired a cook for lambing season. She lived in a small house up the hill. The lambing sheds were made of poles, dirt and hay with compartments just big enough for a ewe and lamb or lambs. Babe Nesheim worked there, too. He and Ethel and two small children lived in the log Harren homestead. Ruby and Sonny were nice little kids. They liked the wooly lambs, but Alice said she didn't want kids around the lambing sheds. She ran them off with a blacksnake whip, and they stayed away.

Claude Harren lived in a trailer house, a mile south, herding the flock that had already lambed. My job was to watch for ewe's preparing to lamb and ride the old bay horse in a circle as a signal. Babe would drive out with the team and get the ewe.

When the lambing was finished, Alice sent me to help Babe fix fence. We had a team and wagon, posts, augers, staples, and ham mers. We drove up and down the steep hills, looking for fence to fix. I didn't like sheep, and I sure didn't like fence fixing, but money is money. I fixed fence. In a month I was out of a job, and Judy and baby John Lee came home from Nebraska for a visit.

On April 12, President Roosevelt suffered a massive cerebral hemorrhage and died. Harry Truman became President to fill out Roosevelt's fourth term. The Allied Forces were pressing hard against the Germans. The Russian Army surrounded Berlin and attacked the city on April 17. Adolf Hitler remained in his bunker with his mistress Eva Braun. He married her on April 29, and the next day killed her and himself. May 8, 1945 was VE Day. The long war in Europe was over.

Uncle Alvin came home from The Veteran's Hospital while I was herding sheep. He was thin, not the husky, robust man he had been. He still walked as straight as any soldier, but he was stiff and slow like a stove up old saddle horse that has been ridden too far and too fast. He wanted a small horse to ride, one he could mount easily when he wanted to ride through his cattle. We loaned him Tuffy, small but mighty. They got along fine.

I went home from Harren's and broke horses. I threw my saddle on a short, gray filly, daughter of Darkie. I was wearing overshoes because the ground was muddy. Lee mounted Darkie to haze. I grabbed the saddle horn and climbed aboard. I kicked the filly. She jumped ten feet and lit bucking. I sailed over her head and lit in the mud. I got up shaking my head and caught the filly. "I can't ride this stupid horse," I said. The gray looked self satisfied and shook her head as if agreeing with me.

"Sure you can," Lee said. "Take your overshoes off. Put your spurs on and get back on. She can't buck you off, if you're set. She's too little."

I eyed the little mare. She looked as innocent as a kitten playing with its tail. "Get on," Lee said. "You can ride her." I removed my overshoes and strapped spurs on my boots.

"I hope you know what you're talking about," I said as I gathered my hackamore reins. I stepped into a stirrup. The filly stood quiet ly while I mounted. I took a deep seat and a strangle hold on the saddle horn. I turned my spurs in and grabbed her sides.

She took a couple of steps, bogged her head and bucked. She headed west across the flat, trying her darndest to throw me in the mud again. I clung to the saddle horn like a cockle burr clings to a horse's tail and let her go. She bucked a quarter of a mile across the flat with Lee riding beside her, yelling encouragement and enjoying the fun. When the filly got across the flat, she was blowing hard and tired of bucking. I turned her back across the field. When she got to the corral, she crossed her front legs and fell. She was plumb tuckered out.

We got along fine after that spell. I rode her for several years, then sold her to Bob Evans. Bob was lame, making it hard for him to get around on foot, but he could hop on this little mare bareback and ride anywhere on the ranch.

In late summer, Lee went to Hastings, Nebraska to work in the ammunition depot, making shells to shoot at the Japanese. I stayed home to care for the livestock.

Range horses were being sold in large herds, trailed to stockyards and loaded on railroad cars for shipment. Lloyd Heeb asked me to help him trail a herd from the Ottumwa country to Nowlin for Pat London, noted horse auctioneer. Pat bought hundreds of horses and shipped them out of the country. We trailed the horses most of the day and drove them into the stockyards about sundown. Pat asked what he owed us.

Lloyd said, "Fifteen dollars," and Pat nearly fainted. "We got them babies here in good shape, and you know it," Lloyd said. Pat had to admit that his horses were fine. He gave Lloyd fifteen dollars. Lloyd handed me my seven and a half, the most money I had ever earned in one day.

Pat next hired us to trail a wild bunch to Murdo. Those horses ran like antelope in every direction but down the road. We were constantly heading them back on the dirt grade. We drove the herd through Capa and headed south. Murdo was twenty-five miles down the trail. The poor horses ran so hard some of them had locked jaws by the time we got them penned in the Murdo stockyards, but they recovered by morning.

With the war in Europe over, auto makers were told they could manufacture 200,000 automobiles, if they could find the material to make them. They could make cars, but all cafes across the land were ordered to black out their neon signs.

In August, the Enola Gay dropped the first atomic bomb on Hiroshima, and the horror of atomic war was born. The Japanese refused to surrender until a second bomb fell on Nagasaki three days later. They surrendered August 14 and the peace treaty was signed aboard the USS Missouri September 2, 1945. Nearly four years of war were over.

I was sitting in Mrs. Earl Morgan's living room in Philip when the news came over the radio. The killing was finally over. Our daily papers would no longer carry stories and pictures of horror beyond our comprehension. Our brothers, our friends, our fiances and sometimes our husbands would be spared the agony of more war. For those whose husbands, brothers, sons or sweethearts didn't return, the victory was bittersweet.

I sat in Lee's Grandma Anderson's living room in Forest City, Iowa and listened to a lovely young woman in a pink dress talk to a lady missionary whose field had been India. The young lady's fiance's plane had gone down somewhere in the mountains of India. She wondered how much chance there was of a pilot ever returning who had gone down while flying over the "Hump" in India. Was it possible that he was alive? I watched her carefully composed face as she tried to show no emotion, and heard the missionary tell her the chances were almost nil.

The ammunition plants in Hastings laid off workers so Lee went to Iowa. In September Aunt Amanda helped me drive our horse herd and cattle north to Dad's place, then I boarded the train and went to Iowa too.

Mickey was a Senior in high school, staying at Bertelsons. Buddy had quit school after he and Wally Russell were expelled for three days for going fishing. Wally went back to school, but

Buddy went to work on construction. Mom was teaching at the Liberty School because the board had not been able to find a teacher. Julian, now called Judy, John Lee and a new baby named Judith Ann, born in July, were living in the tiny house by Mitchell Creek.

Essie took Judy to our place to get some furniture. She drove the pickup into a ditch and punctured the radiator. They walked to Steiens and called Simon Elrod to pull the pickup to town. We hadn't decided where our road should be, but it would be treacherous at best. Essie helped Judy paper the walls of her living room, and Judy, John Lee and Little Judy settled down to wait for John to come home.

Gas rationing was lifted and highways were crowded with vehicles. Fred Foster had moved his family from Minnesota and opened a garage in Jake Oberembt's Conoco Station and Gamble Store. Jake was gone.

Herb was in Charleston, South Carolina, learning to fly a C-54 four engine transport plane. He was to start flying cargo.

Lee was staying with her Grandma Anderson and working in the Forest City Produce, picking pin feathers out of chickens. We called it "The Chicken Factory." I went with Lee to see if I could get a job picking chickens. We stepped inside the door, and the smell of a thousand wet chickens nearly knocked me over. I said, "I don't know if I can stand to work in this place."

She laughed at me. "You'll get used to it."

I did. In three days, I didn't notice the awful odor any more. I grabbed a naked chicken and followed it down the line. The chickens moved on a chain. You moved with the chain until you had picked out the pin feathers and went back and followed another chicken. The work was boring, but the pay was good.

Forest City had a group of German war prisoners. They worked at the canning factory, cutting corn off the cob and putting it into cans. One day, someone looked out a window and said, "Hey, the German POWs are going by." Most of us ran to the window to watch the German soldiers march up the street.

A woman who didn't go said, "Look at that, one German running to look at another." Almost caused a fight.

At lunch an older lady asked me how old I was. I said, "Twenty-five."

She said, "Don't make me laugh. You're not a day over eighteen." I guess I looked immature. "What nationality are you?" she asked.

I said, "Norwegian." She wouldn't believe that either. "You can't kid me," she said. "You're Irish."

Perhaps one of my long ago Viking ancestors captured an Irish lass and took her home for his bride. One of them must have captured an Indian or Spanish bride, too, because people laughed at Judy when she claimed Norwegian blood. She was accused of being part Indian or Italian. Mickey, with her blond hair and blue eyes, was the only one who looked Norwegian out of all of us, even though my mother and father were full Norwegian.

After a couple of hours picking pin feathers from naked chickens, we were happy for coffee break. I didn't think a human being could eat in the stinking place, but we did. We brought our lunch and ate in a pleasant room away from the smelly chickens.

One day foreman Melvin Juhl, (Melvin was married to Uncle Charley's niece, Clara), asked me if I would work on the ruffer. The regular operator was sick. I agreed. It would be a change. I held a wet chicken against a bumpy, rubber cylinder and dirt, feathers and unmentionable stuff flew everywhere, especially all over me. I was glad when the regular operator came back. Forest Olson asked me if I would like to work in the freezer.

I said, "I sure would," anything to escape the chicken picking room.

Forest Olson, Uncle Charley's nephew, was foreman of the freezer crew. The freezer was cold, but not frosted. We wore caps, gloves, underwear and coats. Dorothy, the only other woman working in the freezer, and I packed Wapsie Valley chickens into crates for shipment to various markets.I learned how to grade chickens, and I don't eat commercial chicken soup to this day.

One day a bunch of us went to the canning factory and watched the German POWs cut and pack corn. The German officer did nothing except tell the soldiers what to do. He wore jodhpurs and riding boots and looked at us like we were dirt.

Lee and I moved to Aunt Spick's house. She was married to Forest Olson, and they had a red haired baby boy named Owen. They lived about a mile from the Forest City Produce. The freezer workers went to work an hour earlier than the pickers did. Forest and I walked to work together each morning in companionable silence, except the morning I overslept. We had to punch a time clock, and I was going to be late. I leaped into my clothes and ran all the way to work. I grabbed my time card. Forest had already punched it in.

According to rumor, some creep was hiding in the bushes grabbing girls. Forest City had bushes everywhere. We were nervous when we walked around in the night. Aunt Spick said, "I wish he would grab Lee or Timmie. He'd think he got a grizzley bear." I didn't want him to grab me. Lee might throw him ten feet, but I would probably faint. He didn't grab either of us, but we were spooky about the bushes that lined every sidewalk.

We ran around with a bunch of the girls that worked for the produce company: Fern and Violet Schlender, Mary Trenary and Mom's cousin, Lenora Hauge who was bookkeeper for the company and owned a car. She took us to The Ice Capades in Mason City. We went to movies and dances, but there were few men around to dance with. Mary's brother, Jim, came home on furlough from the Army. Jim and Buster, who was just out of high school, thought it was fun to escort six girls to the movies or a dance. Jim always held hands with the girl on either side at the movies, but he seemed partial to Lee.

I walked several blocks in snow nearly to my knees to eat Thanksgiving dinner with Great Aunt Susan Hauge and daughters Murrie and Lenora. Since wearing slacks would have been impolite, I wore a dress. My silk stocking clad legs were about as cold as the snow when I arrived at Aunt Susan's house.

The Chicken Factory ran out of poultry right after Thanksgiving so we boarded a bus and headed for South Dakota. The bus was so crowded we had to stand until someone got off so we could grab a seat. South Dakota had as much snow as Iowa did. The bus went north to Faulkton before coming back to Pierre and then to Midland.

We were surprised when Babe Nesheim boarded the bus at Faulkton and took the seat next to ours. He told us his wife had left him. We didn't believe him, but his story proved true. Ethel had taken the children and moved away.

We got back to Midland to a rash of celebrations. Uniforms were everywhere. Banquets and parties welcomed the boys home. Brother Hank was discharged from Fort Logan, Colorado, November 4, 1945 after three years, seven months and twenty-nine days in Uncle Sam's Army. He spent two years and eight months in the Pacific Theater, running soldiers and supplies from ship to shore on a landing barge while Japanese bombs fell so thick they shook the islands and the ocean turned red with blood.

For this he received a good conduct medal, World War II Victory Medal, Phillipine Liberation Ribbon with one bronze star and the Asiatic Pacific Service Medal. I never saw any of them. He also received malaria from which he never completely recovered. He was paid $36.10 travel pay. He got a total of $455.75 and was happy to be home. I was shocked when I saw him. His once black hair was as white as the driven snow, even though he was only twenty-six years old.

People crowded the streets of Midland again.

Mickey and Little Judy Sanford at Dad's farm.

Mickey with the Sanford's dog, Mutt and her puppies.

CHAPTER 15
The Golden Years

The long years of war were over. Rain was falling. The depression turned tail and ran. Prosperity knocked on every door. Some things were in short supply. There wasn't enough lumber to build all the houses and barns people wanted to build or enough automobiles to go around, but jobs beckoned from every corner. People were working again and building again. Hope sprang anew and life was good. The golden age of prosperity and growth was here.

The Archie Joy Enterprises/Tri-State Insulation Company hired returned service men. Kenneth "Kink" Anderson and Ambrose "Bruce" Jennegas fresh from the US Air Force and US Army went to work for Archie Joy. Archie also hired me.

About a week before Christmas, Aunt Tina, a friend of Archie's wife Fern, said to me, "Archie Joy needs a secretary. He said for you to come and see him."

I gathered my courage and went for an interview. He visited a couple of minutes and hired me to be bookkeeper and secretary for *The Archie Joy Enterprises* and *The Tri-State Insulation Company*, two separate companies with two sets of books. I, who had never wanted to work in an office, was working in one. I knew how to type, but I knew nothing about bookkeeping or shorthand. I didn't need shorthand. Archie had a dictaphone. He said I didn't have to worry about the books, Severt would teach me.

Severt Dale, the manager, was an expert accountant. He taught me how to keep track of every cent and make the books balance. I took Kink Anderson's place as bookkeeper, and he was happy to get outside. I was paid $.45 cents per hour, soon raised to $.50 cents like the men received. We worked sixty hours per week, ten hours a day, and were paid time and a half for over forty hours. I learned to keep books, be a secretary, grade wheat, sell lumber and building material, seed and feed and load cement. Sometimes I actually enjoyed my work.

Archie Joy had the biggest little business in Midland. Certainly, he hired the most people. The steady crew consisted of Severt, me, Kink, Bruce, Tom Gillaspie, Joe Schilling and Tim Walters. Tri-State Insulation had crews and a couple of salesmen, Clarence McKinley and Honey Russell. Ed Hartl and Max Hoeppner worked part time helping grind paper into insulation.

Sometimes bolts or burrs went through the hammermill and came out red hot which probably explains why the insulation sheds all burned. Archie couldn't get enough paper for insulation so he shipped in loads of surplus canon plugs from the Ammunition Factory at Hastings, Nebraska and ground them into insulation. The insulation shed was north of town in a cow pasture. There was no motel there then, no store, no highway, just cows.

Archie spent about half of every week on the road, selling insulation and making other business contacts. Severt came into the office where I was industriously working on my books. "You'd better save some work for when Archie gets back," he said. "He doesn't like to see anybody not working." So I learned when to work and when to loaf. The rest of the crew already knew that. When the cat's away the mice will play. When Archie was on a trip, the men often dropped their hammers and wrenches and sat in the office, pestering me.

The first time I tried to balance my books, I ran into trouble. Severt watched me struggling with my adding machine and my columns of figures. "Sometimes Archie writes in the books," he said. "Then you can't balance them until you find out what he did."

I searched until I found the place where Archie had doodled in my books. I deleted his figures and asked him to "Please" keep his pen on his own desk. He never wrote in my books again.

Every Friday when Archie came back to Midland, he dictated about a dozen letters into his dictaphone. I transcribed the letters to paper, scraped off the wax, and the cylinder was ready for the next batch. I sent out bushel baskets of circulars in every direction, advertising what we had to sell.

Highway 14 still ran down Midland's Main Street. Farmers and ranchers for miles around traded in Midland. The streets on Saturday night were crowded with families buying groceries, going to the movies and dances. Burkhart was gone. Kennedy's Bar was full of customers. Orland Kieffer's Midland Pool Hall was filled with pool and card players.

Buster came to visit, and since we had no livestock to care for that winter, Lee and Buster hitch-hiked to Hot Springs and worked in The Catholic Hospital until spring. I stayed with Aunt Tina and Uncle Charley.

Mickey was staying with Uncle Alvin and Essie. Sometimes Uncle Alvin had trouble getting up the muddy riverbank with his pickup. Then one of his passengers would stand on the back bumper to give the wheels more traction. Mickey hopped on the back bumper one muddy day and grabbed the pickup box. The pickup roared across the river and hit the far bank with enough momentum to take it up the slope and enough bounce to knock her off her perch. She caught one leg in the bumper and was dragged up the bank in the mud. She was stretched out and muddy, but not hurt.

Lennard Blucher, a senior in high school like Mickey, stayed at Bertelson's and helped with the chores each morning before riding Essie's horse to school. Mickey walked. She was walking down the road to school one day when Lennard caught up to her.

"Want a ride?" he asked. Mickey climbed up behind him and grasped the cantle with both hands. The mare didn't like her double load. Mickey hung on as the horse danced along. Suddenly, the mare ducked her head and bucked, throwing Mickey off, kicking her a solid whack on one thigh as she went down.

"Well, I guess she won't ride double," Lennard said and galloped off to school. Mickey limped after him, leg hurting like blazes, getting angrier with every step.

Lee and Buster hitch-hiked home in the spring. He went back to Iowa to help his father plant oats and corn. We moved to our delapidated house on Mitchell Creek. Lee brought an eight- year-old Lakota girl home with her. Wilma Swallow had been born with no sockets in her hips. The little girl was destined to have several operations. The Sisters at the hospital wanted her to have a few weeks of vacation before her surgeries began. She stayed several weeks with us, then went back to Hot Springs.

The snow melted. Rains came. The grass turned green. Foals and calves frolicked on the hillsides. Farmers roads got muddy. Mickey graduated from high school in May and went to work as a waitress in Danny's Cafe on the north side of Main Street.

Lee hired out to herd Harren's lambing flock. Colon Harren, home from the army, worked for Claude and Alice, too. Babe Nesheim worked in the lambing shed. While Lee rode over the greening hills and valleys, I sat at my counter top desk and wrote sales slips, put figures in my books, wrote letters and wished I was riding over the prairie, even if I had to herd sheep, although I didn't envy her on rainy days.

Archie and Fern Joy had five children. Vernon was about twelve. He was followed by Richard, Donnie, Ardis and baby Doris. You could stumble over a Joy kid around the elevator or lumberyard most any time of day.

Vernon liked to help around the shop where Tom and Joe worked on the trucks. I was working on my books when I heard a crack like a rifle shot and a scream that raised me out of my chair. I ran to the door. Vernon ran around the corner of the elevator, still screaming, blood streaming down his face. Pat Zeiman ran from the locker plant across the alley.

Pat grabbed the shrieking boy and laid him on the office floor.

He put a cloth over Vernon's forehead where the blood was pouring out. Vernon had been taking the tire off a truck wheel when the rim exploded, smashing into his forehead. Archie took Vernon to the hospital in Kadoka, and before long Vernon was back working on the trucks.

Richard and Donnie would rather play. They each had a BB gun. One day when I went to the bank, I saw them skulking along the east side of Johnson's Store in the old Murray building. John Sanford walked down the sidewalk toward the Midland Co-op Store. I wondered what the Joy boys were up to.

Richard aimed his gun. Pop! A beebee hit John in the hip pocket. He jumped three feet straight up. He turned around, but Richard and Donnie were gone, streaking for the back of the store. They peeked around the corner to see if anyone was pursuing them.

I laughed most of the way back to the office. "Richard and Donnie are down by Johnson's Store, shooting people in the rear with their BB guns," I told Archie.

Archie called Charley Schofield, the burley town cop, and told him to pick up his sharp-shooting boys. Big Charley soon appeared at the office door with two frightened little boys. They promised never to shoot people again.

Lee and I helped Dad and Uncle Alvin when they moved cattle or branded. We were driving a herd west from Dad's dam when a cow decided to go east instead of west. I was riding Darkie. Lee and Babe were in his car. Darkie loped around the cow, but the stubborn critter dodged around and refused to go back. She loped along the fence, determined to go her own way. Babe drove beside Darkie.

Lee leaned out the window and yelled. "Rope her and drag her back."

"I can't rope anything," I said.

"Nothing to it," Lee said. "Just whirl your rope and throw it like a baseball, straight at her head."

I was the South Dakota cowgirl. She was an Iowa clodhopper, and she was telling me how to rope a cow. I tied my lariat to my saddle horn and whirled the loop around my head. I threw the loop straight at the cow's head. The rope sizzled through the air and settled neatly around the critter's neck. Darkie set her feet. Old bossy whipped around like a catfish on the end of a line. I couldn't believe my eyes. I had roped a cow. I was a roper.

We were still looking for a good place to cross the draw south of our house. The Model A got stuck in the middle of the draw. I hitched Flash and Fly to the car. Lee got behind the steering wheel. Flash didn't like to pull heavy loads. Fly tried to pull, but Flash see-sawed. Fly couldn't pull it alone. The car stayed stuck, and I got angrier. I let loose with some Frank Schroader language, and the team buckled down and pulled the car out of the mud hole.

We finally followed the draw southwest across a small dam grade and down a short, steep slope, crossing the draw above a ten foot deep washout. Our trail climbed the steep breaks and connected with Uncle Walt's road to Midland. Our trail was rugged, but most of it blew clear of snow in winter. Today, a gravel road runs to the house and a wooden bridge spans the draw.

Our Model A was wearing out. The knuckles on the ends of the steering rods were so loose that they popped off every time the car made a sharp turn. Then the Model A would go its own way. Someone had to crawl underneath the front end and put the knuckle back on the ball. The dear old pickup was getting dangerous so we sold it. We were afoot or horseback. We needed an automobile.

Lee found one advertised in Uncle Walt's Sioux Falls Argus Leader. She hitch-hiked to Sioux Falls and drove back to Midland in a 1938 green Lincoln that had been sawed in two and turned into a pickup with a wooden box. Twelve cylinders purred under the hood, if you could keep them all hitting at the same time. The speedometer was broke. I found out the Lincoln would fly low when I drove the twenty-eight miles to Philip in twenty minutes. I knew I had to ease up on the gas.

I was approaching the Bad River bridge from the south with Mac, the dog, riding in the box. I glanced over my shoulder to see how Mac was fairing. Mac looked happy with the breeze ruffling his fur, and I ran into the bridge. The collision broke a hole in the radiator. The water ran out while I was driving to Fred Foster's Garage where he fixed the radiator.

While I was working, Lee went to the Murdo Sales Barn and bought two broncs, a cream gelding, and a blue roan and white paint filly. They were two-years-old and fairly tame. I was happy to see them, as though I didn't already have enough horses to break.

I broke a pair of two-year-old colts to ride that broke out as gentle as sheep dogs. Monte was Sugar's colt. Little John, so named because he was so tall, belonged to Fly. I could catch them anywhere with a bucket of oats or a sugar lump. Soon, I could ride them anywhere I wanted to go, bareback or with a saddle. Monte became my favorite saddle horse. He loved to cut cows. If I showed Monte a cow I wanted cut out of the herd, he ran that critter out and put her where I wanted her. Monte wasn't a rope horse. If I took a rope down, Monte had a fit.

They had a couple of half sisters that weren't so nice. Both were bay and jittery as gazelles. One was a beautiful red bay with a blaze face and white hind feet. I never got her to wait quietly for me to mount. She wanted to dash away, preferably before I hit the saddle. Fortunately for me, neither of them bucked or I would have gone ten feet in the air. I rode them a few months and sold them at the Fort Pierre Sales Barn.

Archie Joy Enterprises got in some of the new sheetrock wallboard and dark green gypsum sheeting. Gypsum board was cheaper than sheetrock so we bought enough to wallboard the ceiling and all but the west wall of our house. It had the framing on the outside. The wind didn't blow through our house so hard anymore.

J.C. Eng and family moved to Midland. He worked for Ole's Stockman's Exchange so Midland had a druggist again. The Eng family lived in the back rooms of the drug store. We soon met them because the drug store was our hang out on Saturday night. There, we bought our ice cream, sodas, banana splits and milk shakes.

Anita, blond, blue-eyed and in high school, took up with us, mainly because we had horses to ride. Anita liked to come home with us and ride for hours. She loved the fresh smell of the earth after a rain and thought the most wonderful meal in the world was the steak and potatoes she ate at our table.

Ole and Millie went across the street and operated *The City Lunch*, a small cafe. Millie ran a tight ship. A sign on the wall said, "We reserve the right to refuse service to anyone." Woe be to anyone that got Millie's dander up. She got upset with Heinie Koch and ordered him from her cafe.

Heinie got off the stool, put his hat on and headed for the door. Millie strode from behind the counter and shoved him. His hat fell off. When he stooped to retrieve his hat, she kicked him in the rump and out the door he went.

Wheat harvest was good despite the grasshoppers still jumping around. People were buying all kinds of building material. Romance came to the office. Archie hired Doris Dale to help me during the summer. She started dating Bruce Jennegas, and they were married the next year.

One summer day, I rode down from checking cattle in the north pasture, unsaddled my horse and went into the house. Lee was cooking dinner. A bashful boy about ten-years-old sat on a kitchen chair. He wore bib overalls, a wide-brimmed straw hat and no shoes. "This is Lyle Dennis," Lee said.

Lyle gave me a shy smile. "My dad calls me Goofy," he said.

"Well, I guess I'll call you Lyle," I said.

The Hank Dennis family lived a couple of miles northwest in a white two-story house set on the flat where the wind had a full sweep. Hope Dennis became a wonderful friend. She had a delightful sense of humor and laughed easily. She was tall and thin, and she loved to dance and square dance. She washed her large family's laundry in a Maytag gasoline washer that she put outside in front of the house in summer. She washed our clothes along with her own.

Lyle had two brothers and two sisters who were younger than he:

Gerald "Peewee", Gloria "Sadie", Howard "Butch" and Judy, who was just Judy. Ivan "Snazz" was a year older. The five older children were all gone most of the time. Kenny and Olivia were married. Leroy, Ronald and Leonard worked away from home.

The next time Lyle came to visit, he brought Peewee with him, and a tradition was started. Lyle and Peewee spent many weekends and a large share of their summer vacation at our house. Sometimes Snazz came along. Sometimes they brought Dean Koch or Butch Quatier or Terry McKillip. Dean rode his Shetland pony out from Midland. The boys scrambled through the trapdoor to sleep in the attic. Lyle and Peewee liked to help ride broncs, fix fence, haul hay and feed the cattle. They were handy boys to have around. They knew how to work.

John Sanford, discharged from the Air Force, came home and moved into the tiny house on Mitchell Creek with Judy, John Lee and Little Judy. He went to work on a road construction crew near Hayes with my brother, Hank.

Captain Herbert Martin was flying for the Air Force in Delaware. His navigator, Arthur "Bud" Callan got him a date with his wife's sister, Nila Barney. Nila worked in Delaware and stayed with Ruth and Bud Callan. Bud said, "Herb is a good pilot, and he's from South Dakota." Nila agreed to go.

They went out for a swordfish dinner where Herb and Nila found they had met before in Hot Springs, South Dakota, when Nila was a nurse to Uncle Alvin. They dated until Nila went home to Igloo, South Dakota, to her parents farm which is now part of the Wild Horse Preserve south of Hot Springs.

Herb was promoted to Major in October and discharged from the Air Force. Like a duck flying south, he headed for Igloo. He and Nila were married October 23, 1946 by the Reverand Sylvan Moe in Rapid City with Bud and Ruth Callan as attendants.

Nila's Uncle Bill Barney and Aunt Helen and Bud and Ruth Callan hosted a bridal dinner for the newlyweds at The Country Club. Herb brought his bride home to meet his family. I thought Nila was as pretty and glamorous as a movie star. They moved into one of the small houses built by Mrs. Hall when Midland was young. Two Hall houses stood between Johnson's Store and The Masonic Temple, now The Midland Library.

Herb and Nila settled into their new home. Mr. and Mrs. Joe Vladyka, retired from the farm, lived next door. Mrs. Vladyka scrounged the store's garbage can for food that might still be edible.

Ruth's little boy, Del, was three. He liked to visit Mrs. Vladyka, and she liked the dark-haired little boy. She gave him grapes from the garbage which upset his mother mightly.

Nila's sister, Joyce, just out of high school, came to visit, too. She liked to ride around with me in the Lincoln. The Lincoln got us into an adventure I wished hadn't happened. Joyce and Noel Eng went with me to get a water tank for Severt Dale. We unloaded the water tank behind Severt's house in Midland just after sundown. I wasn't sure how to get out of the alley, but a trail ran south, passing in front of Kristenson's house. They had retired to Midland from a farm northwest of Midland. I drove the Lincoln cautiously down the trail. The trail ran under a clothes line I didn't see. The wire caught on the lights atop the Lincoln cab. We heard a screech. I slammed on the brakes, too late. The wire broke.

We jumped out of the car as Mr. and Mrs. Kristenson came out of their house, boiling mad. We apologized and offered to fix the clothes line. Mr. Kristenson glared at us. "No, just get out of here."

Mrs. Kristenson said, "You had no business driving down our road in the first place." She was right.

Uncle Alvin and Herb argued about whether prices were going to fall into the basement as they had after World War I or whether prosperity was on the way. Herb was for prosperity. A good Hereford cow was worth between eighty and ninety dollars. Uncle Alvin said, "In a couple of years good cows will sell for forty dollars." Herb disagreed, and he was right. The United States went into a period of unprecedented growth and good times.

The new Jet aircraft were setting astonishing speed records. We heard the amazing planes break the sound barrier with a clap like thunder as they flew over. Some people said the boom cracked plaster and concrete and broke the plumbing loose.

Automobile factories geared up to make the millions of cars, pickups and trucks that millions of people were eager to buy. People signed up at the dealers and waited months to get a new vehicle.

Change came rapidly the fall of 1946. Buster went into the Army and was sent to the Army of Occupation in Italy where he stayed for eleven months. Mickey quit working at Danny's Cafe and went to college at Augustana in Sioux Falls. She stayed at the dormitory and got acquainted with Aunt Ida McCone, one of Dad's sisters.

Lee caught learning fever, too, and hitch-hiked to Chicago to enroll in the famous Art Institute. She was surprised when the first nude model walked in, but she got used to drawing nudes.

The streets of Midland were full of strangers. Farmers and ranchers came from Texas, Nebraska, Kansas and Oklahoma to buy a piece of South Dakota land. A Texan told me that South Dakota bankers didn't know how to loan money, and South Dakota farmers didn't know what this land was worth. I guess he was right. By the time South Dakota farmers and South Dakota banks discovered the the value of our good earth it seemed like half of it belonged to Texas, Nebraska, Kansas and Oklahoma farmers.

The Midland area got its share. Ed and Chick Fenwick came from Nebraska to settle north of Midland. Art Larson, Thurman Adkins, Jack Mahler, Roscoe Riggle, Fred McCarroll, Vernon Sivage, Jack Lawrence, Ernie Hackerott, Jessie Jones--some came to stay; some stayed only a short time.

Harvey Madsen sold the place north of town along Highway 14 where Jerry Jones lives now to Texas lawyer Thurman Adkins. Adkins stayed a few years and sold to R.T. Jones. The R.T. Jones family sold to Jerry Jones and that ranch was back in South Dakota hands.

The open range was also disappearing. New barbed wire gleamed in the sunlight. We could no longer ride from Uncle Alvin's pasture at the Calhoun place ten miles south to Steien's without opening a gate.

Lee got a job working in a drugstore and learned to sketch nude models with a chunk of charcoal. She got acquainted with some horse owners and rode the park trails in Chicago with them from bar to bar. I stayed most of the winter with Aunt Tina and Uncle Charley. I kept a saddle horse and the cream gelding and paint mare Lee bought in Murdo in the stock yards so I could break them to ride. I worked with my broncs after work and on Sunday.

Keith and Leonard Elrod, in seventh and eighth grades, wandered over to the stock yards from their house on Mitchell Creek and found me and the horses. They were eager to help train, water and feed with me. We led the horses to the Elrod place to water when the stock yards water was turned off for the winter.

The Artie Elrods had moved to town from the old Elrod homestead three miles south of Midland. Keith wanted to be a bronc rider. He learned to ride when he was nine and went down the long slope to the Schofield ranch on Brave Bull Creek where he played with Hank and rode the Schofield horses. Hank, a few years older than Keith, taught him to play "Stud Horse" which became their favorite game. The object of the game was to suddenly yell, "Stud Horse", then wheel and kick backward with both feet like a stallion does in a herd of horses. Hank would yell, "Stud Horse," wheel and lash out with wicked hind feet before Keith could get out of the way. When Hank's boot heels connected with the seat of Keith's pants, Keith went down. Keith hardly ever caught Hank, but he never quit trying.

The Elrod boys helped me scotch hobble my broncs and get them ready for the saddle. The paint mare tried to kick us with one hind foot tied up, but she couldn't get the other hoof up high enough to connect. I didn't have a hazer or snubber so I rode around in the stockyard pens. Babe Nesheim rode outside with me, occasionally so the broncs were soon lined out and on the way to being gentle saddle horses. Once I loped the cream horse across a patch of ice hidden under a thin layer of snow. He fell and banged my knee so hard I thought it was broken, but in a few days it was all right.

Keith and Leonard helped me gather hay that was spilled by the hay crews loading bales into boxcars. Many cars of hay were loaded out of Midland that fall. Shorty Woitte loaded seventeen cars for Harold Gorton. We found an ample supply for the horses.

The winter was mild until about Christmas. Mickey came home for Christmas vacation. She stayed one night with Herb and Nila and got so cold that she couldn't sleep. She got up and sat by the stove, shivering.

She went with Hank and Earl "Lou" Root to the New Year's Eve dance in Belvidere. They cruised back to Midland in the black Pontiac to get something to eat, but Midland's cafes were all closed. Hank parked beside my Lincoln just as I was getting in to go to Aunt Amanda's house.

"Let's go to Philip and get something to eat," Hank said. The Highway Cafe in Philip stayed open all night.

"Nope," I said. It's after two o'clock. I'm going home and go to bed."

Hank backed the Pontiac away from the curb, and they roared west. The Pontiac sailed along the highway, tires humming. About a mile west, the car left the road and hit an approach, flying through the air, hitting the ground front-end first where it bounced over, coming to rest on its wheels.

Mickey was caught between two big guys. Hank wasn't moving. "Go for help, Mickey," Lou said. "Hank's dying."

Mickey climbed over Lou and out the door. She ran to town, down Main Street and into The Stroppel Hotel. She was bleeding from a nasty gash on one leg. Someone took her to the Midland Hospital to be treated. Someone went out to get Hank and Lou. Hank had a cut on his lip, but neither of them were hurt as badly as Mickey was.

Hank and John Sanford were working on construction near Hayes so they were out of transportation. Hank borrowed the Lincoln. Anti-freeze was hard to find. I drained the Lincoln at night and refilled the car when I wanted to drive it. Hank didn't want to drain the radiator every night and refill it every morning so he put kerosene in the radiator.

The kerosene didn't freeze, but it ate holes in the radiator hoses, which nobody noticed. I drove the Lincoln home one night, and the water all drained out. The motor got hot and exploded about a quarter of a mile from home. I left the mighty Lincoln on a flat in Uncle Walt's pasture where the lovely automobile rusted for over fifteen years before someone removed it.

Some days, I went out at noon to feed and water the cattle on Mitchell Creek. I got caught at Aunt Amanda's place January 2, 1947, when a blizzard whistled in and dumped a heavy load of snow. The wind screamed for three days. I sat in Aunt Amanda's living room and watched the snow zip past. On the third day, the wind let up enough so I could see the trees like ghostly skeletons in the dimness along Mitchell Creek.

I told Aunt Amanda I was going to walk up the creek and see how the cattle were faring. I dressed in my army surplus parka, and tied the hood tightly. I went out, struggled through the snow and headed up the creek. I heard the wind shrieking through the tree tops, but I was sheltered from it. I sank to my hips in snow as soft as feathers.

I waded through powder for a mile, and came to our fence. I found the cattle, sheltered against the creek bank. Sifting snow covered their backs. I went back to Aunt Amanda's warm fire.

One Saturday night, I went to the movie, "The Circular Staircase" with Glen Muirhead and Buddy. We sat on the edge of our chairs barely breathing as the killer stalked the heroine. The suspense was delightfully frightening. After the movie, we got in Buddy's car, and he drove to Aunt Tina's house and stopped. "I'm not walking you to the house," Glen said. "It's too dark over there."

Midland's street lights were few and dim. The front porch was in deep shadow from vines that climbed the pillars. Aunt Tina always hooked the front screen door at night. She left the back door unlocked so I could get in. I got out of the car. I looked toward the house with its trees, clinging vines and flickering shadows. I didn't want to go into the dark cave that was the back entry. No telling what might be lurking in the shadows. My imagination painted terrifying pictures.

I took a deep breath, ran through the gate and onto the porch. I grabbed the screen door and jerked. The hook let go, and I dashed into the house and went to bed. In the morning, Aunt Tina wondered what happened to the screen door hook.

Spring was coming. Soon Lee would leave her charcoal and drawing board and return to South Dakota.

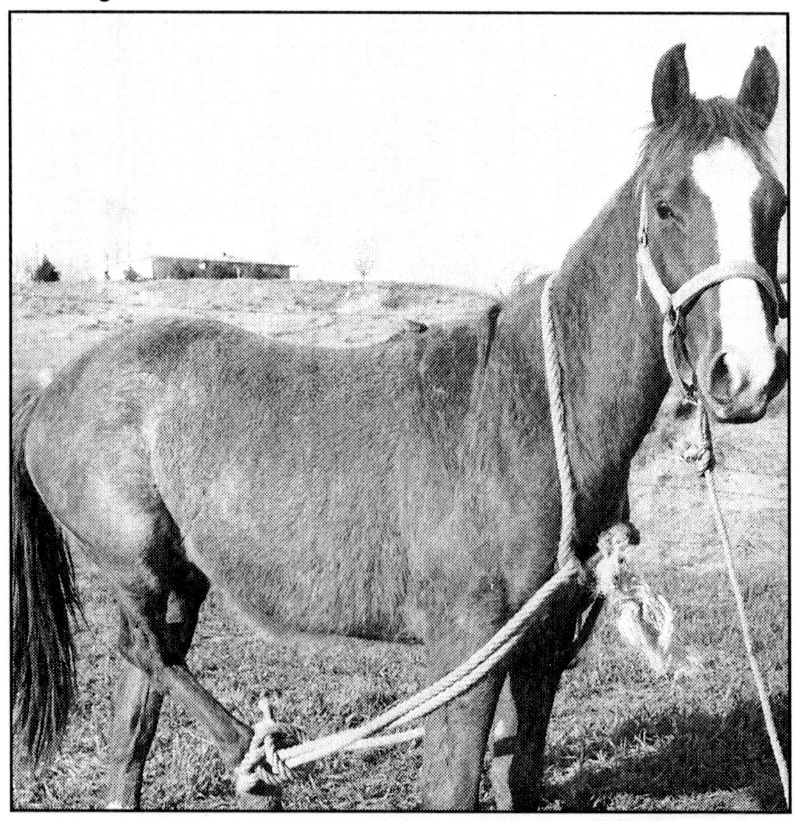

Horse wearing a Scotch hobble, waiting for the next move.

Pronto and part of his harem.

Little John at two years old was already a tall horse.

Nila's sister, Joyce.

Mickey, what's a waitress doing in the middle of the street?

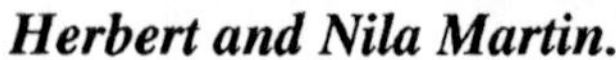

Herbert and Nila Martin.

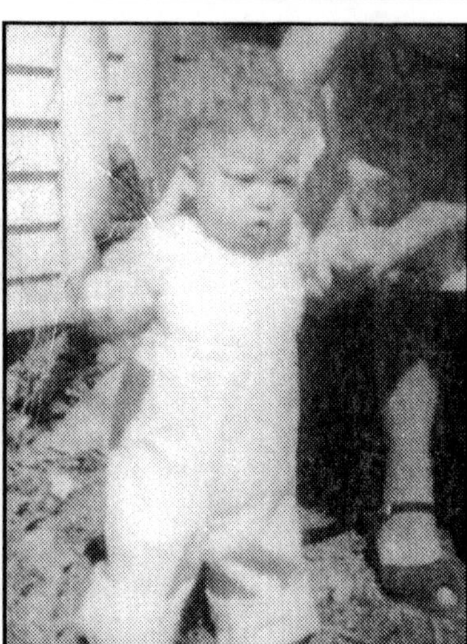

Herbie Marttin

CHAPTER 16
Breaking Broncos and Other Nonsense

Lee drifted back with spring, and we moved to the homestead again. Colon Harren came out to help us round up cattle one day. I gave him my newly broke cream horse to ride. Colon mounted and galloped north. He was almost to the buttes when the cream ducked his head and threw Colon off. The cream had never bucked with me. Colon mounted again and rode more carefully. A couple of months later, Colon bought the horse.

That honest cream horse got some rough training, helping me break broncs. I put a two-year-old appaloosa in the corral to start training. He was a handsome, soggy brute, and he glared at me, if I even looked his way. We got the hackamore on him, and tied the lead rope to the cream's saddle horn. The appy ran on the rope and knocked the cream horse off his feet. The cream scrambled back up, facing the appaloosa. He braced all four hooves and kept the rope tight. The appy pulled, jerked and threw a fit, but the cream never turned his back. I left and came back a couple of hours later. The horses still faced each other, both on their feet and the rope barely taut between them. Appy was broke to lead and Cream was a rope horse.

I still thought I could handle most two-year-olds, but Appy hated me from the time I put a hackamore on him. He had a lot of Morgan blood and the makings of a fine saddle horse, but he was set on killing me, or at least breaking my leg before he'd let me near him. I said, "Okay, good-bye, bronco," and sent him to market. I was bluffed out by another appaloosa, and I have not liked them since.

Lee bought a beautiful bay and white paint filly that I couldn't get along with either. The filly preferred to lead, walking on her hind feet while she slapped at my head with her front hooves. Her hooves were harder than my head so she got a truck ride. While I was working, Lee haunted the Sales Barns, buying cheap horses for me to break. I didn't care, but sometimes I couldn't do it.

We hired Hank to build a dam across the draw a few hundred feet west of the house. The dam was full of water, but it would go dry before summer was over. We needed to find a source of water before the small pond went dry. Aunt Amanda said we could get water by digging a well in the bottom of the creek.

We took a spade and shovel and headed for the creek. Digging was easy in the sandy creek bottom, and we struck water at about four feet. We dug our well six feet square and six feet deep and fenced it. We had ample water that ran in fast. The only problem was that every time the creek ran, the rushing water filled the well full of silt. We had to dig that well many times.

We quit milking, except for a bit to drink, and bought bum calves to put on the cows. Lulu Belle, the black white-faced cow, raised two five hundred pound calves one summer. Betty Ann fed three calves and two pigs. We bought two white pigs to fatten and butcher when fall came. The small pigs followed the cows around the pasture. One day, I saw a white pig sitting on his haunches, having lunch while Betty Ann grazed on the hillside.

Those pigs were a grand nuisance. We hung a bucket of milk in the well to keep it fresh and cool for supper. One evening, I went to the well to get the milk and found two white pigs in the well. They had tried to reach the milk and fell in the well. The pigs squealed at me and clawed at the sides, trying to get out. They had spilled the milk, and I felt like leaving them in the well, but I helped them out, and they ran, still squealing, to the corrals. When fall came, the porkers were big and fat, but we didn't have the heart to butcher them. Instead, we sold them to Dad.

One Sunday, Babe Nesheim took us to Uncle Alvin's north pasture to get the horses we had left there after helping brand calves. We drove the horse herd into the big corral at the Calhoun place. I threw a saddle on Sugar. She was fat and sassy. I cinched the saddle tight. Lee invited Babe to take the first ride, and he couldn't refuse.

Babe gathered the reins and stepped aboard. We could see what was coming. Babe hit the saddle and Sugar exploded. She ducked her head and bawled. She kicked, squealed and pitched. Babe was riding high, until the saddle went up on her shoulders. She threw Babe and the saddle over her head. We laughed like hyenas as Babe picked himself off the ground. Having had her fun, Sugar let me ride her home.

It seemed like I spent more time on horseback than on foot. I got up at four in the morning to ride and train horses before going to work, and I often rode a bronc to work. I got a lot of horses broke to ride that way.

One evening, I was riding Pronto home from work, going along what is now the north side of the city park. Then it was grass, weeds, and no trees. A little bonfire crackled merrily near the road. Pronto's ears shot forward. His head went up. I talked to him, trying to ease him past the flames. Natalie Doud rode down the trail toward Pronto, headed downtown on her bike. Pronto snorted, stuck his head between his knees and unloaded. I catapulted into the air and landed on my rump in the weeds.

Looking scared and surprised, Natalie wheeled past. I mounted and headed Pronto up the trail again. As I passed Berniece Koch's house, she hollered from her porch, "Are you all right?"

I said, "Yeah, I'm okay," and rode toward home, my dignity badly ruffled.

Herb invested money saved from his years in the Air Force on two second hand trucks. He bought a GMC and an International from Archie Joy for $1,000.00 each. He sold his Nash to Kink Anderson, painted Herbert Martin on the sides of his trucks and was in the trucking business. He hired brother Buddy to drive one truck, and they hauled baled hay to Rapid City.

Herb also rented 160 acres from Uncle Alvin on the Calhoun place and planted barley. The barley grew thick and tall with plump kernels. In late July, his bumper crop of barley waved and rippled in every breeze. A hard wind passed by and harvested his crop for him, blowing all that money away with it.

In early spring, Uncle Alvin started disking his fields, getting the ground ready to plant. One morning, he didn't feel too chipper. Essie offered to go to the field and disk, although she had never driven the tractor before.

"You can go out and start disking," Uncle Alvin said, happy for a little more rest. "I'll come out after while. Slow down for that big ditch that runs into the river." He cranked the F20, and Essie headed for the big field west of the house.

The old tractor putted around the field while Essie watched the black earth flowing behind her. She drove half a mile west, turned north and drove another mile as the soil churned, and small weeds disappeared. She turned east, then south. She listened to the roar of the tractor and heard a pheasant rooster crow. Suddenly, the ditch loomed, like an iceberg coming out of a fog.

Uncle Alvin had warned her about that ditch, but he forgot to tell her how to slow the tractor down. Before she could figure which lever to pull, the F20 hit the ditch. The front wheels left the ground. Essie grasped the steering wheel with all her strength and bounced on the seat. The front wheels crawled up the other side of the ditch. The big hind wheels hit the bottom. Essie bounced higher as she clung with all her might to the steering wheel. The tractor climbed out of the ditch and rolled on around the field. Essie figured out how to slow the tractor before she got to the ditch again.

Before harvest began, Uncle Alvin got Essie to help him clean the thousand bushel steel grain bin. The day was hot. Essie swept the moldy wheat, mouse cards and dirt into piles. Uncle Alvin scooped the piles out the door. When they were finished, they were hot and dusty. Sweat caked the dirt on their faces. They went to Midland to wash off the grime in a hot plunge at The Stroppel Hotel. (No bath tubs or running water in ranch houses then.)

While they were gone, a storm came up. A fierce wind tore across the land with clouds and rain. When they got home, the steel granary was gone. They found the bin a couple of hundred feet east in Bad River, all bent out of shape.

When Uncle Alvin combined wheat, Herb rode the towering combine. Uncle Alvin drove the tractor pulling the monster machine. Essie drove the truck and hauled wheat home and shoveled the grain into the bin. When the grain piled too high to shovel more grain, Essie got into the bin and shoveled the wheat back. The bin was an oven with the blazing sun heating the outside temperature to over a hundred degrees.

All the animals knew enough to stay out of the heat. The cottontails were shaded up. Rattlesnakes were coiled in any bit of shade they could find, but Essie was throwing scoop shovel after scoop shovel of wheat into the bin. Her wide straw hat shaded her face, but that didn't stop the sweat from running down her face and dripping off her chin.

After a few truck loads of wheat, a shovel full of farmer's gold felt like a hundred pounds even through the shovel was a new light aluminum model. The scoop was the largest size one could buy, just right for Uncle Alvin. Essie's arms felt like sticks. She was so tired she could drop, and she couldn't keep up with the wheat spilling out of the combine hopper, so Uncle Alvin and Herb decided to teach her to run the combine. Essie climbed on the huge machine and rode around and around the field. The sun was hot, but at least a breeze blew. Herb shoveled wheat into the bin. He could throw a scoop of wheat, full and running over, into the bin and keep ahead of the combine with ease.

We finally figured out that we had too many unbroken horses eating grass in our pasture. Mom, Banker Lovald and Frank Schroader were right. The market for draft horses was gone. A buyer offered a cent a pound and range horses went to market in droves. We rounded up about twenty head and delivered them to the Midland stock yards. I hated to sell the horses for a cent a pound because I knew most of them would end up in dog food cans. The buyer gave $42.00 each for Mom's team of bay mares. At least, they went somewhere to work for a farmer.

In June, Lee and I went to The Rapid City Range Days and watched the rodeo and horse show. The horses jumping over fences, brick walls, and other barriers fascinated me. I traded a load of baled hay for an Argentina jumping saddle and went home to train a jumper.

We built a primitive post and rail jump and set it two feet high. I saddled Little John with my new saddle and mounted. Little John cantered toward the jump. He eyed that pole in front of him, skidded on all four hooves and stopped. I nearly went over his head. Lee gave me a switch. I circled and headed him for the jump at a gallop.When he was almost there, I could feel him tense. "Hike!" I said, and cut him across the rump with my switch. He sailed over.

Lee tried Monte, but he thought jumping over poles was a ridiculous waste of time and refused to participate. Lee decided jumping barriers wasn't fun either, but I was hooked. We bought three 4x4s sixteen feet long, rounded the sharp edges with a draw knife and painted them white. Lee built two white hen coops with "knock off" tops, a fake brick wall and a brush jump holder that we filled with tree branches. I had a jumping course, of sorts.

Little John took the post and rail jumps and headed for the brush. The brush jump and the brick wall struck terror in his heart. He loped toward the brush jump, set all four hooves and skidded. I kept going. I mounted again and headed for the brush jump with Little John at an easy canter. He eyed the jump, and I felt him getting ready to set his brakes again. I popped his rear with my switch and yelled "Hike!" Surprised, Little John sailed over the jump a full two feet higher than necessary.

We practiced all summer. Little John decided those jumps weren't so frightening. He was a natural jumper and usually cleared the jumps by a foot or two. He jumped gracefully, landing as lightly as a gazelle.

We made one investment that Banker Lovald approved. We bought twenty-three Hereford heifers from Colon Harren. Those white-faced beauties made our cow herd look twice as good and our need for hay, twice as large. We hired Harold Gorton and his hay crew to put up a quarter section of hay in our north pasture.

I went to the hayfield after work to see how the haying was coming. Most of the hay was down. Mr. Gorton sat in his pickup, watching the hay stack grow. Two army surplus jeeps with seven foot mowers on the back bumper whistled around the field so fast the mowers hummed instead of clicking. Two of the new hyddraulic stackers, mounted on truck chassis turned backward so you had to steer opposite of the way you wanted to go, roared down the windows. Bucker teeth snapped and flew, and the hay stack grew like a giant loaf of bread.

I thought, that's the way I want to make hay. One of the wild young men driving a jeep was Kandus "Shorty" Woitte. Shorty was sparking my blond, blue-eyed, baby sister, Mickey, to the dismay of most of us. Judy and I thought something should be done, but we didn't know what. We hoped she would get tired of him.

The first time I saw Shorty was at a basketball game. I went to the game in The Legion Hall with a friend. The Midland Town team played after the high school game. When the town team trotted out on the floor here was this cute little guy I had never seen before. He zipped around the floor like a cottontail dodging a coyote. I turned to my friend and said, "Who is that little guy?"

"His name's Whitey," she said. "He's on a hay crew from Minnesota or someplace." Midland was loaded with hay crews.

I wondered why they called him Whitey when his hair was black and his eyes as brown as a chocolate bar. I found out later that his last name was Woitte, pronounced Whitey, and he was called Shorty.

Mickey waited tables at Danny's Cafe. She stayed with Aunt Tina and Uncle Charley and sat on their front porch with Shorty until all hours. We kept a wary eye on the situation. Our silly brothers, Hank and Buddy, encouraged the romance. Hank hauled Mickey and his friend, Shorty, to dances from Hayes to Midland to Philip and Belvidere. Shorty was their friend, but we didn't know him from "Adam's off ox," as Mom would say. Some of those haymakers weren't guys you wanted your little sisters going with and our little sister was only seventeen. We took comfort in the fact that she would go back to Augustana for her sophomore year when fall came.

Archie Joy Enterprises was humming like a well-oiled sewing machine. He bought car loads of west coast lumber and sent trucks to Rapid City for building material every week or two. New houses were going up. Barns, sheds and granaries were being built, painted or repaired.

The wheat harvest was abundant. The railroad couldn't haul wheat away fast enough. Farmers had to call the elevators before bringing a truck load of wheat to market. Much wheat was now harvested by custom combiners. Uncle Alvin called one day and asked if he could bring in a load. I asked Archie. He consulted his bin record and nodded. "Yeah, he's a pretty good old horse. Tell him to bring it in."

With the coming of fall, the hills along Bad River blazed with red top grass. We hauled hay three miles home from our north pasture on Sundays. September first came and went, and Mickey didn't go back to Augustana. She kept working at Danny's Cafe and going with Shorty Woitte who stayed in Midland to load out boxcars of baled hay. We hoped he would run out of hay and go back to Milbank where he belonged.

What we didn't know was that Mickey had given Shorty an ultimatum: "Either we get married, or I go back to Augustana and forget you." Shorty didn't want to be forgotten. He didn't have any money, but he didn't want to lose Mickey. He borrowed $10.00 from Colon Harren to buy a wedding ring. He didn't have a car so he borrowed Colon's car. Mickey turned eighteen in December, and in February, they slipped away to Kadoka and tied the knot.

Before we figured out what to do about the romance, Mickey

was married to her little haymaker, and we all love Shorty. They soon learned to squeeze the Indian until he rode the buffalo or Jefferson until he ran into Monticello, depending on which nickel they had to spend.

Shorty took his bride home to Milbank way over on the eastern side of South Dakota to visit his mother, his sister, Nina, and his brother, Willard, and family. Mickey and Shorty moved to Huron where Shorty got a job in the packing plant.

Fall brought changes for Herb and Nila, too. Herb and Buddy trucked some baled hay to Rapid City, but trucking jobs were scarce. Herb's barley crop had failed. Nila was pregnant. He decided farming and trucking were not for him. He had to find a better way to support a family.

He sold his GMC truck to Dad, drove the International to Rapid City and enrolled in The School of Mines. He left Nila in Midland to await the birth of their first child. Ruth Callan and Del stayed with Nila.

Ruth called me the morning of September 16, 1947 and said she had taken Nila to the hospital. I rushed to The Midland Community Hospital and heard a baby crying as I walked through the door. Dr. Mehra who was from Iran and his wife, Aileen operated the hospital.

Herbie was a robust baby with a mound of curly, blond hair and blue eyes. Nila and Herbie came home in a few days. I stopped to visit and admire my new nephew one day. Nila got a bottle of milk from the refrigerator. She said, "Dr. Mehra said to give Herbie milk straight from the refrigerator." She stuck the icy nipple in Herbie's mouth.

"I warm milk for a baby calf," I said.

"I'm going to warm Herbie's milk then," she said, and she did.

Herb came and got Nila and Herbie and took them to Rapid City. Nila's Uncle Bill Barney persuaded Herb to buy a lot on St. Patrick Street, the very south edge of Rapid City. Herb built a basement house across the street north of Ruth and Bud Callan's new house. South of St. Patrick Street was rolling cow pasture.

The School of Mines wouldn't accept Herb's previous year and a half of the credits. He had to go the full four years. This time he chose Mechanical Engineering, and buckled down to study and build a house. He used his truck for a car with his name painted large on the doors. The name of Herbert Martin became known all over Rapid City.

That fall, a couple of truckers from eastern South Dakota, Hefter Dahl and Richard Pattee, stopped at the office, and Archie sold them The Archie Joy Enterprises. Dick and Hefty were like Mutt and Jeff. Hefty was short and heavy; Dick was over six feet tall. Pattee soon got disenchanted with the partnership and made things so unpleasant for Hefty that Hefty bought him out. Hefty and his wife moved into the ground floor apartment in The Okaton State Bank building. That picturesque old building, constructed in 1909, is now ready to fall into its basement.

Archie sold me along with the business and hired Janey Elrod, wife of Donald Elrod, to keep The Tri-State Insulation Company books. I lost one set of books and shared my office with Janey. She used Archie's desk.

Hefty bought bronze, naked lady bottle openers from a slick salesman. He gave one to each employee and one to Archie. Archie hid his bottle opener in his desk drawer. Janey dearly wanted one of those bottle openers, but Hefty wouldn't give her one. Janey came to work one morning and dug Archie's bottle opener out of the drawer and put it on the desk. When Archie came in, he put the bottle opener back in the desk drawer. Janie put it back on the desk as soon as he left. Archie came into the office and saw the naked, bronze lady setting on his desk again.

"You can have that, if you want it," he told Janey. So Janey got her bottle opener.

Around Christmas time, Hefty gave Archie a calendar that had a picture of a lovely lady, scantily clad, for each month. The legend read, "Turn backward, turn backward, oh time in your flight. Make me a boy again, just for one night." The calendar so embarrassed Archie that he threw it in the waste paper basket and probably ground it into insulation.

Janey and I shared office space amicably, but Janey had a phobia about cats. I thought that strange since kittens are such adorable little creatures. One day, Richard stepped into the office, carrying his cat. I glanced at Janey. Her face was drained of all color. No sheet was ever whiter. She looked scared to death.

I said, "Richard, get that cat out of here."

"Why?" Richard hesitated in the doorway, petting his cat.

"Take him away, now," I said, getting up. Richard backed out the door with his cat, and the color slowly returned to Janey's ashen face.

Bab Bathel worked for Hefty, mostly hauling baled hay to Rapid City and building material back. His truck pulled a twenty-four foot semi-trailer. One day, Babe was going west a couple of miles to get a load of bales. As he walked out the door to weigh his truck, he said, "I'll be back in forty-five minutes to weigh my load."

I looked at the clock and thought, "Sure, you will, more like two hours." Forty-five minutes later, Babe pulled onto the scale with a full load, six bales high, weighing a hundred pounds each. He loaded the bales by hand from a bale stack.

Babe waited on Billie Hancock one day while I was opening the day's many letters. Hancocks had purchased Danny's Cafe. Billie complained because she didn't get any letters. After she left, Babe said, "We should write her a letter. You write it, and I'll sign it." I agreed and we composed a letter to Billie.

Dear Billie:

Thirty days hath Septober, Octember, June and Nowonder. All the rest have thirty-one except my grandmother and she has a little red tricycle. And on the other hand, she had a foot."

There was more silly stuff, none of it original. Then we signed the epistle "Bad Bascomb and The Bashful Brunette," and sent it off to Billie.

The winter was fairly mild, and we were happy to see spring come with its green grass and new baby livestock.

Timmie on the pinto stallion, Red Cloud.

A man from Michigan who brought this white mare from us.

Martin Linder on Tar Baby in 1949. He broke her so he 'd have a horse to ride to school.

Harold Severson showing off one of the Severson Angus herd bulls at the Severson farm in Clark, South Dakota.

George Oldenberg and his buried water tank. George moved a lot of snow with that scoop in 1949.

Bud Severson on Cherry, a horse we sold him for $50.00.

CHAPTER 17
The New Wells

We bought a hundred Buff Orpington chicks and moved our hen-house to the flat northwest of our house. We tore the barn and corral down and used the boards from the barn to build a windbreak on the north. Lee built a smaller barn from railroad ties. Our barn yard was now sheltered from the north wind and a lot handier.

Colts and calves gamboled in the north pasture, but Mitchell Creek was between the farmstead and the pasture and could turn into a raging little river that I didn't like to ride across. Being caught at home wasn't bad, but riding down from the pasture to find deep water denying me acess to the house was disturbing. I rode Little John into the creek once, and he had to swim. Little John didn't mind, but I didn't like it.

Lee said she would fix a way to cross. She tied a hay rope between huge elm trees on either bank. The heavy rope hung a few feet above the tumbling water. Lee straddled the rope with one hand in front and one behind and worked herself across. The rope sagged alarmingly close to the water when she reached the center, then uphill again and she dropped to the ground.

I said, "I'm not crossing the creek on that contraption."

Lee laughed. "You might have to. It's easy, try it."

I shook my head. "Nope, not me."

But one day, I rode down from the north pasture and found Mitchell Creek rolling toward Bad River, bank full of muddy water. I didn't want to ride into that angry stream. I rode to the rope bridge. I didn't like it either, but I was hungry. I unsaddled my horse and turned him loose. I eyed the skinny rope bridge and the water rolling beneath it, too close. I took a deep breath and straddled the rope. I inched forward as the rope sagged closer to the roiling water. At midpoint my feet almost touched it. Then I started going up and made it to the other side. I stepped off the rope and walked to the house ten feet tall. I had conquered the rope bridge and the mighty creek.

When the creek ran, the well in the bottom of the creek filled with silt, and we had to dig it out again when the creek went dry. Digging that well out once or twice a year was a tiresome task. Lloyd Heeb offered to witch a well for us. He said he could follow the water vein from the bottom of the creek up on the flat so we could dig a well that wouldn't fill with dirt every time Mitchell Creek ran.

Holding his willow stick between his hands, he trotted across the flat, dodging this way and that. "There she is," he said, grinning. "I can feel the pull on the stick." He followed the vein to a spot a few feet south of our corral. The willow stick mysteriously turned down.

"There it is, you know it," Lloyd said. "Dig right there and you'll hit water." We hoped he was right. We had borrowed Uncle Walt's test auger with the twenty-foot handle. We drilled down, taking turns on the auger and hit water. We couldn't believe our eyes when we pulled that dripping mud out of the hole, but Lloyd wasn't surprised. He knew the water was there.

"Let's go eat supper," Lee said. "Tomorrow we'll dig the well."

After supper, we sat around swapping wild tales. A mouse peeped over the rim of the dish pan sitting under the kerosene stove in the corner. Slowly, I reached for the .22 rifle, leaning against the wall. The mouse popped down, out of sight. We sat like statues. The mouse climbed on the dish pan rim and surveyed the room again. I aimed and pulled the trigger. "Boom!" The mouse disappeared.

Lloyd hooted and slapped his leg. "She shot that son-of-a-buck right off the dish pan."

That mouse didn't bother us anymore, but there were plenty to take its place. One mouse chewed a hole in the wall, crawled into the house and ran into the head strap of a new halter that was laying on the floor. Instead of climbing over the halter, the stupid mouse chewed a round door in it and crawled through it.

We gathered spades and shovels and set out to dig our well. When we were down too far to throw the dirt out, Lee dug dirt loose, and I hauled it up in a bucket and dumped it. At about twenty feet a stream of water gushed into the well. Lloyd was right. We had water. We were elated.

We lowered two chunks of concrete culvert into the well for casing, put a pump in the well and bought a water tank. We situated the tank so stock could drink from inside or outside the corral. We never had water problems on Mitchell Creek again, but we did in the north pasture. The dam was going dry.

Mr. and Mrs. John Remillard rented Frank Dinsmore's place joining our north pasture on the east. They ran a couple hundred Herefords, and they were getting short of water, too. John's saddle horse didn't like to be caught so John would take after him in the pickup. He'd head the horse toward the corral and pepper the old bay with buckshot until he ran into the pen.

Mrs. Remillard was near-sighted and wore thick glasses. I ate dinner there one day and found two iron burrs in my plate of fried potatoes. They were too hard to eat, but I managed to get them off my plate without Mrs. Remillard seeing me.

When we told Aunt Amanda about our water situation, she said, "There's an old homestead well in the draw below your dam. There used to be a post to mark the place. That well had good drinking water. If you find the right place, you'll get all the water you need."

We took a bucket, a rope and a couple of spades one Sunday and went looking for that post. We followed the draw for about a quarter of a mile below the dam and found a post stuck into the ground. The soil around the post was damp. We dug down three feet with a post auger and hit water.

"There's water down there all right," I said, grabbing a spade. I started digging, throwing the damp earth around the growing hole. Lee knocked dirt loose with the other spade. The hole got bigger. At about two feet, we discovered that we were digging inside an old well. Spade marks were plainly visible on the walls, spade marks left by a long ago homesteader.

"We're digging right down the sides of the old well," Lee said, mopping the sweat off her face. "We should hit water before too long."

The original well was about four-feet square with hard shale sides. As the hole got deeper, water seeped in around our feet. I climbed out of the well and pulled buckets of mud up as Lee filled them. At about six feet, a stream of water as big around as my arm shot across the well, nearly hitting the other side.

"Wow!" Lee said. "We hit the vein. Look at that water come in." I helped her out of the well, and we watched the water pour in and cover the bottom of the hole. The water crept up the sides of the well. In a few minutes the water was three feet deep. We pulled up a bucket of clear water and tasted it. The water was cold and good. We had a fine well.

Now all we needed was a pump and a tank, and we had neither. We would have to pull water up with a bucket, a daunting task for around sixty head of livestock. We were admiring our well, when John Remillard walked across the draw. He stared into the hole. "Looks like a good one."

"Yup, now all we need is a tank," Lee said.

"I need water, too," John said. "My dam's dry, and the well is no good. If you let me water my cattle here, I'll put a pump in the well and put a tank here. I can put a motor on the pump and pump for all the stock." He also agreed to stack our hay with his overhead stacker, a good deal all around.

We threw open the gates between the pastures and fenced the well. John never pumped the well dry, although he watered over three hundred head of cattle and horses in his big, round tank.

After our Lincoln blew up, we didn't have a car. Lee went to Iowa to visit her folks and drove home in a black Plymouth she bought from Buster. I learned not to trust second hand Plymouths from that little auto. The Plymouth eventually settled into a draw and rusted away.

Little John and I had been practicing jumping, and we were getting better. I decided to enter the jumping classes at *The Rapid City Range Days* in June. I didn't have English riding boots or pants, but I had a pair of black western riding pants and a black jacket. I bought low heeled Acme cowboy boots and pretended they were English riding boots.

We borrowed Fred McCaroll's one horse trailer, loaded Little John and headed west. The show was held at the fair grounds just east of the city. We unloaded Little John, tied him to a manger in one of the barns and fed him some hay. We couldn't afford a box stall. Little John had never been in a barn before. He didn't like his roomy manger. He didn't like the noisy crowds nor all the strange things to scare the wits out of a country horse. Lee and I went from barn to barn and admired all the pretty horses.

When show time arrived, I saddled Little John and rode onto the race track to await our turn in the first jumping class. Little John rolled his eyes at the people and the noise and the strange things fluttering here and there. I jumped him over the race track fence. He didn't hesitate, but he didn't like the Lakota warriors in their fancy feathers dancing in the arena.

I rode around the race track to limber him up and get his mind off the Lakotas. He was on a spanking trot when we came face to face with a small black bear tethered to a post. Little John nearly fainted, then snorted and whirled around to tear away from this terrible creature that was only about 1/20th as big as he. The bear tried to climb the pole as Little John retreated down the track.

The first horse to jump was a chestnut mare, ridden by an arrogant millionaire from Denver. She was poetry in motion, a perfect score, no faults. Little John walked reluctantly into the arena, star ing at all those white jumps. His head was too high. He didn't like the noisy people in the grandstand. He cantered his circle and headed for the first post and rail. He sailed over that jump, then over another post and rail. Cantering easily, he approached the hen coop. I could feel his hesitation. He didn't want to jump that glittering white hen coop. I guided him straight at the jump. He started to brace his legs to stop and changed his mind, launching himself into a slab sided leap that threw me sideways. My left foot jammed hard against the stirrup. The stirrup gave way, and I came a cropper on the hard ground.

I picked up my stirrup and led Little John on the ignominous walk out of the arena. A lady said, "The poor girl lost a stirrup." What she didn't know was that those stirrups are made to let go so the horse won't drag his hapless rider.

Sunday night in the Stakes Class, Little John did better. He didn't refuse until he came face to face with a picket fence. Little John had never seen a picket fence before. We ended in fifth place and went home with a fancy pink ribbon.

Our cattle herd was growing. We could never mow enough hay with a team and five foot mower to feed them. Ted Barney, Nila's dad, said he had just what we needed, "A John Deere tractor and a seven foot mower." We bought the outfit and hauled it home. The old, green John Deere putted around the field, and the mower laid the grass down, but it was a bear to start. You cranked the John Deere by whirling a giant flywheel on the side. That took muscle.

It was our summer to improve, and Lee needed help so we hired Keith Elrod to work for the summer. Keith was a husky sixteen-year-old, eager to earn some money. I bought a spool of barbed wire, and Keith and I went to the north pasture to build a fence on each side of the dam, making two pastures. Keith couldn't hit a staple. He held the staple against the post and whacked at it a couple of times with the hammer, hit his finger and threw the staple as far as he could. He littered the grass with shiny, new staples.

I said, "Keith, quit throwing the staples away. You're supposed to drive them into the post."

"I know that, but I can't hit a staple," he said, throwing another one down. He finally got his hammer to hit a staple and quit throwing them away.

Keith tried sleeping in the attic, but he felt every two-by -four under the mattress and decided he couldn't sleep there. He wanted to ride from home every day, so I loaned him Little John and said, "You'll have to put him in the shed, or he'll jump out and come home."

"Okay," Keith said, loping over the hill toward town. He led Little John into the pen behind their house near the bank of Mitchell Creek. The board sides of the pen were about six feet high. Keith decided Little John couldn't jump out of the high pen. He unsaddled and went to the house. The next morning, when he came to saddle up, Little John was gone. He had jumped the corral fence and three barbed wire fences. He was home eating grass with his friends.

Shorty quit his job at the packing plant when spring came and went back to work for Harold Gorton. He and Mickey lived in one of Gorton's tiny trailer houses, and he gave them $10.00 per week to buy groceries. Shorty baled flax straw in Minnesota when snow was still on the ground. They came west with Gorton and crew to bale hay in the Midland area. When fall came, Harold Gorton headed for Minnesota, owing Shorty over $600.00, which he never paid. Shorty and Mickey had bills to pay and no money to pay them.

They rented the tiny house by Mitchell Creek that Johnny and Judy had lived in for $12.00 per month. Shorty went to work at Oscar's Mobil Station, selling gas, fixing tires and greasing vehicles. Shorty liked his work and he liked getting paid.

Lee's Plymouth broke down, and she dumped it in a draw to rust away. We went to Iowa to visit her folks and found a red Dodge truck with a fourteen foot box. Trucks were still hard to find, and the Dodge was like new. We borrowed $2,000.00 and happily drove the Dodge home. We were going to be truckers. We could haul hay and cows and horses and make a bunch of money. We could have made money by selling the truck for the $500.00 profit we were offered, but we kept it instead.

Lee immediately drove to the Wall Sales Barn and came back with a load of the wildest horses I had ever seen. When a pair of grulla mares with colts saw me come through the south pasture gate, they headed north in full flight. They ran for two miles and hid behind Saddle Buttes at the far north end of the pasture.

In August, a bunch of us put on a rodeo at the Midland stockyards. Frank Hall furnished the bucking horses. A large arena was fenced with a single strand of rope. The broncs were saddled in a pen and chased out with a cowboy on board. Lloyd Heeb and I were pickup riders, but we never picked a man off his horse. The poor cowboys had to ride until they either fell or jumped off, then we chased the horse back to the pens.

I rode Monte down the row of cars lining the south side of the arena and stopped to talk to Mrs. Dahl. "When are you going to ride a bronc?" she asked.

"I'm never going to ride one," I said.

"But I just came to see you ride."

I shook my head. "Not me." She was put out, but you couldn't have got me on one of those big brutes that acted like they ate dynamite for breakfast if you gave me a million bucks, cold cash. Frank Hall's horses bucked hard. I had learned to be careful what I threw my saddle on.

Sawmills worked along the Missouri River, turning cottonwood logs into rough lumber before the building of the Oahe Dam which would put all that land under water. We needed more corrals on our little ranch. We bought a truck load of cottonwood planks and set to work. I dug holes till I felt like a badger. When we finished we had a large square corral, a round corral and a loading chute. We also built corrals and loading chutes at the north pasture. We could brand and load out without bringing stock home.

Bud Severson drove over from Clark to deliver an Angus bull we bought from him. Uncle Alvin and Dad and the neighbors looked askance at us for putting an Angus bull with our cows.

That just wasn't done then. "We better not let him out of our pasture," they told us. They should have told the bull. He sired bigger calves and climbed bigger fences than the Hereford bulls did.

We got acquainted with Bud Severson when he answered our horse ad in *The Western Horseman* magazine. Bud came and bought a horse or two several times. Bud raised registered Angus cattle, and we got our Angus bulls from Severson Brothers.

We asked Bud if he wanted to practice barrel roping. Being a horse show freak like us, he agreed. We loaned him a horse. I went first on the little gray mare that I later sold to Bob Evans. I loped her past a 15 gallon steel barrel and dropped my loop over the barrel. When the rope tightened, the barrel jumped ten feet in the air and lit with a bang. The gray mare panicked. She bolted straight for a barbed wire fence.

I dropped the rope. The coil caught my saddle horn, and the fence came up with blinding speed. I didn't have time to bail off. The gray mare hit the fence straight on. The top wire broke and she fell through, getting a small cut on her chest. I was unhurt. I had one of the hardest working guardian angels in the business.

September 4, 1948 a baby girl came to live with Uncle Alvin and Essie. Ethlyn Juanita was blond with blue eyes and looked like Uncle Alvin. Ten days later, Nila Martin went to the hospital in Rapid City and delivered a baby girl, also blond and blue eyed. They named her Linda.

We halter broke the two black mares and a gray part Arabian that Lee bought in Wall, but they were flighty. The gray mare flinched every time I touched her. I told Lee, "I'm not riding those horses. They're too wild." I'd had enough of horses that would like to stomp me into the dust of the corral.They scared the wits out of me. I wanted nice, gentle ponies that would eat sugar lumps out of my hand without taking a couple of fingers.

A farmer from southern Minnesota saw our ad in *The Western Horseman* and bought the gray and one black. He said he was going to hitch them to a cultivator and cultivate his corn with them. We delivered the goosey mares to his farm, and I bet he cul tivated the fastest corn in Minnesota.

In October, Archie Joy got his business back from Hefty Dahl. Severt Dale had quit and was farming. Archie went into partnership with Charley Nemec, and they hired Pat Calhoon to manage the new Midland Grain and Lumber Company.

John Sanford and I drove Dad and Uncle Alvin's cattle to the Bad River ranch in November. We gathered the herd of about two hundred cows and drove them out the south gate of the Calhoun pasture. We headed for the Steien place nine miles south where the herd would rest for the night.

When the last cow went through the gate, John let out a bellow and tore across behind the cattle, whirling his rope and scared the cows into a stampede.

"Hey, what are you doing?" I yelled for him to stop.

"I'm getting these babies moving so we can get to Uncle Walt's place," he said.

"You can't run cows." I was disgusted. "You have to let them amble along at their own speed."

"I didn't know that," he said. We let the herd calm down and got them all safely to winter range on Bad River.

The weather was warm. Our hay was stacked along the corral fence. We were ready for winter, we thought. Our cows still grazed in the north pasture, but we weren't worried. If the weather turned sour, we would go up and open the gate and let them drift home.

Ivan and Lyle Dennis the spring of 1949. Darkie is doing a reluctant rear.

CHAPTER 18
The Blizzard of '49

The mighty blizzard that roared in on January 3, 1949 was probably the grandaddy of all blizzards. The screaming wind lasted longer than any winter storm in recorded history. The famous blizzard of 1888 that nearly wiped out the livestock industry in South Dakota and took over a hundred lives in South Dakota alone lasted twelve hours. The blizzard of 1949 raged for the good part of four days, building from January 2, 1949 until January 5, 1949. For nearly eighty-two hours, the wind howled and snow fell, fourteen inches on top of the six or eight already on the ground.

It's a wonder any cattle survived. Many did not. Cattle were buried in snow all over the western ranges as the wind roared past at forty to seventy plus miles an hour.

January l, 1949 was a warm Saturday, so warm that we didn't need jackets. Snow started to fall about mid-morning, but nobody worried. The forecast was for light snow, nothing serious. Lee and I were in town the afternoon of January 2nd. The ground was already covered in six inches of snow. The air felt strange. We decided we should let our cattle out of the north pasture so they could come home to the shelter of Mitchell Creek. Babe Nesheim offered to drive to the pasture, so I jumped in his car and we headed across the snowy prairie. We threw the gate open and went back to town. I figured the cattle would drift to the-gate and head for Mitchell Creek. I wasn't worried about them. Neither was Lee. We should have been.

We headed home and left the truck up on the high hill so it wouldn't get snowed in. The wind rose and began to blow snow around. I saddled Pronto and pulled wood from the creek to the house. We chopped and sawed several days supply and stacked it by the heater. I put the axe and saw in the house. Aunt Amanda had warned us to keep our axe and saw in the house because if your axe got buried in snow you would be in big trouble.

We awoke the third of January to blowing snow so thick and fast, we could barely see the outline of trees along the creek. I built fire, and we settled down to wait out the blizzard. We didn't worry about the cattle. We were confident they would find the open gate and drift to the creek. They didn't.

The wind continued to howl and scream for three more days. On the fourth morning, I opened the door to a world that was covered in white as far as I could see, white, not cold. The temperature climbed to 44 degrees. Pronto ran around in the corral, but not a cow was in sight. We figured they were in the breaks along the creek.

I took the truck and went to town so I could get groceries and catch up on my book work at The Midland Grain and Lumber Company. Lee rode out to find the cattle and bring them home.

I followed the ridges and dodged snow drifts until I reached the fence between Steiens and DeYoungs. Herb and Harold laid the fence down, and I drove across and on to town. I did my book work, got groceries and drove back. We left the Dodge parked on the hill and walked between there and our house for the rest of the winter.

Lee was home with the cattle, but she was short two of our fifty head. She hadn't found the cattle along the creek in the shelter of the high hills and trees. She found them, after hours of riding through sometimes belly deep snow, in the southeast corner of Frank Dinsmore's place, stuck against the barbed wire fence. Instead of coming south, they had drifted southeast with the bitter, angry wind. A blue roan cow got stuck in a snow drift halfway across the pasture. She reared, turned her head to the wind and died. A Hereford heifer fell through the fence and was stuck in a snowbank.

We went to town the next day, planning to load the heifer in the truck and bring her home. Babe Nesheim and Babe Bathel offered to help us put her in the truck. The truck plowed through the snow as we followed the ridges across Adkins' pasture. Lee backed up to the heifer. We tried to scare her into the truck, but she couldn't lunge out of the snow. We tried to lift her into the truck, but she was too heavy. The wind came up, skittering snow across the prairie. Babe Nesheim shot the cow, and we left. Those were our only casualties of The Blizzard of '49.

After two warm days, the temperature plummeted. Our fire went out at night. When the chunks burned down and the coals blinked out, the house grew steadily colder. Frigid air seeped through the walls. Cows crowded close to the house at night, trying to draw heat into their cold bodies. Sometimes, we woke and heard the snow squeaking as a cow shifted from one miserable foot to another. I got up to build fire one morning, and the temperature inside the house was 35 degrees below zero. I built a roaring fire and dived back into bed. I covered up my head and waited for the house to warm up.

We got twenty-four inches of snow in January, and the temperature averaged eleven degrees below zero. Blizzard followed blizzard, blowing newly opened roads shut tight. Four times the wind blew a hurricane. County snow plows couldn't keep the roads open. Heinie Koch's bull dozers worked out of Midland, roaring day and night to break through the huge drifts. The dozers left the roads and followed ridges because drifts in draws were too deep to plow through.

Babe Nesheim drove one of Koch's bull dozers. Ranchers stalled in town followed the dozers home, sometimes leaving their car or pickup and walking the last miles home over the hard snow drifts. Roads were opened and by the next morning the path was drifted shut again. Bulldozers took until the middle of February to free the last farmer in Pennington County from his snow jail.

The blizzard caught most of western South Dakota unaware. The wind started blowing in the Wall area Sunday afternoon, but hadn't yet reached our territory. Teachers were caught in country school houses. Travelers were stranded in motels and hotels.

Myrtle Fleming, teacher of the Lucerne School twenty-two miles northeast of Philip, went to the school house Sunday afternoon. Since she batched at school during the week, she had plenty of food and coal. She was alone at the school house when the blizzard winds roared and screamed across the prairie. She had no phone. No children came to school. Five days later on Friday afternoon, she walked west to Eugene Noack's ranch.

He told her there would be no school for weeks because getting children to school would be impossible. He thought if she went west to Highway 73, she could catch a ride as soon as the snow plow went through. She walked over the drifts, but no plow had been through. No cars moved on the asphalt road.

Myrtle Fleming struggled on. She got to the Lloyd Buchert ranch and ate lunch. Mrs. Buchert asked her to stay, but Myrtle wanted to reach a telephone. Mrs. Buchert loaned her a flashlight, and she headed home over the glittering snow. She crawled on hands and knees over steep and icy snowbanks arriving home at two thirty Saturday morning. She had walked twenty-two miles over huge snow drifts, mostly at night. She was one tough woman, and mighty thankful to be home.

In tiny Wicksville, population 13, between Philip and Rapid City, 71 motorists were stranded. They found shelter in three homes, a store and two gas stations. They played cards, told tall tales, and read every magazine they could lay their hands on. One station ran low on coal and burned used tires in the stove. The snow plow rammed through a cut near Wicksville that was over a thousand feet long and twenty feet deep. Interstate 90 now runs a few miles north of Wicksville.

So many people were crammed into hotels and motels in Wall that they took turns sleeping in the beds. Some slept during the night, others during the day. By the second day one hotel door was blocked with snow, and they had to tunnel out. People slept on floors, in chairs and on counters. The lucky ones got the rooms. They played bridge, whist, hearts and gin rummy as they waited for the wind to die, and the snow plow to come.

Snow drifts hid the train in a cut near Wall. The mail and much of the freight came on the railroad. With the trains stopped by snow, mail didn't come for a month. Frank Dinsmore followed the dozers to Moenville three times in January, driving his mail route from Midland.

The Moenville country didn't have telephones. People listened to their radios for news of friends or relatives stranded in the snow or in towns. Planes flew missions day after day, looking for SOS signs in the snow. Georgia Jipp and her father flew out of the Philip Airport, taking farmers and ranchers stranded in town to their homes and dropping notes and food. They hauled people to hospitals and medicine to farm homes.

At Martin, planes had to be shoveled out of the snow. Pilot Edison Ward spent Thursday afternoon and Friday flying expectant mothers to Martin, Pine Ridge and Rosebud hospitals. The pilots saw dead cattle, some still standing, smothered by the fine snow that iced their nostrils shut. Fences disappeared under snow. Only the tops of trees stuck out. Houses were nearly buried. One could walk from a snow bank onto the roof of the house. The mighty blizzard filled draws and creeks and leveled spaces between hills with fifteen to twenty feet of snow.

One rancher put his cattle in a shed with a hay roof. As snow drifted into the shed the cattle tramped it down until the snow was so deep they stood on four feet of solid snow. They barely had room to stand, but they had food. They ate the roof.

John Ostlein from the Moenvlle country was a Norwegian immigrant and an expert skier. He borrowed skis and skied around his neighborhood to help anyone in need. He rescued a neighbor's herd of thirty bewildered cows stuck in a snow corral. Happily, John freed the cattle and led them to their home corral. John was helping a neighbor get home during the evening when their car stalled in a drift. John put their four year old son on his back and skied six miles to their house. The house was cold, so John built a fire, then skied back to the car and helped the rest of the family get home. All winter, John helped his neighbors, skiing up and down steep hills and across flats.

Willard Bloom, who lived south of Quinn, found one of his cows in the top of a plum tree. The cow was standing on twenty feet of snow, and had been in the tree for fourteen days without food. Willard dismounted and walked over to scare her out of the snow corral she had made around herself. With an angry snort, she broke out of her white pen and chased him back to his horse. He lost twenty-four of his sixty-five head of cattle.

Curt Anderson was working on the Cheyenne Indian Reservation for Western Farm Management, staying in a cabin on Rudy Creek. When the big blow was over, he saddled his horse and rode out to search for cattle. He found thirty cows locked in a snow corral. They had taken shelter in a protected spot and tramped around until the sides were too deep for them to get out. Curt rode his horse in and out of the snow corral until he had a trail for the cattle to follow his horse out of their prison.

Many ranchers and farmers had hay stacks, but their tractors and loaders were buried in snow with no way to get them out except by shoveling. Getting feed to stranded cattle was often an impossible task. Drifts were deep and wide. Most farmers didn't have snow moving equipment. Heinie Koch, who lived in Midland, had two dozers and opened roads into farms and to haystacks, but they couldn't keep up with the blowing snow. Air Force planes flew over and dropped hay to starving cattle.

Heinie Koch was a daring pilot and flew over the country, looking for distress signals and stranded cattle. He flew in groceries and medicine and took people to the doctor. Like other pilots, he spotted hungry cattle and notified the Air Force. The pilots saw hundreds of dead cattle caught in snow too deep for them to escape from.

Brother Hank and Uncle Alvin hauled hay with trucks from the north pasture to Bad River. They made the forty mile trip once each day, if possible. They were ready to head out the afternoon of January 2nd, when Hank said, "My truck needs a little a little fixing. Can you wait a half hour?"

Hank tuned up the GMC and slammed the hood down. A gust of wind whirled snow into the air. The wind rose chasing snow across the ground. "We better wait till morning," Uncle Alvin said.

They spent most of the next three days in the house, watching the snow whip past. Cattle walking between the house and chicken house were moving shadows in a hazy, white world, but they found shelter in the trees and breaks along Bad River. When the blow was over, Hank and Uncle Alvin hauled hay again. They needed to haul hay every day, but they couldn't always get through. Getting hay to the cattle was a nightmare of shoveling snow and breaking axles. There was plenty of hay, but hauling it was a constant battle with wind and snow. Hank broke an axle crossing a draw and had to get under the truck in the snow and repair his vehicle.

Ranchers on the prairie had much harder conditions to contend with. Drifts filled corrals and sheds, and grew around buildings. Chicken houses were often buried, the snow insulating the chickens from the cold.

Our cattle were surviving. One evening about sundown, we saw someone walking across the flat west of our house. We stood by the hay corral fence, watching him stride toward us. Harold DeYoung walked up to us and said, "Road's open." Then he turned around and went home. He truly was a man of few words.

I made it to work often enough to keep up on my book work at The Midland Grain and Lumber Company. They sold tons of cow cake. February turned warm. Snow melted, making icy patches. I rode Pronto around, looking through the cattle and wished he had neverslip shoes, but he didn't fall. I dragged logs up for our heater with Pronto, too.

Ronald Dennis wandered down with Peewee and Lyle one

Sunday. He was a big husky kid, and he grabbed a pitchfork and helped me throw on a load of hay. The first few forkfuls went all right, then he stuck the fork deep in the stack and reared back, trying to load half the rack with one fork of hay and broke the fork handle. He grinned and shrugged like "I can't help it, if I'm so strong." It always made me mad when men showed off their strength by breaking my pitchfork handles. I could break a pitchfork handle too, but I didn't. I had to have fork handles to feed cattle. If some Neanderthal broke a fork handle, that meant I had to go to town, get a new handle and fix the fork.

The Dennis children went to school in Midland because the Eureka school west of their place was closed. Hank Dennis had trouble getting them to school because the road blew shut about as fast as it was opened. Toward the end of January, Lyle and Peewee Dennis rode down to see us.

"Dad wants to know if you'll take us to town with the team," Lyle said. "We haven't been to school all month." Lyle said Hank wanted us to haul Hope, the children, cooking utensils, clothing and blankets to town. "Dad rented us a house at the M&M cabins." Lyle grinned.

We had a team, but we didn't have a bob sled, or even a wagon anymore. All we had was the hayrack, and it had rubber tires. The team couldn't pull the hayrack all the way to Midland and back in the deep snow. Midland was about six miles from the Dennis place, six miles of snow so deep the draws were nearly level. Huge drifts buried fences. You couldn't even find a gate, if it was in the way of a snow drift.

We told the boys we would see if we could borrow Uncle Walt's bobsled, a relic from pioneer days. We weren't even sure the old sleigh would hold together long enough to get to town and back. The tongue was still strong though, and we could use our neck yoke and double trees. The bobsled's box had long ago rotted away. Uncle Walt found some old boards and built a box. We hitched Big Bertha and the bald-faced bay mare to the sleigh and rode it home. We spread hay on the bottom of the box and headed for the Dennis farm.

The day was clear and cold. Snow squeaked and crackled with every step the horses took. The sled glided over the snow. It sure beat a wagon when snow reached from horizon to horizon.

At the Dennis house, we loaded cooking equipment, blankets and clothing. Bundled up in coats, caps, mittens, overshoes and scarves, Butch, Judy and Sadie climbed into the bobsled and snuggled down for the adventure of their lives. Lee and Hope settled into the hay, and I turned the team southeast across the white, trackless prairie. Lyle and Peewee walked behind the sled, climbing on to ride when they got tired.

Sadie, Butch and Judy snuggled under the quilts and peeked out. Where gates were drifted over, we took the fence down or drove over it on the solidly packed snow. We skirted the deepest draws on the DeYoung place, crossing at the shallow end. The country telephone line marched across the prairie, the twenty foot poles going into a draw and disappearing under snow, to emerge again hundreds of feet away.

We unloaded Hope, the kids and their gear at the small house Hank had rented. They stayed in Midland until spring when the snow melted and roads were passable once more. We drove the team home in the gathering twilight and returned Uncle Walt's bobsled to the hillside. That was the last trip the old sled made.

I decided all that snow would be a good place to ride the black Morgan mare Lee bought in Wall. She was a beautiful horse, but she didn't want anything to do with humans. We had tied her to a log so she was halter broken. We sacked her out, saddled her and hung Lee's chaps on the saddle horn. She tore up some snow trying to throw the flopping thing off, but it stayed. I rode her in the round corral, around the mound of snow that had piled in the center. I rode her around a few times and unsaddled.

On Sunday forenoon, Martin Linder rode out to see how we were standing the winter. He was riding Tar Baby, a Morgan mare we loaned him to ride to school from his dad's farm about four miles west of Midland. Tar Baby wasn't broke when he got her, but she would be by spring. I asked Martin if he wanted to ride my black mare.

He said, "Sure," and threw his saddle on her. He mounted and she threw him off in the snowbank. He got up mad at the silly little mare that thought he couldn't ride her. He offered to give her a good ride.

I saddled Pronto and we headed north to check on the horses in the big pasture. The black mare didn't buck even once. The range horses were getting thin from pawing through snow for grass and eating snow for water. By the time the black mare had traveled ten miles in deep snow, she was peaceful and quiet. I hoped she would break out gentle.

With March and April came warm days and the promise of spring. I drove the Dodge truck to work, and we thought we needed a vehicle for Lee to drive. We bought a 4x4 army truck from Burns Garage. About all that truck was good for was making deep ruts in the prairie, ruts so deep they will probably be there for a hundred years.

The snow melted and cascaded down the draws and into creeks and rivers. Mitchell Creek ran deep and covered the flat nearly reaching our house before it retreated again to the creek.

The snow in the corrals melted, leaving the big corral ankle deep in slop. The snowbank was gone from the round corral. I threw my saddle on the black mare and rode her in the round corral. She moved quietly, not offering to buck.

"I'll let her out in the big corral," Lee said, opening the gate. She was always being brave for me.

I urged the mare through. She snorted at both sides of the gate and walked into the large corral, picking her way carefully. I kicked her ribs. She hunched her back, ducked her head and unwound. I grabbed the saddle horn, socked my spurs in and hung on. I sure didn't want to fall off into that muck. The little, black mare bucked all over the corral until she was so tired, she had to quit. She didn't buck again, but I never rode her outside of the pen.

We hauled her to the Fort Pierre Sales Barn when spring came. I rode her into the ring. She walked to the fence and stood in one spot, eyeing the people in the seats. I let her stand quietly and hoped the ring men would keep their whips down and she wouldn't explode. She was a beautiful animal, and, being ridden by a woman, the bidders figured she had to be gentle. She brought a fair price, and I often wondered what happened to the buyer when he climbed aboard and kicked her into a lope. Because of that misconception I was sometimes asked to ride a horse for other sellers. Some guy would lead a horse down the alley and say, "Hey, will you ride my horse? He'll bring more money then." I always rode the horse through the ring, but I never claimed the animal was gentle.

By the time spring was peeking around the corner, a lot of cattle had ribs showing and badly needed warm weather and green grass. I was riding at Uncle Alvin's ranch and came upon one of Dad's cows standing in the middle of Bad River with the icy water running around her knees. She looked exactly like the painting *The Last Of The 5,000.* Her skin was tight against her bones, a pitiful sight. She didn't live to see the grass grow green.

The grass did come. Flowers bloomed. We drove our cattle to the north pasture. Colts and calves frolicked on green hills once more. We were ready for a new season. We were ready for more room, too. Tired of living in a one room shack. Lee said she could build a room out of the dugout room, if we moved the kitchen back to it. We dug the room about six feet wider. Lee shored it up with rocks from the prairie, and we poured a cement floor. We borrowed a couple of handyman jacks and jacked the house back to fasten to the stone room. Lee put on the roof and paneled the living room with real knotty pine boards. Thus we added a living room and bedroom to our house. We even had a clothes closet. Lyle and Peewee Dennis could sleep on a cot in the living room now instead of climbing into the attic. It was a fine addition.

When Little Judy, my niece, who was now four and lived in Aberdeen, came to visit, she loved the new living room. She stood in the doorway, admiring the walls for a moment, then said, "My, you got your knots matched nice."

Those rooms were a lovely addition to our house, but when rain came, water ran down the sloping roof, under the walls and through the rocks to puddle in the middle of the living room floor.

Little Judy and her brother, John Lee, spent many summer days with us. Judy liked to ride the horses and play around the yard. She came into the house for supper one evening, washed her hands and came to the table. "Judy, your face is dirty," I said. "You have to wash your face, too."

She went back to the washstand and looked at the wash dish for a moment, then said to Lee, "Will you wash my face? I already washed my hands and I don't want to get them wet again."

In March, Martin and Edith Schofield moved from Pete Fosheim's place about twenty-five miles north of Midland to Harry Schofield's ranch on Brave Bull Creek. They had traded a small Caterpillar to Pete for twenty-three Hereford cows. Martin hired us to haul the cow's from Edith's dad's place to his dad's ranch.

We hauled one load while the ground was still frozen. We loaded the rest and headed out. I was driving. Lee and Martin rode along. Everything went fine until we turned in at the Schofield gate. The road sloped for a mile down to the buildings nestled on the meadow above Brave Bull. Patches of snow stuck to the hills. Ice under the muddy patches made them even slicker. I eased the truck down the hill and headed across the flat toward the corrals. The truck hit a wet spot and slid slowly south. The wheels caught on a hard rut and laid the truck over on the side.

The cows spilled out of the box and headed south while Martin and Lee walked on top of me. I was scrunched behind the steering wheel. Martin weighed about two hundred pounds, and he was scrambling around, trying to get the door open and trampling on Lee and me. He pushed the door open and climbed out ready to run after his cows.

"Hey, Martin, wait," Lee said. "Hold the door open so we can get out."

"Oh, oh," Martin said and laid the door wide. He jumped to the ground, and Lee scrambled out. I crawled out from under the steering wheel and followed. Martin ran after his cattle, heading them toward the corral. We helped him herd the cows home and put them safely in the pen. We went back to the truck. The Dodge wasn't damaged, and we waited for Martin to come with his dad's little Ford tractor. Martin hooked a cable to the truck and tipped it back on the wheels. I wasn't the only one to tip the Dodge over.

Lee tipped the truck over in Iowa with a load of horses and her Grandma Andersen as a passenger. Roads were slick and muddy from rain. The truck skidded over, tipping the horses out. Lee and Grandma were not hurt, but Grandma got her long hair full of gravel. Aunt Spick spent an hour combing the gravel out of Grandma's hair. Buster wondered if Grandma had clean underwear on because she always warned him to put clean underwear on in the morning in case he got in an accident.

In June, Mickey went to the Midland Hospital where Dr. Nishamura delivered a baby girl,named Kandace Ann.

Fly's foal that spring was a beauty, a black and white paint filly. We named her Stardust Queen. Her father was Red Cloud, a showy chestnut and white stallion that Lee bought after we sold Pronto to a horse breeder from east of the Missouri River. Buyers also showed up from Minnesota, Michigan, and Illinois. Unfortunately, horses weren't worth much. Two well broke saddle horses might buy one cow. Now it takes two or three cows to get one horse.

About the middle of the summer, a man from Illinois showed up, looking for paint horses. He had come mainly to look at Red Cloud. "He has a beautiful color," he said when we showed him the horse. Red Cloud had been wire cut at some time and one hock was enlarged, but he wasn't lame. The man shook his head. "You should have mentioned the hock in your letter." He looked down at us from his superior height, and we looked foolish. We didn't know that. We thought you looked at a horse and if you wanted to buy it, you did.

He smiled. He was a nice man. He published a magazine called *The Illinois Horseman*, and was looking for horses for a riding club in his town. He bought Red Cloud, Redwing and Blue, parting with $250.00 for Red Cloud and a lesser amount for the mares. He loaded his horses and went back to Illinois.

We were going out of the paint business. We'd had two paint studs and didn't get many paint colts from either of them. Paints were going out of style anyway. Palominos were the rage now. We wanted either a Thoroughbred or a Quarter Horse for our next stallion. Lee went to a horse sale in Whitewood and came home instead with a registered Half-breed mare named Miss Sheridan. Miss Sheridan was seven eighths Thoroughbred, deep chestnut, and a beauty. I had no trouble breaking her to ride. Lee also bought me a new saddle with a Little Wonder tree, a pancake seat and a low cantle. For a while, every time my horse jumped, I lit behind the saddle.

I turned Miss Sheridan into the north pasture and when I caught her a couple of months later, she tried to dump me. I sold her first colt to Whisler Brothers for their nephew. Her next colt broke his leg and had to be destroyed. Her last foal was a lovely Palomio filly. I was taking the horses to the north pasture when the foal turned into a patch of buckbrush, caught her neck in a barbed wire fence and cut her jugular vein. She also died. I sold Miss Sheridan to Bud Severson, and she went to Clark, South Dakota. Her life was better there.

Just before haying season started, Lee went to Iowa and bought a woman-killing baler from her dad. Women usually rode those mad machines, poking baling wire through the hay for another female to poke back so the first one could tie the wires. Then the bale popped out the back end of the machine, and another bale was ready to tie.

We baled a field of hay for Davy Heeb south of Ottumwa with our clanking old baler. Lee drove the tractor pulling the baler, and Lloyd Heeb and I rode the baler. After we finished Davy's hay we pulled into Lloyd's place and baled hay on shares. Baling hay is hot, dusty work and not much fun. Sweat ran down our faces. By the time the sun was low in the west, we were all ready to go home, and we still had two trucks to load with bales. Our truck held a hundred and twenty bales. Lloyd's snub nose held about forty more.

Lee drove the trucks around the field. Lloyd and I walked along on either side of the truck and threw those ninety pound bales until I had to climb on the flatbed and stack them. By the time we got 260 bales loaded, I was tired, cranky, ornery and anxious to get home. Lloyd tied the bales down, and we headed for Mitchell Creek.

The road was narrow with square corners. I drove too fast around a corner and the load shifted, and the whole thing slid into the ditch. I braked and we got out. Lloyd stopped behind us. We looked at the mess beside the road. I said some unkind things about people who couldn't tie a load of bales so they stayed put.

Lloyd was tired, too. He blew his stack. He told me where I could go, how I could get there and what I could do after I got there. It rocked me back so hard I nearly broke the heels off my boots. Lee never said a word. She just stood there like a totem pole and listened. I thought, "Boy, you sure had that coming." Lloyd helped us load our bales, and we went home.

We baled a stack of hay at home one fall day. Aunt Amanda pitched hay into the baler while Lee and I tied bales. Aunt Amanda was sixty-four years old, but she pitched hay into the baler all day and thought it was fun.

No intelligent rancher sells hay, but we did. We hauled baled hay to Onida, Rapid City, Hot Springs and Sun Dance, Wyoming. We sold a load to Tri-State Milling in Rapid City and Nila's cousin, Rex Barney, and a couple of husky young men came out to stack bales. Rex told Nila he thought they were going to have an easy hour of work. We were afraid they would think we were too slow, so we threw bales off as fast as we could. We always had a bale waiting. Rex and his buddies worked themselves into a sweat.

I drove a load to Sun Dance, going on the steep and winding

Black Hills roads past Spearfish in the dark. Coming back in daylight scared me. Lee said, "No use getting scared now. You drove through here in the dark once."

Uncle Walt decided he wasn't going through another winter like 1949. He put his ranch up for sale and prepared to move to Midland. He bought some lots at the west edge of town, tore down the homestead shack north of his place and built a house. The house is now the home of Mickey and Shorty Woitte.

We stopped one day to see how he was doing. His house was all enclosed and new rafters lay across the top. "I could nail those rafters in place in an hour, if I had somebody to hold them," he said.

We held the rafters in place while he nailed. In an hour he was ready to nail on the roof boards. He was almost eighty years old when he built this home. They moved in that fall.

We wanted to buy Uncle Walt's place, but we couldn't figure out where to get the money. By the time Uncle Walt and Ralph Jones got through haggling over the price of 3,000 acres and twenty good Hereford cows and a bull, Uncle Walt had dealt off one of Aunt Amanda's milk cows in the deal. She only got to keep one. She was slow to anger, but I think she would have liked to kick two male hind ends all the way to the barn. She moved her milk cow to the small barn with the hay roof that Uncle Walt built south of the house. She staked her cow by the railroad track or on the meadow west of the house during the day and fed her hay at night. For a few years she milked her cow twice a day and dreamed about being back on the ranch on Mitchell Creek.

When spring came, we moved our cattle to the north pasture, and new colts and calves began to arrive. This winter had been fairly mild, but we did get some snow. By April, Bad River ran deep, and several feet of water roared over the Brave Bull bridge. At the Bertelson ranch, they were expecting more than baby calves.

Bud Adams on Silver Moon.

Mickey and Kandy on Stardust Queen. Kandy's first horseback ride.

(Right) Essie and Uncle Alvin holding Little Alvin and Ethlyn. (Below) Betty and Gary Eng on Stardust Queen.

CHAPTER 19
Calves, Colts and Babies

Essie was pregnant with her second child and ready to give birth any time. With the river and creek so deep, Uncle Alvin couldn't drive across to take her to the hospital in Midland. Essie worried about getting there in time. Heinie Koch said they could call him, and he would hop into his plane and fly over and take Essie to the hospital. Essie still worried as the day drew nearer.

"Don't worry," Uncle Alvin said. "I've delivered lots of calves. I can deliver a baby without any trouble."

On April 17, 1950, Essie went into labor. Bad River roared past nearly bankful. Water still rolled several feet deep over the Brave Bull bridge. They decided to go south to the Tom Jones' pasture, then follow the trail to the road from Belvidere to Nowlin. At Nowlin, they could cross on the Bad River bridge and go to Midland, a trip of about twenty miles.

"I'll start the pickup," Uncle Alvin said, heading for the door. "You get Ethlyn ready."

He drove south, climbing the Bad River Breaks, and turned west across the flat. He got out to open a gate, and Ethlyn pulled the choke out. The motor flooded and died.

Uncle Alvin jumped into the pickup and tramped on the starter. The starter buzzed, but the motor was silent. Uncle Alvin stomped on the starter and cussed the pickup. Essie had never seen him get excited about anything before, but he was excited now. He may have delivered a thousand calves, but he didn't want to deliver even one baby. He hit the starter again, and the motor roared to life. He grinned and put the pickup in gear.

He drove to Midland, left Ethlyn with Aunt Amanda and took Essie to the Midland Hospital where Dr. Nishamura delivered a blond, blue-eyed baby boy. Essie wanted to name her son Alvin Oscar Jr. Alvin held out for Donald Alvin. They reached a stalemate, so Uncle Alvin went down town to the Midland Bar and told bartender Dave Owens about the name impasse.

"Oh," Dave said, "He's got to be Alvin Oscar Jr. You better name him Alvin Oscar." Uncle Alvin went back to the hospital and told Essie she had won the baby naming contest.

That summer Archie Joy moved the Tri-State Insulation Company and his family to Miller, South Dakota. Charley and Virgie Nemec moved into the Joy house. Pat Calhoon died of a heart attack in May. He was only a few years older than I. John Buchanan took his place and managed The Midland Grain and Lumber Company. I worked the rest of the summer, then quit and went to work full time on the ranch.

We leased the Wenger place about a mile east of our pasture and some land across Highway 14 east of the Wenger farm. Lee hired Hazel Stickler to mow hay. Hazel was working in Millie's Cafe, but she said she would rather mow hay for $4.00 per day than wait tables for the same amount. She took off her waitress apron, donned a straw hat and climbed on the old John Deere. Hazel mowed a pile of hay.

We sold the wicked hay baler and bought an overhead hydraulic stacker, mounted on an International truck chassis. We stopped in Murdo one day, and my old school mate, Willard Burns, sold us a little, green army jeep for $500.00. The jeep was a wonderful machine. It would roar through snow and mud belly deep, pull a load of hay or go gayly off to town when a car hid behind the house to keep out of the mud. The little, green jeep could double for a saddle horse and carry a few sacks of cow cake in the box.

Later we mounted a mower on the back bumper and turned it into a mowing machine. We were set to make the hay fly.

That summer The United States was at war again, this time in Korea. Harry Truman was President. Leonard and Ronald Dennis went to Korea. Dwayne Dale and Ole Nelson fought there. War reached into our homes and into our hearts once more, a scant five years after the end of World War II.

We hauled our hay home and stacked it in the hay yard. We moved our cattle to the Wenger place to winter where the grass was thick and knee deep. We tried to feed the happy cattle a load of hay in the middle of the winter, but they were so full and satisfied that they turned up their noses at the hay. The winter was lovely, but we were happy to see spring come.

Our Buff Orpington hens hid nests under the hay rack, beside posts and in the shelter of trees. They hatched plump tan chicks and taught them to chase bugs and grab worms. The ducks and geese swam in the dam and in the creek and were fiercely protective of their babies. Baby animals gamboled on the hillsides, and one more grandson came for Mom and Dad.

Ted Henry Martin was born March 19, 1951, the third child for Herb and Nila. On July 27th another grandson arrived. Rex Dean Woitte, Mickey and Shorty's second child joined Kandy, their first.

Herb graduated from The School of Mines with a degree in Mechanical Engineering. The Army Air Force immediately grabbed him. Major Herbert Martin was stationed at The Ellsworth Air Base east of Rapid City. He was Commanding Officer of the Motor Vehicle Squadron for a time, then became Executive Officer of the Operations Squadron. Bud Callan was not so lucky. He was navigator of a plane that was missing in action in Korea. He was never found.

Uncle Charley Myrland died in May. He was 87 years old and told us he longed for his heavenly home. Aunt Tina was alone after 59 years of marriage.

We fenced our north quarter during the summer. Herbie and Linda Martin were visiting us and helped, carrying hammers and fencing pliers. Herbie was four and took his job seriously. Linda wanted to stand under the shiny barbed wire, and I was constantly moving her. We finished and had our hay quarter.

I saw a cow across the fence in Ernest Nemec's pasture one day. I rode after the stray and was chasing her into her own pasture when I saw Ernest coming across the prairie in his pickup.

"Oh, oh," I thought. "You better get out of here. He'll give you heck." I shut the gate. The pickup roared closer. I swung into the saddle as Ernest and young Ernie pulled up beside the fence. Ernest visited a while, then asked if I had a horse gentle enough for his kids to ride. I sold him a black pony and delivered it a couple of days later.

I bought a buckskin Quarter Horse stallion from Lloyd Heeb for $125.00. His name was Yokley's Silver Moon. He had been brought up from Texas. I ran Silver up on a calf so fast the little critter bawled for his mother. Silver was gentle, but he would unload if something scared him. I was riding him and had about six feet of rope dangling. I went to coil the rope and it caught under my saddle fender. Silver felt the rope pull and heard the buzzing noise and bucked me off.

In June of 1951, Buddy's draft number came up. He became Private Albert Martin in the US Army. He was lucky. He was sent to the European Theater and spent his time in Italy and Austria. Some of his friends were fighting in Korea. Leonard Dennis and Ole Nelson were seriously wounded. PFC Ole Nelson took shrapnel in one arm. As he walked to the Aid Station, he came upon a soldier with a knee so blown apart that the leg was almost torn off. With his good arm, Ole managed to get the soldier's pack off. They struggled toward the Aid Station with Ole holding onto his fallen comrade. From there they were transported to a Military Hospital in Osaka, Japan where Ole recuperated for three months.

Captain Rupert Nelson flew a C119 two engine plane, hauling cargo. He lost a motor and went down in The Sea of Japan. The plane went down about twenty miles from shore. Most of the men were rescued, but Captain Nelson was not. Danny Eng lost his life in Korea. Midland again felt the effects of war.

I mowed hay across Highway 14 with the Jeep. We put a power-takeoff on the jeep and mounted a seven foot International mower on the back bumper. It was the most comfortable hay outfit I ever used. I sat in the shade and ate graham crackers and watched the hay fall. We loaded the hay with our stacker and hauled the loads home to our hay corral. We figured we were ready for a winter and a half.

We had given Lyle and Peewee Dennis a homely bay mare for riding the hay rake one year. They broke her to ride and had taken her to Uncle Alvin's north pasture. When they wanted to get their horse back, we rode up and ran the horse herd into the corral. I caught the mare and threw my saddle on her. I cinched her down a little quick, and, when Lyle started to mount, she jerked loose and bucked across the corral.

"Wow!" Lyle said.

That silly little horse couldn't throw a cat out of a greased saddle, I thought. I ran and caught the reins and swung aboard. She squealed like a pig in a woven wire fence, ducked her head and came undone. I found myself a foot above the saddle with plenty of daylight showing under the seat of my pants. I reached down, grabbed the saddle horn and pulled myself back on the seat. I hung on with everything I had while she tried to unload. She scattered horses all over the corral and finally came to a standstill, blowing like a steam engine. I rode over to the boys, stepped off and handed Lyle the reins.

Lyle and Peewee looked at me with eyes as big as hen's eggs. They were properly impressed, and I made up my mind I wouldn't do that again.

That fall, Lee and I went to Philip and bought a 1952 tan Chevrolet from Dorothy Brothers. I drove the new car back to Midland and we picked up Mickey and Judy and kids. We cruised down Main Street and saw Shorty walking home from the post office. I slowed up and Mickey and Judy yelled, "Hey, Handsome, do you want a ride."

"No, no, I'm going home." Shorty didn't even look at us. He skeddadled down the street.

We drove around the block, laughing, and got to his house about the same time he did. I pulled up beside him and stopped. He looked at us and said, "I knew it was you all time." We didn't believe him.

We decided we didn't need the John Deere and its rusty mower since we had the Jeep and mower so we dealt the outfit to John "Bud" Gillaspie. Bud and Avis and three small children came after the tractor and mower one Sunday. We were working on the Dodge truck. The clutch had gone out, and Lee was going to put it back. I drove the Dodge under the big cottonwood east of the house. We fastened a log chain around the motor and hoisted it into the tree. Lee put the new clutch in. The motor was poised above the truck, and we were contemplating the job of lowering the motor back into the truck, and getting all those bolts lined up right when Bud and Avis came.

Bud grabbed a wrench and helped us get the motor fastened in place. Meanwhile Little Ronnie and Little John found a two-wheeled cart to play with. Evelyn toddled along, trying to help push the cart up a small hill. The cart got away and backed over Evelyn. We were happy to see the old John Deere leave and have our Dodge truck mobile again.

The pasture east of Highway 14 wasn't fenced on the west side, but we wanted to let the cows eat off some of the grass so Lee moved our small trailer house there and herded the cattle off the highway. She had made the neat, little house from masonite panels, and it had all the comforts of home on a tiny scale. We were there on December 8th when the first snow of winter came--about ten inches of white stuff that buried the grass. When we woke up and saw all that snow, we knew we better get our cows home before a blizzard hit.

I drove home across the prairie to get a saddle horse. I couldn't drive across the creek, so I parked the car on the north side. Wind came and snow buried the new Chevy. I saddled Silver and rode after the cattle. Lloyd Heeb who was wintering his cattle on the Linder place west of town rode along to help drive the herd home. I broke trail and Lloyd drove the cattle. Lee drove the Jeep. The cows were happy to get to Mitchell Creek with its trees and sheltering high hills.

I brought Big Bertha and the brother of the bald-faced bay mare home to haul hay to the cattle. He was almost a dead ringer for his sister. Big Bertha was their mother. They were the last draft horses we broke. Every morning, I pitched a load of hay on the rack, and we hauled the load to the feed ground. I liked to feed the cattle with a team. Lee drove the team while I pitched hay to the cows as they ran from bunch to bunch to be sure the next forkful wasn't better than the one they left. The Jeep pumped the water.

Butch Dennis, a little red-haired guy about eight-years-old, was helping me feed one day. I had tied the lines together and looped them over the post in the center of the rack. The team moseyed along as I threw off the last of the hay. Butch held the ends of the line, and thought he was driving. I pushed the last of the hay out the back end of the rack. Butch hollered "Whoa!" in his high-pitched voice.

The squeaky command startled the horses. They broke into a trot. Butch yelled, "Whoa!" louder and the horses trotted faster. I sprinted across the rack and grabbed the lines. The horses dropped back to a walk. They seemed relieved to hear a familiar "Whoa" and know I was in command of the hay wagon.

We had a dandy winter shaping up. A foot of snow already covered the ground. We hadn't had any big wind, but we felt a little uneasy. Keith Elrod went to work for Johnny Roberts. Johnny had bought a ranch east of Highway 14 from Thurman Adkins who went back to Texas. Roberts paid $25.00 per acre and bought a large herd of calves to winter. He already had a herd of registered Hereford cattle. He was about to get an education in South Dakota weather.

Monday morning, January 21, 1952 dawned bright, clear and still. Curt Anderson was working on the Tom Jones' ranch about eight miles south of Midland and said he could hear people in Midland talking. Nothing stirred. If a feather dropped, it would have fallen straight to the ground.

We fed the cattle early and had just finished putting the team away when the wind hit. The blizzard came with blinding force, instantly cutting visibility to zero. We couldn't even see the trees along the creek. I had never before seen so much snow in the air.

The wind caught ranchers unaware; children in school; travelers whereeever they were. The temperature dropped rapidly. The blizzard of 1952 turned out to be among the worst on record in South Dakota, rivaling the legendary blizzard of 1888.

The Dennis children, Lyle, Peewee, Sadie and Butch walked across the pasture west for a mile to school while the brilliant sun scattered diamonds across the snow. The Snook children, Gene and Carl stayed home. Their father had heard the weather forecast. When the blizzard suddenly blanked out the world, Eleanor Rhodes, the teacher, and the pupils were prisoners in the school house. Mrs. Rhodes and her daughters, Delores and Beverly used one room of the school house for living quarters. She had a cookstove and food so waiting out the blizzard would not be a hardship.

Lyle didn't want to wait out the blizzard with Mrs. Rhodes and all those girls. He said he was going home. Mrs. Rhodes objected. "Don't go, Lyle. You'll get lost in the blizzard."

"No, I won't," Lyle said. "I'll follow the fence home. I can make it." The fence ran straight east for a mile, then north past the Dennis house. Lyle was a husky sixteen-year-old. He didn't think walking home in the screaming wind would be a problem.

He put on his overshoes, coat, cap and mittens and stepped out into the teeth of as wild a blizzard as South Dakota had ever seen. The wind hit him like a boxcar. He turned his face away from the wind and struggled to the school yard gate. He crossed the road, climbed the fence and headed east.

The northwest wind hit him slantwise, colder than an iceberg. Sharp, driving snow bombarded his face. He plodded east along the fence, unable to see anything except the swirling white that stung his face like a thousand bees. His hands and feet grew colder. He wished he had stayed in school. He struggled on until he reached the fence corner. He turned north into the vicious teeth of the storm. His hands and feet were numb.

The wind was like a giant hand pushing against his cold body. He slogged north until he reached the mailbox beside the road and knew the house was near. He could see ghostly snatches of its outline appearing and disappearing. The shrieking wind tore at his clothes. He crawled through the fence and the wind pushed him to the house. He staggered inside. His hands were icy clubs inside his mittens. His father put a tub of snow on the porch and made Lyle sit with his hands and feet in the snow until the frost left them. Lyle suffered through the ordeal. Fortunately, his hands and feet survived the harsh treatment.

The blizzard of 1952 took several lives. Two little girls died trying to get home from school. A man and his hired man lost their lives, trying to bring two of the girls home. Thor Fosheim, 75, a rancher in the Moenville country, saddled his horse and rode into the storm to search for his cattle. Minnie, a daughter living with him, worried when he didn't return. The wind was so fierce she didn't dare go outside, but kept lamps in all the windows.

Tuesday morning, she bundled up and went out into the bitter wind. She searched for several hours around haystacks where she thought he might have taken shelter. She gave up, started home and found a dark object near a gate about a quarter of a mile from home. The frozen body of Thor Fosheim lay in the snow. She fixed a sled and pulled the body home. Roads were so blocked with snow that the funeral was not held until January 29.

Tillie Dinsmore and two-year-old Vincent were home in their two story house about a half mile west of the Midland School House on the hill. When Tillie opened the front door to look outside sometimes she couldn't see the yard gate a few feet from the house. She worried about Frank who had left on his mail route that morning, and the three older children who were in school. Evening came and no one came out of the storm. She and baby Vincent waited. By Tuesday morning, a snowdrift reached the top of their two-story house, and the howling wind still blew.

Wednesday morning dawned bright and clear, and Tillie finally found out what happened to Frank and the children. When the blizzard hit, the teacher sent the children home. Blaine, Cherelyn and Ruby, all in grade school, went home with the Hunt children who lived a half block from the school house. The Dinsmore children stayed at Hunts until the blow ended. Ida Hunt sat them down with her seven children for a pancake dinner. She fried pancakes and the kids ate. Blaine embarrassed Cherelyn by getting into a pancake-eating contest with one of the Hunt boys. The Dinsmore children spent two nights at Hunts and walked home over the snowdrifts when the wind quit.

Frank Dinsmore started on his mail route in his Ford car that Monday morning. He was at Ottumwa when the wind hit and a wall of snow blotted out the landscape. He turned around and headed back to Midland, fighting to keep his car on the gravel road. He battled the wind for six miles, then ran off the road and was stuck tight in a snowbank. He got out of the car. He could see nothing but a solid, white wall, but he knew the abandoned Kunkle buildings were nearby. He struggled to the house and went inside. Wind whistled through broken windows, blowing snow on the floor. The temperature was dropping rapidly. Frank walked and stamped his feet and beat his hands together to keep from freezing as the wind screeched and howled around the house.

He had no water, but he had two sandwiches and some graham crackers that he rationed to himself during his grueling two days and nights as a prisoner of the storm. On the third day, he saw the sun shining so brightly the snow was turned to a field of diamonds. The wind had dropped to a stiff breeze. He found a piece of cardboard and used it to shield his face from the brisk wind. He headed south, walking two miles to Highway 14 where he headed east along the asphalt. No cars came. The highway was blocked with snow. He saw the Noble farm buildings about a mile south so he went there and found warmth, food and water.

Ed Owens started north on Highway 14, headed for Hayes on his mail route. He was about nine miles north of Midland when the wind hit. The Holden family lived close to the road on the west side. Ed struggled against the wind to the house and knocked on the door. Gladys Holden invited him into the house. Gladys and the children were wondering where Fred was. Fred and his truck were stranded at the Ernest Nemec ranch a couple of miles southeast.

Hotels and motels were often full of stranded travelers. Leif Hansen, owner of the Fort Pierre Sales Barn, was stuck in his car on the highway. He spent a cold two days beating on his car to stay warm before he was rescued by a snow plow. Bill, Verna and Tom Lammon were in the process of moving back to South Dakota from Montana. Bill, Tom and their dog Mark were holed up in a hotel in a small town east of Rapid City. Verna was in Montana, preparing to load the truck and head for Midland. She was about to load four horses, some heifers, a few goats and their furniture when Bill called and told her not to come.

We had ninety-six cows and two bulls to feed. We were shooting for a hundred cows, but we lost one so by spring we had ninety-five and were getting low on hay. Lloyd wintered his herd on the Linder place west of town and stayed at The Foley Hotel. He walked out to see how we were wintering, and said the snow was so hard it was like walking on a sidewalk. He had been getting up before sunup and driving his truck out to feed his cattle. He said, "I pull on that air horn when I leave town and wake everybody up. I want them to know Lloyd Heeb is leaving town."

His air horn was loud. Tony Mosseau, who operated a repair shop and worked until at least midnight every night, said, "That darn Lloyd blows his air horn and wakes me up every morning."

I pulled wood out of the creek and chopped and sawed fuel for the kitchen heater, but we were modern in the living room. We had an oil heater. The tank held about five gallons and had to be filled every day, but that was easy compared to sawing wood.

The Dennis kids dug a snow house in a thirty -foot snowbank south of their barn. They played in their sixteen-foot square house all winter, but towards spring the snow began to soften. Sonny, Olivia's little boy, fell through the roof, and they had to dig him out.

For entertainment that long cold winter, we played a lot of whist and Canasta. We had a telephone by that time and Hank or Hope would call and say, "Come up and play cards." We'd saddle Silver and a buckskin quarter mare and ride to the Dennis' house and play cards for a few hours. One night as we rode home, a billion stars glittered. They looked like they were so close I could reach up and grab one. Not a breath of air stirred. The horses trotted home with snow squeaking and crackling with every step. We didn't feel cold, but the thermometer said twenty below when we got home.

Kenny and Doris Wheeler were visiting the Dennis' family one Sunday when we were there. Doris and Kenny and their two small red-haired girls didn't even wear overshoes or heavy coats. Doris said, "It's warm in the car."

I thought, "Yeah, but it won't be warm if you get stuck and have to walk or stay with your car till help comes." Texans sometimes learned about South Dakota winters the hard way.

Jesse Jones who lived up Ottumwa way watched his Angus cows starve to death with hay about two miles away under the snow. When spring finally came, he went back to Texas.

We ran out of hay in April and borrowed some from a stack Ralph Jones had on the meadow across the fence from our place. We hauled hay back the next fall.

Johnny Roberts over east of the highway was getting short, too. His calves were dying. Keith Elrod headed for town in Johnny's jeep one day and cut a fancy dido that turned the jeep upside down. Keith didn't get hurt, but the jeep was a mess.

By the middle of April we were looking hard for green grass and so were the cows. Melting snow formed pools in the creek so we didn't have to pump much water for the stock, but we, like every one else, were longing for spring flowers and green grass. The weather warmed as April wore on, and patches of green appeared. The cattle spread over the hills, looking for the green grass that poked through the ground.

We decided to move our herd to the north pasture where there was more to eat. We moved the tiny trailerhouse into the Jones pasture as close to the south end of our pasture as we could get and waited for more snow to melt. I opened the gate, mounted Silver and headed the cows north. They moved slowly, spreading out on the hills to chase the grass. I herded them to the flat where the trailerhouse was parked. I stayed in the little house with Silver staked outside. The cows grazed north, and I hoped the snow would melt so I could get them out of Ralph Jones' pasture.

One day, Clinton Harry and Wayne Haerer, two Jones' cowboys, appeared on the horizon. They rode up to the trailerhouse and stopped. Clinton said, "Are you taking up a homestead?" They grinned like they had just stolen a watermelon and it was good.

I was caught like the monkey with his hand in the sugar jar, but I couldn't get any further north. The weather stayed warm, and the snow melted fast. In a week, I had the cattle inside their own pasture and hoped we wouldn't get another storm.

One part Brahma cow was heavy with calf and weak as a new born cottontail. She waddled to a draw and lay down and couldn't get up again. I hoisted on her tail. She tried to get up, but fell back to the ground. Lee hauled her some hay and fed her cake. I lugged water to her from the dam. She took her ease for a week. Then one day I rode to the pasture and found her standing proudly, nursing a new baby calf.

Lee hauled cake from town, a couple of hundred pound sacks at a time, to the pasture with the jeep until one day she didn't get started early enough, and the frost went out of the ground before she got to the pasture. She buried the jeep to the axles in the mud in the Jones' pasture.

Fortunately for all cattle raisers, we got no more snow. The sun shone warm, raising the temperature into the seventies and eighties. Water rushed down the draws. One day the temperature rose to ninety-five degrees and snow literally turned to water in minutes.

Spring was greeted with joy. The floods of spring were not.

CHAPTER 20
Spring 1952

Spring came with such a rush, one could almost see the grass grow. It was a blessing. One more blizzard would have finished a lot of weak cattle. We were lucky. We only lost two. Some ranchers were not so fortunate. They lost whole herds. If you drove by the Roberts' place you could see dead cattle everywhere. Johnny Roberts sold his place to R.T. Jones from Texas and went back to Colorado.

When enough snow melted so we could find our tan Chevy, we dug the car out of its snowy cocoon before the creek swallowed it. Water rippled off the hillsides, ran down the draws and filled dams to overflowing. Rivers raged out of their banks and covered the lowlands.

Mitchell Creek spread over the flats and ran through our corrals, coming almost to the house. Bad River covered the lowlands and rushed toward Fort Pierre. Flooding rivers and creeks poured into the Missouri River where no dams held back the flood. The Missouri River couldn't contain all the water that dumped into it from the Cheyenne and Moreau Rivers. Fort Pierre got the rolling flood from Bad River as it tore through into the already overflowing Missouri. The Missouri swelled and deepened until the raging water covered the low part of Pierre and most of Fort Pierre.

We drove to the high bluffs above Fort Pierre to see the flood. Parked high above the flood waters, we looked on the destruction going on below us. The water rolled by about two miles wide. Much of Fort Pierre was in deep water. A blue bus sat on the street between *The Hop Scotch* night club and a store building with only about a foot of blue sticking above the water. Cars left on the street were submerged. People could have driven their cars to higher ground, but nobody thought the water would crest so high. An army duck roared over the water, rescuing people caught in the flood.

The balmy weather with bright blue days and warm nights turned the prairie green. As grass grew on hills and valleys, the winter weary cows gained strength. Winter wheat sprang to life. Calves and colts kicked up their heels on the hills and meadows of our north pasture.

Human babies arrived, too. John Eric joined a sister and two brothers at Herb and Nila's home. Budd Lee was born to Mickey and Shorty and Juliana arrived at the Bertelson house.

Lee and I went back into the hog business. We bought several Chester White sows from Willie McGary who lived north of Belvidere and found a few more sows at the Ernie Hackerott farm northeast of Midland. We had enough money to buy lumber for Lee to build two farrowing houses. The four-foot high houses had three pens each with a door at the top so we could look in on the hog family. The white sows weren't fierce like the red ones. They were gentle. I could pick up a small pig without the mother threatening to tear my arm off.

We didn't pen our hogs so we soon had pigs running all over the farmyard and up and down the creek. Fortunately, they didn't find the neighbors in any direction. Iowa farmers called hogs "mortgage lifters." Our pig families multiplied and grew fat and eased the financial burden. Some happy hunter thought a white pig in the weeds was a deer and shot the porker. I could have sold the pig and bought him glasses.

Bountiful rains fell that spring and summer. Grass grew tall. Mowing went fast with the seven footer humming behind the jeep. Lee drove the stacker and I wielded the pitch fork to pile the hay into stacks. The hay stacks built up to just over twenty feet high. The first time I had to come down off a finished stack, I was in trouble. I looked at the ground. It was too far to jump. "How am I supposed to get down?" I asked.

Lee rested the stacker teeth on the hay stack. "Nothing to it," she said. "Get on, I'll give you a ride down."

"Nope, I'm not riding that wobbling thing," I said.

"What are you going to do, stay up there all night?"

I looked at the ground. I looked at the stacker basket. I couldn't stay on the hay stack. I threw my pitch fork to the ground and stepped gingerly onto the stacker teeth. I walked to the back of the basket in the exact center and grabbed the frame. Lee backed the stacker away from the stack. I was poised twenty feet in the air on the wobbly basket. It was worse than the ferris wheel. She pulled the lever and down I came. I never got so I liked that ride, but it was a fast way to get to the ground.

One day the stacker motor lost its power, and I drove it to Tony's Shop in Midland for repairs. Tony fixed the motor, and I drove back to the hayfield. The stacker still wouldn't push a load of hay. Disgusted, we drove back to see Tony. "That motor still doesn't have any power," Lee said

"I don't know what's wrong with it," Tony said. "Get Hank to look at it."

My brother Hank went with us to the hayfield. He listened to the motor. "There's an air leak in the manifold," he said and got out his tools. He took the manifold off, cut a length off a used tail pipe, took it to town and got it reamed down. He forced that piece into the manifold and put the motor back together. The motor hummed like new.

We broke a lot of stacker teeth. When Lee went to town after new ones, she often brought back a pint of ice cream for me. Sitting in the shade of the hay stack, eating chocolate ice cream when the temperature is a hundred degrees is pure bliss. I ate the whole thing.

When we finished haying at our place, we moved our equipment to some land Claude Harren had rented from John Sohls and put up a large stack for Claude. Claude brought out a long rope and held one end while I held the other to measure the stack.

"It sure was funny watching you and Claude measure the hay," Lee said. "Claude measured the stack long, so he wouldn't cheat us, and you measured it short so we wouldn't cheat him." We probably came out about right. We rented that pasture from Claude to winter our cattle. The pasture had good breaks, ideal for winter pasture.

One summer day, the neighborhood kids asked us to come to a meeting at Snooks to organize a 4-H Club. Most of the neighborhood kids were there: Gene and Carl Snook; Lyle, Peewee, Sadie, and Butch Dennis; Pat, Ted and Eddie Fenwick. County Agent Kenneth Wanless took the kids to the basement to pick their leader. The adults waited upstairs for their decision.

Gene trotted upstairs and said, "The Dennis kids want Lee or Timmie for leader, but they won't say which one."

"I'll do it," Lee said and became the 4-H leader.

I helped the kids with their livestock projects and had as much fun as they did, washing and grooming calves for the County Fair. A Hereford calf was mighty pretty with a bath and freshly curled face.

Gene wanted to do a dinner exhibit for the fair. She said, "I have my vegetable and bread, but I don't have any meat." She wanted a jar of chicken to complete her menu.

Lee said, "Come over and help can chickens and you can have a jar."

On a hot August day, Gene came and helped pick stinking wet chickens. She helped cut them up and pack jars, working hard most of the day. She went proudly home with her jar of canned chicken.

Colon Harren came out to help round up some cows one day, and I gave him Monte to ride. Colon stepped on, and Monte froze to the spot. He wanted to buck, but he didn't know how. Colon slammed his heels into Monte's ribs. Monte looked alarmed and started spinning like a top. He spun until his legs got weak, and he sank to the ground. Colon stepped off, and Lee and I laughed like fools.

Monte's next victim was Lee's cousin, Marvin Schroader from Keister, Minnesota. He was lately home from the Korean War and came to visit. Marvin wanted to ride a horse so naturally, I saddled Monte. Marvin mounted and kicked Monte. Monte went into his spin.

"Hey, what's wrong with this horse?" Marvin asked. "I want off." But he couldn't get off while Monte was doing his whirling dervish act. When Monte's spinning mechanism wore out, he sank until his belly touched the ground. Marvin got off. Monte simply refused to let a man ride him.

Marvin's brother, Moon, wanted a ride so I saddled a lovely black filly with a blaze face and white hind legs. She was green broke. Moon got on the filly and I mounted Monte. We rode over the hills and valleys in Steien's pasture south of our place. We started down a hill. I kind of forgot to tell Moon not to lope her off a hill. He let her canter down the a hill, reins halfway to her knees. Halfway down, she kinked her back, bogged her head and began to crow hop. Moon grabbed the saddle horn. When I caught up to him, he gave me a dirty look, and we rode home.

I bought a handsome three-year-old chestnut Thoroughbred gelding at the Fort Pierre Sales Barn. Robin Hood was a bit over fifteen hands and gentle to ride. He had a white star on his face and white stockings behind. Robin Hood never bucked. I rubbed an inch of wet snow off his back and threw the saddle on and he didn't even hump his back. He made a fine cow horse and was the best rope horse I had, but he was nervous. I could never catch him in the pasture.

I bought a book about training hunters and jumpers by an expert Russian horseman and set out to teach Robin Hood to jump the right way. I started him on the longe rope. He learned to walk, trot, canter and then to jump on the rope without a rider. Soon he would take each jump without a moments hesitation. I started riding him over the jumps, and he seemed to enjoy the sport as much as I did. He never refused a jump, but I made mistakes.

For example, I saddled Robin Hood and headed for the hen coop. Robin Hood was half over when he saw the rope. He jerked sideways away from the rope with me perched up in the stirrups like a hen about to fly. Robin Hood went over the jump, but I lit on the rope.

The REA turned the electricity on and lit up the country. We threw out our kerosene lamps, and lanterns. People bought electric refrigerators and electric ranges for their kitchens. Mom bought an electric range and gave us her bottle-gas cookstove, which was a lot better than our smokey three burner kerosene stove. People still put meat in the Zeimann Locker Plant in Midland when they butchered.

We hired an electrician to wire our house. He fell through the sheetrock ceiling of the living room, lighting on the floor in a pile of plaster and a cloud of dust. He apologized, finished wiring the house and fixed the hole in the ceiling. The guy who went up the ladder to install the yard light on the tall pole by the corral stuck his head between the wires and made enough of a connection to knock him back across the ladder. His face turned white, and I thought he was a goner, but he shook his head and got up.

His boss said, "I'll bet he won't do that again." The young man finished the job carefully, and we could throw a switch and light up the whole farmyard like daylight.

We installed an electric motor on the pump, so I didn't have to crank the jeep and back it up to the well to fill the tank anymore. I just threw a switch, and the little motor went to work. We had electricity and a telephone. We were getting modern.

Mickey and Shorty bought the Griffith house three blocks north of Main Street and moved into it. A cistern in the back bedroom provided drinking water. Midland's city water wasn't good to drink. Shorty hauled water to fill the cistern from the well on the flat north of town. He worked at Oscar's Mobil Station, pumping gas, fixing tires, and greasing vehicles. He worked long hours and many Sundays.

Judy and John Sanford lived in Watertown with their children: John Lee, Judy and Dena Marie called Dee. Dee was born in 1950. The Sanfords moved from Midland to Mobridge to Watertown where John drove a milk delivery truck when dairies still delivered milk and cream to individual houses. Little Judy and John Lee spent summers with Grandma and Grandpa Martin, Lee, me, and Woittes. Dee started coming along as soon as she turned four. The kids loved riding the horses, and Little Judy thought Stardust Queen was her horse.

Lloyd's snub-nose truck broke down, and he asked me to pull it to *Dorothy Brothers Garage* in Philip for an overhaul. He hitched his truck to the Dodge with a stout log chain, and we headed for Philip. I drove down Main Street past Pohle's Cream Station, dragging the snub nose behind me. A bunch of men stood on the sidewalk with nothing better to do than ogle those passing by.

Skipper Durnell said, "There goes Calamity Jane and Wild Bill Hickok." Lloyd thought that was the funniest thing he ever heard. I didn't find it comical. I would rather have been Wild Bill.

Sometimes the snub nose startled Lloyd. He was hauling a load of cows for Ralph Jones and shifted on a steep hill. The truck reared up on its tail. Cattle slid to the backend and spilled out. A few were killed. The ones able to move ran off into the breaks.

One lovely October day, Lee said, "Let's go out and get a deer." We were tired of eating eggs for every meal. Meat would taste good, but I was a little shy about poaching a deer. Lee said she would take the car and I could ride a horse up the creek. We'd surely see one. I agreed to go.

I saddled Little John, took my 32 rifle and headed west along the north side of Mitchell Creek. Lee got her rifle, got in the car and headed north. If one of us got a deer, we were to go up on a high hill and signal.

A few clouds floated in a sky of deep blue, a perfect autumn day. The leaves on the trees were turning to yellow and gold. The prairie grass was brown. I rode through the breaks for about two miles till I hit Snook's fence without seeing a single deer. I turned north and rode to the gate into Snook's pasture. Still no game. I went into the pasture and started down a steep draw toward the creek.

Halfway down the draw, Little John's ears shot forward. A four-point buck watched us from across the draw. I raised my rifle, aimed and pulled the trigger. I had my meat. I hurried down and gutted the deer. I cut off his head, threw all the evidence in a washout and kicked dirt over it, all the time worrying about someone popping over the hill. I washed my hands and my knife in a puddle, tied my rifle under my right saddle fender and mounted.

Breathing easier, I loped Little John up the slope toward the gate. I came over the hill and nearly ran into Clair Snook and Verlyn Hagan in Clair's pickup. The pickup stopped.

"What are you up to?" Clair asked.

"Not much, just riding around," I said, scared to death they would go down the draw and find my deer. We talked a bit, and they kept looking at me with funny expressions. "Well, I've got to be going," I said and headed toward the gate. They turned around and went back toward Hagans. I began to breathe a little easier as Little John loped toward the highest hill in the pasture.

Lee saw me and drove to the hill. She hadn't seen any deer. We loaded the deer in the trunk of the car and skedaddled for home. I didn't feel good about shooting that buck. I didn't mind shooting the head off a grouse so we could have meat for supper though. We raised the little wild chickens of the prairie. Poaching a deer seemed different somehow. Perhaps it was because I was raised to be a law-abiding citizen, and I'd poached a deer and very nearly gotten caught. I told Lee I wasn't going to poach any more deer. She laughed. We had personally outwitted the game warden, and she loved it. The Schroaders, like hillbilly bootleggers of the Ozarks and "the revenooers", had a running battle with game wardens. Frank and Dewey Schroader poached the pheasants that ate in their cornfields all the time.

Lee told a tale about Uncle Dewey's run-in with a couple of game wardens. Dewey picked up his shotgun and sauntered into his corn field to get a pheasant rooster for supper. He got his rooster , but at the same time a couple of game wardens showed up. He couldn't get away. They had him with the goods.

"You can't hunt pheasants out of season, Dewey," one warden said. "Give me your gun."

"Nobody takes my gun," Dewey said. The game warden reached for the gun, and Dewey rammed him in the stomach with the gun butt. He hit the other game warden and stalked off to his house. Later the sheriff called and said, "Would you come in and pay your fine, Dewey? We won't take your shotgun." Dewey went in, paid his fine, and went home, ready to poach another pheasant when he got hungry.

We moved our cattle to the winter pasture on the Sohls' ranch on a lovely autumn day. We parked the little trailer house on the south side of a hill where the draw ran down to Ash Creek. We were ready for winter with a good place to stay, if we needed it.

Snow came early in November, about six inches deep and stayed. It fell intermittently that winter, adding four or five inches at a time, but we had no serious blizzards. The wind mostly blew itself out after a few hours.

Marjorie Pickles was teacher at Eureka, living in the school house. Gene and Carl Snook walked two miles south on the hard packed snow to school one cold morning. Gene and Carl, cold from walking, cheeks rosy red stepped into the school house expecting to get warm, but instead found a chilly school house. Marjorie couldn't get the new oil burner to work, and the place was getting colder by the minute.

Finally, Marjorie gave up on the oil stove and went down to the basement where two ancient coal burning furnaces were located. She found a small pile of coal and some kindling and made a fire. The school house got warm. Carl and Gene felt pretty smart because they got to school and the Dennis kids hadn't. They were the only kids in school that cold day.

Gene and Carl rode a horse to school one day and got caught in a spring blizzard on the way home. The wind hit suddenly, sending snow flying through the air so thick they couldn't see the trail. Gene, who was ten, tied the reins together and let the horse go. Turning their faces away from the wind, the children trusted the horse to take them home. The horse floundered on through the storm, until suddenly, the corral gate stopped him. They were home.

Lee had gone to Iowa to visit her folks and ran into the storm on the way home. She hit deep snow west of Sioux Falls on Highway 16. Four other cars were blocked by the same snowdrift. They could go neither forward nor back. Lee had something to eat. We always carried a box of Hershey candy bars in the glove compartment in case of such an emergency.

Two guys from California were driving a convertible. They had no overshoes and wore only light jackets. They were freezing cold when they walked back to Lee's car and asked if they could get in with her. Soon the people in the other cars came, too. No one had any food. Six people sat in the Chevy and ate chocolate bars while they waited for the snowplow. The wind quit about sundown and a plow appeared.

Mickey Woitte in the kitchen of their home.

Robin Hood clears the hen coop with Buster Schroader riding.

Robin Hood jumping a hen coop.

Little John going over the brick wall with Timmie Martin riding.

Shorty Woitte with Budd Lee, Kandy and Rex.

Timmie on Silver Moon.

CHAPTER 21
Back to Work Again

Charley Nemec drove out to see me one day in late winter. "We got the Midland Grain and Lumber Company back," he said. "We let Al Schimming go. Do you want the job of managing the company?"

"No, Charley," I said, "I couldn't do that and take care of this ranch, too."

"Well, will you come in and manage it until we decide what to do with it?"

So I went back to work for Charley Nemec. Archie was never there. He lived in Miller. Being boss was quite an experience. I had a secretary. Maggie Mulcahy was efficient and wondered if I would fire her since I knew how to do what she was doing. Of course, I didn't fire her. I needed her to do all the things that secretary-bookkeepers do. I'd never had a secretary before. Never since either.

Bob Yanish and Rex Huston worked there with little to do because we were in a slack season, and Mr. Schimming hadn't figured out a way to keep them busy. He required a bare minimum of labor. They were paid $250.00 per month instead of by the hour whether they showed up for work or not. Rex said Mr. Schimming was a fine man to work for because he took them out for supper every now and then. I didn't.

Charley was a wonderful boss, but he was too tender hearted.

Rex got "lit up" one night and hung over. He forgot to come to work the next day. He walked into the office the next morning with a sheepish grin on his face, and I said, "You're fired, Rex."

Rex went to Charley and asked for his job back. Charley came to the office and said, "You could give Rex another chance. He says he won't miss work again." So Rex came back to work.

Some positive changes had been made since the first time I had worked there. The old weighing room had been converted into an office with room for paint and hardware items. Maggie had a chair with wheels so she could scoot about the office from desk to counter and back. The manager had a larger desk and a big padded chair with wheels.

I could sit in my padded chair and watch Maggie work. The boys sat out front and waited on customers when we had any. Winter is a slow time. I didn't let them sit and play cards like they did when Al Schimming was boss.

We got a load of wheat now and then or sold a bit of lumber or a load of cow cake. One farmer brought in a load of wheat that was liberally sprinkled with mouse turds. At that time, the government allowed one turd in three probes of wheat. I took a sample and got a couple dozen mouse calling cards.

"I can't buy this wheat," I said. "It's full of mouse turds. Take it home and feed it to the chickens." The farmer was upset. He thought I could run his pickup load of dirty wheat into a car and by the time his wheat got mixed with another 100,000 pounds of wheat the turds wouldn't be noticeable. I thought he was a big turd, but I didn't say so.

One Texas tornado from north of town came in after planting time and wanted to sell a truck load of wheat that had been treated with pantogen. Pantogen treated wheat has pink kernels . The poison is so deadly that if you find one kernel in a probe you have to condemn the load. You take three probes. A probe is a brass rod about three feet long with holes to let wheat run in. You jab the probe into the wheat, close the holes and pull it out. This load had so much Pantogen-treated wheat that I didn't have to probe it. I could see pink kernels all through the load. He was upset when he had to take his wheat home, too. He thought we should mix his poisoned wheat in a carload. I don't know whether he would want to eat the bread.

In late February, Archie and Charley sold *The Midland Grain and Lumber Company* to Gust Larson. Gust, Lucy and their boys, Larry, Scott and Charley lived in St. Paul where Gust worked on the railroad. Lucy had been little Lucy Bonhorst when we went to the same Rally Days in grade school. Gust grew up in the Van Metre country down Bad River from Midland. Gust was a Marine during World War II.

They bought the Conklin house and a small acreage about half a mile west of town. Oscar Parrotts moved out and the Larson family moved in. Several years later, Gust and Lucy built a new house.

Gust brought five-year-old Charley to the office one day. "This is my youngest son, Randall Charles," he said. Charley gave me a charming smile and a candy bar.

Gust took over *The Midland Grain and Lumber Company* March 1, 1953. He made some changes. He let Rex go because he didn't need two hired men sitting around when he didn't have enough work for one. Maggie left, went to school and became a lab technician at *The Bennett Clarkson Memorial Hospital* in Rapid City. I was the bookkeeper, and Gust found jobs for Bob.

Bob and Elaine and their three children lived a mile south of town near where the city dump is now. Bob was a hard worker. He built their house and a small chicken coop and raised a few chickens. About the time his chickens got big enough to eat, raccoons sneaked up from Bad River and opened the chicken house door. The little bandits stole a chicken or two every night no matter what Bob did to lock them out. One night the whole family of racoons dropped by, and about thirty chickens disappeared. Bob was walking by Bad River and found his chickens stuffed into a crevasse in the river bank.

When Gust and Lucy went back to Minneapolis/Saint Paul for a few days, they left the boys with me. Larry was never any trouble.

Mostly he sat around worrying about what his little brothers would do to embarrass him. Charlie stuck a black, game piece from a bingo game up his nose. It scared the dickens out of me. Our Aunt Tina and Aunt Amanda had warned us about the horrible results of sticking things up one's nose or into one's ears. "If the object were a seed, it might sprout and grow out of the appendage," she warned.

Lee calmly told Charley to lie on the couch, took the tweezers and pulled the game piece out of his nose. Then to my horror, she gave it back to him, "in case you want to stick it up your nose again." Charley said he didn't think he would.

Scott was a small carpenter. He took our new hand saw and tried to saw the half inch thick iron trailer hitch off the car. He didn't saw far into the hitch, but the teeth of the saw went every which way. Lee caught him and put the saw away. Scott found a hammer and pounded the bottom out of a twenty gallon crock. We were glad when Lucy and Gust got home.

One time when I stayed with the boys at their house, Larry got out his new boxing gloves and challenged me to a match. Larry was a husky twelve-year-old. He forgot to duck and ran into my right fist. The roundhouse blow caught him squarely on the nose. I didn't mean to hit him so hard, but the fight was over.

When the men were hauling wheat, trucking lumber and building material or building granaries, I was the one who weighed grain trucks and stuck the probe in for a sample. I tested the wheat and watched as the dusty grain poured from the truck into the pit.

The worst job was loading cement. When some guy came in and wanted a hundred sacks of cement I was the one who said, "Back up to the shed, and we'll load it on." Some guys looked at me like they wondered who was going to throw those hundred pound sacks onto the truck. I threw the sacks onto the truck bed while the farmer stacked them in the front of the box. If he wanted lumber, I helped load that, too. I got so I could tell how long a board was by looking at it. Steel posts and barbed wire were a rough combination. A roll of barbed wire is 80 pounds of stickers, about like picking up a cactus. I wore skin-tight buckskin gloves. They saved a bunch of scratches. I did everything but drive trucks and build granaries.

We brought our cattle home in the spring and started calving in April. We put the little trailer house between the dam and the corrals, making a cozy place to rest and cook dinner instead of riding home.

One delightful Sunday, Lyle, Peewee and Snazz Dennis came to visit. After dinner, Lee spread a blanket on the ground in the shade of the trailer house so she could take a nap. The boys wanted to break horses. We had a pair of dandy two-year-old paint geldings ready for the saddle. Snazz said he wanted to ride one, and Lyle volunteered to ride the other. Snazz was going first. I saddled the bay and white paint first, and Snazz got on. He rode around in the corral and the paint went fine. We decided to take a ride in the pasture. I mounted Robin Hood and we started out.

We rode around the end of the chute and headed north. The bronc turned toward the dam and began to pitch. He bucked around the trailer house and saw Lee asleep on the blanket. The startled horse jumped over her, and she woke up looking at a horse's underside. The paint bucked to the fence and stopped. Snazz dismounted, and Lee told us to take our horses back to the corral. Snazz led his horse back to the pen, walking ten feet high. Lyle and Peewee were impressed. Lyle said he guessed he wouldn't ride his bronc.

Spring rains fell in abundance. Cows were calving, sows were pigging, a few colts appeared in the north pasture. The geese and ducks hid nests away as did a few Buff hens, all trying to keep their eggs or babies dry in the frequent showers. Since I worked full time, Lee did the calving. She stayed in the trailer house during the day. Heinie Koch hadn't started building dams so Babe Nesheim, who operated one of the cats, drove out and helped her. They fell in love and decided to get married in June.

Rain was dripping May 1st when we got a phone call saying Uncle Alvin had been in a car accident. He was driving home from

Philip in the late evening when his pickup ran off the highway and hit the east bank of Jack Daly Creek. The railroad section men found him when they went by on the hand car. He had a head wound and was unconscious. Lee and I were supposed to go to the Bertelson ranch and tell Essie that an ambulance had taken him to *St. Mary's Hospital* in Pierre.

We drove to the railroad gate fronting Uncle Alvin's place and parked the car. His M Tractor sat by the gate where he had left it so he could drive it home if the mud was too deep for his pickup or the river was too high to cross. Lee climbed on the seat and started the tractor. I stood on the drawbar, holding onto the seat as she drove across the muddy flat to the river. Muddy water several feet deep ran down the river. Lee eased the tractor into the river and water closed around the wheels. With water running over the top of the small front wheels, the tractor roared across the river and up the other bank.

We left the tractor and walked to the house, dreading the task of telling Essie. We knocked on the door. Essie opened it, and Little Alvin and Ethlyn started talking. I looked at them, not knowing what to say. Juliana, about a year old, grinned. I said, "It's nice weather for ducks."

Essie laughed and said, "It sure is."

"Alvin had a car wreck," Lee said. "He's hurt bad."

"How bad?" Essie asked.

"I don't know," I said. "They took him to Pierre in an ambulance. Uncle Walt and Aunt Amanda are waiting to take you down."

We hurried the kids into coats and headed for the tractor. I carried Juliana. Lee took Essie and Juliana across the river, then came back after us. I put Alvin on Lee's lap and stood on the drawbar with Ethlyn. "Hang on to the seat," I told Ethlyn. The kids thought it was a great adventure as the water coursed along inches below our feet.

Gray clouds still threatened more rain for our soggy ground. Lee drove to the car with Juliana on her lap and Ethlyn and Alvin riding the drawbar. Essie and I walked, the mud caking on our feet.

Lee and I went to see Uncle Alvin, but I don't think he knew we were there. He died May 4, 1953. Little Alvin said, "They put my daddy in a big, black box."

Lee and Babe were married in June at the Methodist parsonage in Rapid City with Curt Anderson and I as attendents. After the wedding, they toured the hills for a few blissful days, then came home to the Mitchell Creek ranch. When Lee told her parents she was getting married, her father was upset. He thought she had better sense. Her mother laughed and gave her $50.00 for a wedding present.

Buster, now called Les or Leslie by his friends, and Beata Schroader were married in June also, as was Donnie Schroader. We went to Keister, Minnesota for both weddings. At Donnie's wedding we sat a couple of rows behind Donnie's parents, Bee and Dewey Schroader. During the ceremony, I notice Bee's shoulders shaking.

"Aunt Bee is crying," I said.

"No, she isn't," Lee said, "she's trying not to laugh."

When the wedding was over, I asked Aunt Bee what was so funny. She said, "When Donnie turned to his bride and said 'With all my worldly goods, I thee endow,' Dewey said, 'There goes his bicycle.'"

We were getting too many horses for our pasture again. I didn't have time to break all the colts. Unbroke horses were hard to sell so we loaded eight head in the Dodge and took them to a horse sale at the Fort Pierre Sales Barn. One was a two-year-old chestnut gelding by Silver Moon out of a Thoroughbred, American Saddle, Morgan and bronco mare. He was built like a Quarter Horse and looked like he could split the wind.

Irving Asmussen who had a ranch in the Agar vicinity bought the chestnut colt. We went to the horse races in Fort Pierre a few months later and this colt was running the legs off the other Quarter Horses. He broke the track record in the 220 and Irving was happily matching him against any horse anyone wanted to run. Lee stood by the finish line to take a picture of the colt in one match race, and the horses went by so fast all she got was their tails.

Brother Buddy was discharged from the Army in June and came home. In November, he married Bonnie Foster. They moved into a mobile home beside Mom's house and Buddy worked with Dad. The farmstead had changed since the dry years. A windbreak of tall trees sheltered the house from the north wind. Iris, yellow roses and other flowers bloomed in Mom's huge flower garden west of the house.

In Iowa, Buster needed pasture because Frank's farm was too small for Frank's hundred head of sheep and all the cattle and horses that grazed the small pastures. Buster wanted to bring his cattle to South Dakota, but we didn't have any spare pasture. Dad came to the rescue and agreed to pasture Buster's small herd of cows of many ages and many colors. Buster unloaded his cattle among the Herefords grazing on the lush grass that covered the prairie like a green blanket.

The Iowa cattle gobbled green grass until they came to the east pasture fence. Beyond that fence corn was growing tall. Cows stuck their heads through the three wire fence and stretched their necks toward the delicious odor of rustling corn. They couldn't reach a single stalk. One cow pressed harder and fell through the fence. Another cow followed until half a dozen cows were gobbling corn stalks.

Buddy rode past, checking cattle and saw cow backs moving among the corn stalks. He drove the marauders out of the field and fixed the wire that had popped a few wires. All summer Buddy chased Iowa critters out of Dad's cornfield. By fall, Dad was fed up with fence crawling cows. He told Lee, "I can't keep Buster's cattle here. They won't stay in the pasture." We drove the herd to our pasture, and they mixed with our cattle where there was no cornfield to tempt them.

The proclivity to crawl fences proved fatal to two of Buster's cows. One was a dandy roan that could fill a bucket with milk. Her calf was nearly as big as a yearling by weaning time. One winter day, the roan cow and a friend strolled up the bed of Bad River. When they came to the fence, they pushed through and continued. The river was dry except for spring fed water holes covered with thin ice. The wandering cows fell through the ice and drowned.

The Korean War was over. Major Herbert Martin was discharged from the Air Force and accepted an engineering position with U.S. Gypsum at their plant in Fort Dodge, Iowa. He went to Fort Dodge, leaving Nila to sell their basement house in Rapid City. After the house was sold, Hank moved Nila and the children and the furniture to a rented house in Fort Dodge. They could get television in Iowa so Herb bought a set. The TV messed up every time a Ford went by.

Lee and I rented the Bertelson ranch from Essie. She, Little Alvin, Ethlyn and Juliana lived in the house. Mary Lou was born later. Uncle Alvin had planted corn on his eighty acre field, and the crop was growing. Wheat didn't look good because of an early summer dry spell. A good hay crop was shaping up on the river bottoms, which had been flooded by high water in the spring.

The last of June, we started haying the lush grass on the river meadows. The hay fields were yellow with sweet clover blossoms, and their heady perfume filled the air. After work and on Sundays, I drove the jeep around the field and watched all that cow feed fall before my sickle bar. The only problem was that by the time I made a round on the forty-acre field, sweet clover several inches thick was wrapped around the drive shafts, stopping the jeep in its tracks. I hopped out, opened my jackknife, crawled under the jeep and hacked the sweet clover loose. Another round and the jeep was plugged again. I spent more time cutting sweet clover off the drive shafts than I did mowing hay. I lay under the jeep with sweat running down my face. Mosquitos and deer flies bit me as I chopped those tough stems in pieces, then pulled them loose and threw them away. There had to be a better way.

Lee studied the problem and borrowed two, three-foot lengths of stove pipe from Essie. She opened the tin lengths and spread the tin flat. Then she wired a sheet of tin under each of the jeep's drive shafts. It worked like a charm. The sweet clover slid under the tin. Not a spear or stem wound around either drive shaft as the jeep roared around the field. The mower hummed. Hay fell and piled in windrows behind the mowing outfit. We rolled up a huge stack west of the barn for the coming winter.

That summer, Ervin "Sonny" and Ruby, Babe's children, came to visit their father. Ruby stayed and entered the Catholic School at Sturgis for her freshman year in high school.

Buster and Beata came for Rapid City Range Days in August. Buster was going to ride Robin Hood in the jumping classes. Little John and I had been going after that elusive first place trophy for years. The second year we went, Little John had looked at all the people in the grandstand and got stage fright so bad he wouldn't jump a thing. I wanted to show Herb and Nila that he could jump so after the show was over for the day and the crowd was gone, Lee set up a jump outside the arena, and I mounted Little John ready to put on our show.

Unfortunately, she set the jump up beside a huge hole where a utility pole was to be planted. Little John cantered toward the jump, ears forward. He lifted into the air, gracefully and was halfway over the jump when he saw the hole. He twisted his big body sharply to the left. I fell into the hole. My head crashed against the hard, sharp edge. I came to in St. John's Hospital with a doctor pounding my knee with a little hammer to see if I had any reflexes. I spent the night with a nurse running in every hour to check my blood presssure. Little John didn't have to jump at all that year.

One year a load of jumpers came from Minneapolis. A smart alecky twelve-year-old girl rode a great little gray jumper named Little David. Little David happily jumped the first row of jumps and kept cantering north. He cleared the four foot arena fence and continued down the race track. Her father considered buying Little John for $500.00, a lot of money for a horse at that time, but we loaded up and went home. I usually won enough money to pay expenses. One year Little John and I got third in Stakes Class, but the pretty bronze trophy with the horse jumping a fence always went home with someone else.

This time Buster and Robin Hood were going to try for that trophy, too. It was the first show for both of them. Buster rode Robin Hood into the arena. Robin Hood cantered his circle and headed for the first post and rail. Head up, ears alert, Robin Hood looked at all the strange things and listened to the unfamiliar noises. He cantered toward the jump, hesitated a moment and sailed over. Buster slipped sideways. Robin Hood stopped. Buster hung straight out from his side, one foot hooked on the saddle. Robin Hood never moved a muscle. Buster pulled himself back into the saddle and completed the course.

The ringmaster said, "That young man made a remarkable recovery." The grandstand erupted in applause, and Buster rode out of the arena, feeling embarrassed.

Little John did a mediocre job. The grand trophy went to a young man from Nebraska, riding an unflappable old army jumper from Fort Robinson named Walnut. He suggested that we come to Scottsbluff, Nebraska and show next year. Another rider told us about the jumping show in September on the old Military Course at Fort Meade in the northern Black Hills. Francis said he had been the only rider last year, and the course was easy, running up and down the gentle mountains of the old cavalry jumping course. He said his horse had no trouble jumping it. Robin Hood and Little John both beat his mare, so we decided to go to the Fort Meade show.

Buster and his friend, Glen Hove, came in September, and we loaded the horses and drove to Fort Meade. Mom and Dad, Babe, Lee and Ruby came to watch the show. We tacked up and rode out to inspect the course. The jumps were post and rail and rock walls, all solid and real. There were no knock down jumps. The horse had to jump out of the arena, go over a rock wall with a rail on top, then follow the course through the pines, up a mountain side and down, then back to the arena. The jumps were rugged, but they weren't high. None were over three and a half feet high. We watched Francis take a practice run around the course his mare ran nearly every day all summer. She jumped easily, staying on a slow canter between jumps.

Buster jumped Robin Hood out of the arena and headed for the rock wall. I followed on Little John. Robin Hood sailed over the rock wall and headed for the next jump. Little John saw the rock wall and was petrified by an obstacle he could have cleared by two feet. I felt him getting ready to set his feet and snapped him with the whip, yelling "Hike!"

Little John set all four feet and skidded. I sailed over his head and came a cropper on the rock wall. My back felt like somebody had hit me with a baseball bat. Little John's knees were skinned from hitting the rocks. A young med student rushed over and felt my back.

"You're all right," he said. "You can go ahead and ride."

I mounted Little John and jumped him over a rail fence. When he hit the ground I knew I wasn't going to ride in the show. I dismounted. Buster agreed to ride both horses. Little John had had enough of military courses. He refused even to jump out of the arena.

Francis started on the course while Buster switched the saddle to Robin Hood. Francis's old mare cantered ponderously around, taking each jump in the long course until she arrived back at the arena. Robin Hood jumped out of the arena, sailed over the rock wall and headed through the pines. He jumped smoothly over the first jumps, then cantered up the mountain, taking each jump eagerly. They headed down the mountainside until they came to a concrete water tank with rails on each side.

Buster felt Robin Hood tense. He could see himself and Robin Hood falling into the concrete tank and being injured. He pulled up and went around the jump. The judges called him back. Francis won the trophy. I was disgusted with my horses. They could have easily jumped the course, but horses don't like surprises. Mom didn't get to see me do anything but fall off my horse. We loaded up and went home where plenty of work waited.

Midland had some changes that summer. Mrs. Charlie Illian bought the small cafe on the south side of Main Street beside the Midland Bar. Today, the bar is gone and the cafe is someone's house. Mrs. Illian called her place Mom's Cafe. I often ate dinner there. I could get a hot pork or a hot beef sandwich for fifty cents and a glass of milk for a nickel.

Uncle Walt was killed in a car train collision in October. While driving his Ford, he was approaching the track from A.C. Behl's place about a half mile west of Midland. A train was on the track near the depot. Apparently, Uncle Walt saw the train at the depot but was hit by a train screaming in from the west. He died October 13, 1953, and another old cowboy was gone.

When corn-picking time came, Hank and Tom Stalley borrowed a corn picker and hitched it to Essie's M tractor to pick her corn. Instead of unloading the corn in the corncrib or the corral where the gate could be shut, they shoveled it off east of the corrals near the south pasture fence.

We moved around a hundred cows into the pasture for the winter. Cows came to the fence and smelled the delicious corn in the golden pile. Heads went between the wires of the two wire fence and pushed until the cows fell through. They were in cow heaven until Essie tore out of the house with a broom and fire in her eye, chasing them away.

Lee fixed the fence. Cows came back to ogle the corn piled so close an ear could almost be reached with a long tongue. Again, they fell through the fence into the feast. Finally, Lee and Babe moved down and stayed with Essie until she sold her corn.

The wheat crop that fall didn't pay for the combining, so Essie lost money on the harvest. She sold all but twenty-five of their hundred and thirty-nine head of cows and paid the bank loan. She sold the rest of her cows a few years later.

Little Alvin turned four in April of 1954. I gave him a cowboy hat, leather roping cuffs, two six guns and a miniature lariat for his birthday. Alvin donned his cowboy equipment and sallied forth, rope in hand, looking for a critter to rope.

His mother raised New Hampshire Red chickens. A New Hampshire Red rooster is the fierce protector of his flock. The rooster chased the Bertelson children back to the house whenever they got too close to the chicken house. His new attire gave him fresh courage, and Alvin headed for the chicken house, rope twirling. The red rooster, guarding his hens in front of the chicken house, glared at the small cowboy invading his domain, while the red hens scratched busily in the dirt.

The red rooster headed out to challenge the intruder. The rope sizzled through the air and settled around the rooster's neck. Like a true cowboy Little Alvin jerked his rope tight. The red rooster wasn't halter broken. He skidded to a stop and pulled back. Little Alvin headed toward the house. The rooster's neck stretched. His feet slid. His wind shut off. He staggered.

Essie whipped out of the house. "Alvin, let that rooster go. You can't rope the chickens. You'll choke them to death." She took the rope off the rooster's neck, and the red rooster high-tailed it for the chicken house, his pride and courage badly damaged.

I rented the Edward's pastures north of Capa from old Mrs. Edwards, a Capa pioneer, and we prepared to move our cattle.

Shower for Lee and Babe Nesheim. Lee and Babe are seated. Shorty and daughter, Kandy Woitte, watch as Rex Woitte tries to help open the present.

Irving Asmussen and the horse we sold at the Fort Pierre Sales Barn. This horse broke the track record for the 220 at Fort Pierre.

CHAPTER 22
Capa

The sun shone brightly on the May morning we moved our cows and calves to the Edward's pastures. We rounded up the herd with the sun barely above the eastern hills to be sure the cows and calves were paired up. We didn't want to leave any babies hiding beside a yucca plant. Meadowlarks sang their cheerful songs as we headed the herd east.

I rode Robin Hood, brother Buddy was on Little John and Leroy Dennis rode drag on Gold Arrow. We stayed on the south side of Bad River for about four miles, crossed the river at Finn's crossing and traveled along the dirt grade to Capa.

The sun was pushing high noon when Lee drove up beside me in the jeep with lunch. Tired baby calves tried to hide in the buck-brush for a nap. Cows bawled for their calves. Little Alvin sat beside Lee, happy and excited to be on a real cattle drive. I set him in my saddle and got in the jeep to eat.

Little Alvin rode proudly, pretending to be a cowboy. He wore his cowboy hat and cowboy boots, but he was about two feet shy of reaching stirrups. As we moved slowly behind the herd, I led Robin Hood and ate my sandwiches.

The Edward's house, barn, sheds and corrals were on the south side of the road in the town of Capa. The pastures were north of the road. We turned the herd toward the small pasture that bor-dered the road. A cow broke from the herd and ran bawling back through town. Her calf was somewhere along the trail, she thought, and she was going back and find the little bugger. I tore after her and tried to head her back, but she dodged about and refused to turn. I roped the angry cow and dragged her to the corrals where I left her, still bawling for her lost calf.

The sun was at late afternoon when we chased the last cow into the pasture. They spread out on the hills to graze or headed for the dam for a drink. Lee went back in the jeep and found the lost calf napping in the brush. She hauled him back to his anxious mother.

We left the horses in the big corral and all piled into the jeep for the ride back. I needed to get the car because I was going to stay at the Edward's place and drive to work from there. With Skipper, my Doberman, on the back seat, I drove back to Capa.

Little John was gone the next morning. He had jumped over the corral fence and headed home. Instead of following the road, he loped straight west, jumping one pasture fence after the other until he was about six miles west of Capa. He stopped in a pasture east of Harvey Madsen's ranch for lunch. We found him eating grass, caught him and I rode him home.

When I rode through the cows the next morning, I found a cow stuck in the mud below the dam. I looped my lariat around her neck, mounted Robin Hood and tied fast to the saddle horn. Robin Hood dug in his hooves and pulled. The struggling cow came out of the mud.

I rounded up the cattle and drove them through the north gate into a thousand acre pasture across the graded road that ran to Capa from the north. A small creek cut through the pasture, running south into Bad River. The creek and some of the draws running into it were boggy enough to stick a buffalo. I had never had experience with cows in bog holes before.

I spent most of the summer at the Edward's place and drove to my job at *The Midland Grain and Lumber Company*. I'd get up about four o'clock and ride through the cattle before going to work. One morning, I rode over the hills and valleys, counting cows and came over a hill, short one cow. I spied her in a draw about a quarter of a mile away. Satisfied, I rode home and went to work. A couple of days later, the cow was still in the same spot. I rode down to see what was wrong. She was dead, stuck in a bog hole.

Later in the summer, I found a cow stuck clear to her belly in wet sand in the bottom of the creek. I tied fast. Robin Hood dug his hooves in and pulled for all he was worth. The cow didn't budge. I dismounted, took the rope off the cow and dropped the reins. I went down into the creek, and Robin Hood ran off and left me. Disgusted, I watched him trot up the hill toward the gate, head turned so he wouldn't step on the reins.

I knelt in the water-soaked sand and dug around the cow's legs, a handful at a time, like a badger digging a hole. The cow watched patiently as if she knew I was trying to get her out of her terrible predicament. Many handfuls of sand later, all four legs were free. She stepped out of the hole and walked up the bank. I followed. Robin Hood waited by the gate, looking innocent. No more cows got stuck.

Mrs. Edwards had moved to Spearfish to live with her daughter. The old Poler Hotel where people had gone for hot mineral baths in bygone days still stood south of the Edward's house. A grocery store-pool hall combination operated by Larry Forsythe was several blocks north. Larry lived in his store. Helen O'Connor operated the Capa Post Office in her house. Her son, Philip, lived with her. Capa had few residents, but in happier days, there was a school with twelve grades, a bank, stores and hotels.

Wilber Olson, his mother and father lived in the large, square Joe Thorne house a bit west of Capa. Today the Thorne house is a derelict reminder of the huge house of other days and different times. Most of the houses in Capa have fallen down or have been moved away.

The Edward's place had plank corrals, a barn and a ditch with running water from the railroad's artesian well flowing through them. A grove of trees were watered with the ditch water. The water was piped into the house. I had never lived in a house with running water. I could take a hot mineral bath in the old fashioned, claw-foot bath tub whenever I wished.

The house was a strange and eerie place. A number of claim shacks had been pulled in and fastened together. The outside walls were covered with tarpaper. The inside was dark and forbidding, even though the house was completely furnished. Most of the rooms with their carefully pulled shades were bedrooms. Mrs. Edwards had rented rooms to people who came to bathe in the hot water, but that was many years ago.

The furniture was from a different era, the horse-hair sofa, the overstuffed chair, the ottoman, the dressers, chairs and cabinets, the bureaus, the whole place was a museum. A great deal of history was wrapped up in the sprawling, ancient house. If rooms could talk, what tales they could tell.

I used only the kitchen, living room, bathroom and one bedroom. A long hallway led from the living room to the kitchen and another from the living room to my bedroom at the end of the hall. I wasn't scared in my ghostly house. Skipper, the Doberman, stayed with me.

Skipper watch dogged the place so well that the West Central Electric crew stopped at The Midland Grain and Lumber Company office and asked me to take my dog to work with me for a few days because they needed to do some work at the Edward's place and Skipper wouldn't let them on the premises.

Skipper guarded my small nieces and nephews, too. We built a woven-wire fence to enclose a large yard around the house on the Mitchell Creek farm. The horses couldn't come to the door and beg for sugar lumps anymore. The cattle and pigs couldn't roam right up to the door either. The fence even buffaloed most of the chickens, geese and ducks.

Mickey came to visit with Kandy, Rex and baby Budd Lee. Rex disappeared, and I went looking for him. Someone had left the gate open. Rex toddled toward the barnyard wih fifteen half grown porkers running to meet him. I sprinted out the gate, knowing the pigs were going to get to him before I did. Skipper whistled past me, going about ninety miles an hour. He hit the pigs head on about the time they reached Rex. White pigs scattered in every direction with Skipper in hot pursuit. I picked Rex up and carried him back to the house.

Rex was an adventurous tyke. I sat on the dam grade watching the kids play in the water. Kandy and Budd splashed and laughed. Rex waded straight into the dam until only his forehead and a patch of black hair stuck above the water. He jumped to get a breath of air. I ran into the water and brought him to shore. My Levis were wet to the waist. I sat down and poured the water out of my boots.

Rex could make my day. He was watching me dig a post hole at the Bertelson ranch one day. I was down about two feet, and Rex was looking worried. "You better quit, Aunt Timmie," he said. "You'll get down to the devil."

Little Alvin liked to visit me, too. He loved to watch the baby pigs. I took him to the barnyard to see the piglets. We stopped beside a birthing house where a bunch of small white pigs milled about. I picked up a small pig for Alvin to pet, and the pig squealed for its mother. She charged toward us, scattering small pigs in every direction. I scooped Little Alvin up and set him on top of the pig house and kicked the sow in the nose. She turned and dashed after her children.

More nieces and nephews arrived that year. Robin, daughter of Mickey and Shorty, was born in July, and Scott Martin, first child of Buddy and Bonnie Martin, came in September.

Herb and Nila and four children came to visit from Fort Dodge, Iowa in July. Lee and I were overhauling the Chevy when Nila and the kids came out to visit. The Chevy had gone through too much snow and too many mudholes. The motor was protesting loudly when Lee decided we could fix it. I parked the car in front of the house. We jacked up the front end and took off the oil pan. Lee had the valves ground, put new rings on six pistons, and we were ready to put the oil pan back.

John, two, and Ted, three, sat down under the front bumper to watch. "You guys get back," I said. "If the car falls off the jack, the bumper will hit your head." John moved back, but not Ted. Ted wanted to supervise from up close. He refused to budge an inch. I shoved him back away from the bumper, and he got up and stalked off behind the car, one angry little boy.

I held the oilpan in place while Lee fastened the bolts. We crawled out from under the car. We found Ted by the back bumper with a screwdriver clutched in one small fist. He had taken all the tail lights off the Chevy.

Nila said, "Ted Henry likes to take things apart. When we were visiting Mom and Dad there were a bunch of people there, and he took all the license plates off the cars and mixed them up. There sure was a mad scramble as people tried to figure out which plates went with which car."

To my utter amazement after our mechanic work, the Chevy ran like a new one.

In August Sadie Dennis and I loaded Little John and Robin Hood in the truck and headed to the jumping competition in Scottsbluff, Nebraska. I pulled up in front of the show office, and Sadie hopped out of the truck and picked up a twenty dollar bill. I had to work most of three days to get twenty bucks, and she picked it up out of the sand.

Buster and Beata came from Iowa. We ran into some acquaintances from the Rapid City shows, including the millionaire from Colorado and his new wife.

The arena was encircled by a high board fence so the horses didn't have to worry about what was going on outside. Little John walked into the arena and made his circle, cantering easily. He cleared the brush jump and a post and rail, then came face to face with a giant black bull's eye painted on a white fence. The black bull's eye completely unnerved Little John. He skidded to a stop, turned around and refused to go near the horrible thing. So I made the ignominous ride out of the arena, one more time.

We watched a rider from Fort Collins, Colorado riding a twenty-five year old cavalry jumper. The black mare cantered slowly, like every bone was creaking. I thought, "If she gets around without crashing a jump, it will be a miracle." The old mare lifted over every jump without a moments hesitation, although she knocked the top off a few barriers.

We switched the saddle to Robin Hood, and Buster rode into the arena. Robin Hood looked at all the strange jumps and began his circle. Head up, he cantered toward the brush jump. A slight hesitation and he was over. He sailed over every jump, collecting a few faults and finished fourth in a field of about twelve horses. At least he paid most of our expenses.

Later I hauled my horses to Iowa and entered the jumping class at the Winnebago County fair in Forest City. The arena was large, the audience a fair distance away and the jumps all post and rail. The first rider was dressed like a cowboy and rode a western saddle. He looked like he was in the wrong place. His horse thought so, too. He refused to jump anything, to the disgust of his rider.

I rode Little John into the arena. He cantered, ears alert, toward the first jump and cleared it. He took every jump with easy grace, jumping the way I knew he could. Buster rode next on Robin Hood. Robin Hood cleared every jump like a deer sailing over a fence. Little John took first place, Robin Hood second.

Aunt Spick told us that a friend in the grandstand said, "That must be Lee Schroader on that bay horse. Nobody else can ride like that." But the rider wasn't Lee. Lee wouldn't ride a jumper. She wanted nothing to do with them. It was a kid from South Dakota.

I entered Robin Hood in the Confirmation Hunter Class at the Minnesosta State Fair in St. Paul. The entry fee was $20.00. I could only afford to enter one horse, so we left Little John at the Schroader farm and headed for St. Paul. Buster was going to ride Robin Hood.

As Buster sat his horse waiting for the class to begin, another rider said, "Hey, you can't ride without a hard hat. Use mine." He handed the hat to Buster. Buster put the hat on. Robin Hood would show in a field of six horses, among them a horse and rider from

England and a horse and rider from Canada.

The difference between hunters and jumpers is that jumpers have only to clear a jump. Only knock downs and refusals count against the preformance. The hunters were judged on confirmation and style as well. They have to move gracefully and safely. Ticks count against the horse. Front foot knock downs are bad and refusals are terrible.

Hunter and jumper classes were held in the Hipperdome. It would be the first time we had shown inside. Sitting above the arena, Beata and I watched Buster ride into the show ring. Head up and ears alert, Robin Hood cantered toward the first post and rail. He lifted over the jump and continued down the row taking each jump with eager grace. He turned and headed down the last row. He sailed over the brick wall as easily as a deer jumps a fence. He cantered on, taking each jump in stride. He was halfway to the last jump when a photographer ran across the ring and stopped beside the jump. The man so startled Robin Hood that he broke his stride and took the jump at a trot with the flash bulb popping in his face. He won fourth place. We were proud of him, but don't know where he might have placed, if the photographer had taken a picture of one of the other hunters instead.

I went home and left Little John and Robin Hood at the Schroader farm. Buster showed them at a couple of fairs in Minnesota, winning first and second at each fair.

The wheat crop was good that summer. I hired a combiner whose crew consisted of his wife. He ran one of the new self propelled combines, and she hauled the wheat to town. If the elevators were full she had to dump the wheat on the ground. Giant mounds of wheat grew beside many fields.

I came to check on the harvest on a day so hot the meadowlarks hopped about with their tongues hanging out. The combine roared around the field, and the combine lady shoveled wheat from the truck to the ground. Sweat poured down her face, making dusty rivers on her cheeks. She looked beat. Trucks didn't have hoists then. The wheat eventually got to The Midland Grain and Lumber

Company.

We were ready for winter that fall with ample hay and good winter pasture. We drove the cattle to the Bertelson ranch where they were sheltered from battering winds by the breaks and the trees along Bad River. They grazed on the thick brown grass that covered hills and valleys, the hilltops were covered with red top grass.

Before going to work, I chopped holes in the ice on the water holes for the cows to drink. I stayed in the small trailer house we had parked south of the corrals. Essie had hired Ervin O'Niell to move her house across the river and set it on the flat south of the railroad track. No more battling the river for Essie.

Ethlyn was in first grade and needed to get to school every day at Midland. Essie arranged for Dick Schofield to take Ethlyn to school. Essie's house was about an eighth of a mile from the highway, and Dick drove right past her house when he took his own children to school. Essie would hang a white sheet on the line in the morning if Ethlyn was going to school, and Dick came to the railroad track where Ethlyn met him.

After a mild winter, the cows started dropping calves in April. A bit of green grass showed in the draws. Birds were just waking up as I loped my horse across the pasture, checking cattle in the early morning before going to work. The sun burst over the eastern horizon in dazzling brilliance of gold and red, showering the earth with light. I often found baby calves hiding beside a yucca plant. I dismounted, ear marked and put paste on the horn buttons of new calves. That is when it hurts them the least. If you get a calf before he is two-days-old, you can walk up and catch him. If he's older than that he can run like a deer. After work I rode through the cattle again, checking for new baby calves.

That spring I was breaking a chestnut and white paint gelding, and he turned into a saddle horse as I rode the rugged hills of Bad River. I sat at the counter in Mom's Cafe one day when Donnie Illian came in and sat on the stool beside me.

"Have you got a saddle horse I could buy?" he asked. Donnie had graduated from high school that spring.

"I've got a pinto gelding you can have for $75," I said.

"I've only got $25," Donnie said, "but I'm going to work for Uncle Harvey this summer. I'll give you $25 down and $25 a month till he's paid for." He was going to work for Harvey Madsen three miles down the river from Midland.

Donnie handed over the $25 and got his horse. It's the only horse I ever sold on easy payments, and Donnie never missed a payment.

When haying time rolled around, Frank Schroader wanted to borrow a team to haul his hay to the barn. Lee told him he could use Big Bertha and the bald-faced bay mare. I loaded the team into the truck and hauled them to Iowa.

Frank hitched the team to his hay rack and pitched on a load of hay. He pulled up under the huge hay mow's door where he could lift half a load and pull it into the mow. When he climbed down the front of the rack, he apparently slipped and fell. The startled horses ran, and the loaded rack ran over him. He died instantly. Buster found the team standing about a hundred feet away, facing the hog pen fence. Frank's death left a large, vacant spot in our lives.

Lee and Babe moved to Iowa to run the farm for Ula. They bought Buster's cattle and trucked them back to Iowa. I wonder if the cows were glad to get back to greener pastures. Lee was eager to grow Iowa corn, but Babe hadn't had much experience with corn fields.

I cut my work days at The Midland Grain and Lumber Company to three days per week so I would have time for my ranch work. I still didn't have enough time. I had about 150 acres to plow with the "M" tractor and a disk plow. My grain drill was an eight-foot Dempster. The "M" was a big tractor in the 1950s, but I hated farming. I didn't like going round and round the field monotonous hour after monotonous hour with the dust blowing in my face. I got out of some of the farming by hiring Lloyd Heeb to plow the west field. I drilled 84 acres of winter wheat in the field.

I bought Essie's F20 tractor and an International mower and quit mowing hay with the jeep. I hired Carl Snook, who was twelve, to ride the hay rake when I mowed the north quarter. The sun blazed down over a hundred degrees in the shade. I bought a huge watermelon one day, and we sat in the shade of the tractor and ate the whole thing.

Herb was transferred to Chicago and moved his family into an apartment. Linda, who was four, found a friend down the hallway. A lady in an apartment across the hall didn't like to have children running down the hall. When Linda came out to go down the hall and visit her friend, the lady popped out of her apartment and shot Linda with a water pistol. After the water pistol attack, Linda was afraid to go down the hall. One day Herb was home. He told Linda she could go down the hall and play with her friend.

Linda opened the door. She looked down the hall. All the doors were shut. She headed down the hallway. The lady with the pistol popped out of her door. Big Herbert popped out of his door. "Now shoot her while I'm standing here," he said. The lady popped back inside her apartment and slammed the door. Linda went down the hall to play with her friend.

Lyle and Peewee had grown up. Lyle joined the Army and Peewee worked on a ranch. As soon as he was old enough, he , too, joined the Army. Now it was the younger kids that came to help me train horses. I always had eager volunteers when I needed cowboys to help. Gene Snook rode with me whenever her mother let her. She helped me drive a small herd of horses to the Bertelson ranch. Gene, Carl and Leland Snook and Sadie, Butch and Judy Dennis came to watch me ride broncs and jumpers whenever they could.

The kids sat on the round corral fence and watched me ride two-year-olds, although the rides weren't very exciting. The colts by Silver Moon didn't want to buck. They wanted to be friendly and eat sugar lumps out of my hand. I had learned how to make a horse gentle so he didn't want to buck. The kids liked watching Little John and Robin jump the barriers the best. Little John never refused a jump at home so the horses put on a good show, jumping the rail, the hen coops, the brush and brick wall and, most showy of all, the six-foot triple liberty. The kids helped me cool out the horses and take off the gear.

I broke a buckskin gelding and a bay and white paint filly to ride. Buck had the makings of a fine saddle horse, and Bud Severson said he thought I could sell the horses at Clark, South Dakota. Sadie and I loaded the horses and hauled them to the Serverson ranch one Saturday. Bud called a neighbor and he and his father came to look at the horses. Bud's brother, Harold, and his wife, Nyla, also came to look at the horses.

The young man rode Buck around and immediately wanted him. I asked $150 for Buck and $125 for the mare. The guy's father said, "You should take $25 off the buckskin for that wire mark on his foreleg."

I said, "Nope, it doesn't hurt him a bit. I shouldn't sell him anyway."

The farmer argued about the price while his son sat on the horse, looking like he might cry. He wanted that buckskin horse, and I wouldn't budge a nickel. The farmer finally pulled out his checkbook and wrote me a check for $150. Later, I wished I had kept Buck for myself.

Harold wanted the paint mare, but he wanted to jew me down a bit, too. I wanted to sell her, but I didn't want to take less money. We argued about what a good horse she was and whether she was worth $125 until the sun was about to go down. Harold wanted the filly, he just wanted to get me down a dollar or two. Nyla listened to Harold explaining why I should knock off $5 until she got tired of it and said, "Why don't you just buy that horse so we can go home?" Harold grinned and wrote me a check.

Aunt Tina moved across town to live with Aunt Amanda, and Essie and her children moved to Aunt Tina's house in Midland where Essie went to work for Ella Sheely cleaning the M&M cabins.

Verlyn Hagan worked for Ralph Jones whenever Ralph needed extra help to work cattle. If Verlyn was going to be home late,

Esther called me and I rode up the creek and helped her milk their herd of ten Brown Swiss milk cows.

I called on the neighbors when I needed help, too. Hank Dennis came to help me round up some dry cows to take to the Fort Pierre Sales Barn one day. I had Robin Hood and Gold Arrow saddled in the corral when Hank drove up. He eyed Gold Arrow suspiciously and said, "I'm not going to ride that horse. He bucked Butch and Judy off."

"Butch loped him off a hill with the reins hanging to his knees and he kicked up his heels," I said. "He won't buck with you. He's never bucked in his life."

"Let's see you ride him," he said.

I mounted and trotted Gold Arrow around in the pen, then handed Hank the reins. He looked a bit skeptical, but he mounted. We rounded up the cows, and Hank said, "There's nothing wrong with this horse. He's a good saddle horse." I knew that, but was glad to have Hank agree.

That summer I mowed hay on Harvey Madsen's place on shares. I cut a large meadow of excellent hay south of Bad River and stacked it in one huge stack. Verna Lammon manned the pitch fork to build the stack while I stacked it with the hydraulic stacker. When the stacker broke down, we got greasey fixing it. That fall and winter, I hauled the hay to the Bertelson ranch in the truck. Sometimes the road to the stack and the one to the Bertelson place was muddy. I would put chains on the back wheels to drive from the road to the hayfield, get my hay, take the chains off until I got to the Bertelson turn-off and put them on again to drive to the stack yard at the Bertelson barn. I got so I could put chains on in about ten minutes.

By June the winter wheat in the west field looked like a bountiful harvest was coming. The ripening wheat rippled in every breeze. Richard DeYoung appeared one day with his measuring wheel and measured my beautiful field of wheat, the full heads beginning to droop.

"You've got three acres too many," he said. "You'll have to disk some under." He measured off a small plot. I dutifully climbed on the M tractor and watched the plump heads of wheat curl under the black earth.

By July the field was a sea of gold. The whole country looked at record wheat harvests. On the afternoon of July 3rd, dark clouds loomed in the west. Lightning ripped across the angry sky. Thunder rumbled. Hail fell and cut a swath a half mile wide that flattened my lovely wheat field until you couldn't see a single stalk. Everything including the grass on the meadows was beaten into the ground. The river pastures and hay meadows looked like a paved highway. Most people didn't have crop hail insurance. I didn't. It surely reinforced my belief that the native grass should be left right side up.

Herb, Nila and kids were visiting from Chicago. Herb's blue Lincoln was parked in front of Dad's house in Midland a few feet away from Dad's new tan Ford. The hail banged and bounced off cars all over town. The Lincoln and the Ford had so many dimples they looked like polka dots on a dress. My car was fine because no hail fell on Mitchell Creek.

Opal Finn lived on Bad River west of Midland where Danny and Deanna Finn live now. During the storm, she got caught between her chicken house and her house. She was battered and bruised before she reached the house and dashed inside.

When Herb and Nila went home, they left Herbie, who was eight, to spend the rest of the summer with me and his Aunt Ruth in Rapid City. Herbie loved the country, especially riding horses. Clair Snook said Herbie could borrow their Shetland pony and child's saddle for the summer. Herbie, his cousin Del and I went after the pony, riding Robin Hood and Little John. Herbie climbed aboard the small black pony and we headed home.

The pony sensed that Herbie wasn't an experienced rider and bolted. He tore down the road, dust flying. Herbie, black hat pulled low, hung on and rode like a wild cowboy. I kicked Robin Hood into a gallop and caught the pony.

"You have to hold your reins tighter, Herbie," I said. I lead the pony home. Herbie learned to control the pony and he never tired of riding. He rode many happy miles, but he needed someone to play with. We often brought Wylie Schwalm or Little Alvin home with us.

Herbie and Alvin never got enough time on horseback. Sometimes I saddled Darkie and let them ride the gentle old mare in the corral. The milk cow's calf watched the small cowboys through the rails of the round corral. The boys decided to rope the calf. They opened the round corral gate and lead Darkie inside. Herbie took my lariat off the saddle and roped the calf. When they tried to take the rope off the calf's head, the little beast ran around the horse, tangling her in the rope. Darkie stood calm, watching the small cowboys work the rope off the calf.

One day they wanted a horse to ride, but I didn't have time to catch one. Darkie and Stardust Queen grazed west of the house. "If you guys go catch Darkie, I'll saddle her for you," I said. "I don't have any oats, but maybe you can catch her anyway." I usually used sugar lumps, but I was afraid they might a get a finger in the way and get bit, if they did.

"We'll take some rocks in a bucket and shake it so she'll think we have oats," Herbie said.

"You can't do that," I said. "If you fool horses, next time they won't believe you."

Herbie and Alvin got a bridle and, reins dragging in the dirt, ran to catch Darkie. When they were almost up to the horses, Darkie and Stardust Queen walked a few steps, then began to graze again. The boys pursued. The horses moved on, always a few steps ahead until the disgusted little boys gave up and trudged back to the house.

Mom and Dad took Herbie to Rapid City to visit his Aunt Ruth and cousins, Del, Karon and Casey Callan. The kids were running down the hill back of Ruth's house when Herbie fell and broke his arm. That ended his horseback riding for the summer. I took him to the Schroader farm in Iowa in late August where we met his family, and he went back to Chicago.

That summer Curt Anderson drove a Caterpillar, building farm dams for Petoske Construction Company. He was working on a dam for Ralph Jones a few miles northwest of my house. Going to work and back to Midland, he drove past my house, through the hay corral and out the north gate, across Mitchell Creek and on to his Caterpillar.

Sometimes when Curt went back to his trailer house in the evening, I was out in the yard. Naturally he stopped to visit. Once when he stopped, I was standing in the corral with a vaccinating gun, looking at Robin Hood. His jaw was swollen, and the vet had told me to give him an antibiotic shot. I was trying to figure out how to give it without having him jump over the corral fence when the needle hit. Curt climbed over the fence. "I'll give him the shot," he said. I handed him the gun. Curt walked up to the horse and "bingo". The shot went in and Robin Hood didn't even flinch.

Sometimes I was riding one horse or another around in the corral or was riding one of my jumpers when Curt drove past the house. Somehow I got the impression that he regarded jumping horses over fences as an idiot's past time.

Curt didn't dance, but we went to movies in the Gem Theater in downtown Philip and at the new outdoor theater on the flat east of the Sales Barn. Midland's Legion Theater closed in 1956.

Ruby Nesheim, Babe's daughter, taught at the Eureka School that fall. She only had seven students: Butch and Judy Dennis, Gene, Carl and Leland Snook, Clifton Hagan and Theresa, daughter of Kenny and Elva Dennis. Ruby talked me into being Santa Claus for the Christmas program. I dressed in the red suit, stuffed a pillow under my coat, put on the white beard and said, "Ho, ho, ho," in my jolliest manner, but everybody knew who I was anyway. When spring came the proud old school house closed it's doors forever.

The dam building season ended, and Curt hopped on the bus and went to Oregon to spend the winter with brother Maurice, his wife Helen and their children, Kirk and Karen who lived in Lakeview.
I looked forward to his return.

Butch and Judy Dennis trying to make Stardust Queen take a show stance.

(Left)Essie Bertelson and children (Front) Mary Lou and Juliana (Back) Alvin and Ethlyn.

(Below) Linda, John, Ted and Herbie Martin, Herb and Nila's children.

CHAPTER 23
The Andersons

I know little about Curt's father, William Jacob Anderson. He was born in Putnam County, Missouri on June 8, 1871. While living in Missouri, he married and his wife bore two sons and two daughters. In 1907 William Anderson left his wife standing on the railroad platform at the depot, boarded the train and came to the homestead lands of South Dakota. He homestead in the Top Bar vicinity north of Philip, and he never went back to Missouri.

William Anderson was neighbor to a young woman homesteader named Olive Seward, who later became Curt's mother. Her homestead adjoined the homestead of Jake and Ruth Valliant who became her lifelong friends.

Olive's ancestors are believed to be descendants of Samuel Seward, D.D., Vicar of the Church at Yeovil, England in 1648. This church was built during the reign of King Henry VIII 1485-1509. Samuel Seward was thought to be the father of James Seward. James was Irish. He married a French woman named Elizabeth. They were the first known ancestors of Olive Seward. James and Elizabeth Seward sailed from England to Virginia in the late 1700s.

Some German or Dutch blood entered the mix when John Seward, born in Hampton Roads, Virginia February 15, 1790, married Pheba Van Schoych in 1816. John fought as Ensign John Seward in the war of 1812 in the 2nd Ohio Regiment. He moved his family from Ohio to Bartholomew County, Indiana and died there on April 10, 1873.

Jacob Seward, Olive's father, married Ella Celestine Brimmer March l, 1876. Jacob and Ella, Curt's maternal grandparents, were married in the bride's home near Derby, Lucas County, Iowa. They lived there a number of years. The five older children were born there. Ella's family came from New York state and settled in Illinois, then moved to a farm in Iowa. Ella was born June 7, 1851, daughter of Abigail Hoxie and William Brimmer.

Jacob Seward enlisted in the Union Army August 9, 1862. He served in "K" Company from Iowa the 34th Infantry. He fought in Mississippi and in the Army of the Gulf and was discharged August 15, 1865 at Houston, Texas.

In April Jacob located a homestead in Dakota Territories. He moved his family to the homestead which was near what is now Onida, east of Pierre. The next five children were born in a dugout located 16 miles east of Onida. Hannah and twins, Olive and Omie were born in Dakota Territory. South Dakota became a state in 1889, so Amy and David were born in South Dakota. David died of whooping cough at eleven months, Olive said because he played on the cold floor.

June 7, 190l Jacob and Ella and four daughters, Hannah, Olive, Omie and Amy headed back to Iowa in a covered wagon with a spring wagon tied behind. A two-horse team pulled the wagon with another horse trailing. Jacob changed horses periodically to rest his team. They arrived in Iowa June 30, after a 23 day trip.

Harvey and John Tyler stayed home to care for about 900 sheep, 20 horses and some cattle on shares. Jacob returned in September to get a carload of sheep to fatten in Iowa. Harvey left so Jacob made a deal with Albert Youngberg to care for his stock also on shares. John stayed until the fall of 1904 when he said he herded sheep and cattle at the same time and all he did was work and he was leaving.

John went to Iowa and helped move the family back to the

homestead in January of 1908. They lived on "The Spring Place" until Jacob built a new house two miles south. He drilled an artesian well at a cost of $1,000 and was lucky that good water came bubbling up. Omie and Amy came home with their parents.

Myrtle married Albert Youngberg who was farming in Sully County. Jacob died in 1911 and Grandmother Ella made her home with Myrtle and Albert. They moved to Newberg, Oregon in 1937 when the depression and drought drove many people from South Dakota.

John Tyler Seward married Nora Bell Tucker in 1910. She died a year later when Evelyn was born. The bereaved John worked on farms until 1914 when he joined a threshing crew. He was threshing in the Mobridge area that fall. With threshing over, he jumped on his bicycle and headed for Nebraska. He rode 600 miles across South Dakota, crossing the Pine Ridge Indian Reservation and into Nebraska. He arrived in the vicinity of Valentine December 3, 1914. Luckily he didn't get caught by a winter blizzard.

John Tyler and Elva May Saxton were married in 1916. In 1937, the height of the depression, they left Nebraska and settled near Yamhill, Oregon in timber country along the east slope of the Tillamook Moutains. They had two sons, Alva and Clarence, and one daughter Evelin. Clarence died in infancy, but John lived in Oregon the rest of his life.

Uncle Harvey Seward spent several years working in the oil fields of Wyoming and helped dig artesian wells near his old home east of the Missouri River. In 1921 he married Esther Schreiber, a school teacher. They settled on a farm in Sully county.

Curt's Aunt Lena married Alexander McMahon, a school teacher, in 1895. They had seven children: Ivy, Irving, Vern, Ernest, Marion, Eunice and Esther. In 1910 they moved to a homestead in the Lady of the Lake District in the vicinity of Sturgis, Saskatchewan, Canada. Lena divorced Alex in 1920, and in 1927 she married Thomas Franklin.

Curt's Uncle Guy ventured off to Saskatchewan, Canada and homesteaded about four miles from his sister Lena's family.

He worked with the McMaHan boys as they helped each other farm. Around 1920 Guy mysteriously disappeared. His team of horses were near the house. The harness hung in the barn. His house looked like he had walked out and gone to work. He never returned, and no one ever found a trace of him. Lena proved up on his claim as a relative. Many efforts were made to locate Guy, but none were sucessful. He had simply disappeared.

Curt's Aunt Hanna married John Jacobs in Chariton, Iowa in 1906. They had eight children, one of whom died at five years and one at twenty-one. John Jacobs took his bride to a farm near Gaylord, Kansas. John claimed he was breast fed until he was four-years-old when his mother in sheer desperation rubbed cow manure on her breasts to discourage him. He said he started chewing tobacco when he was six and continued the habit all of his life. In 1906 John and Hannah sold the farm and moved to a farm north of Canton, Oklahoma. In 1940 the government forced them to sell that farm so a dam could be constructed across the North Canadian River. John bought 80 acres eleven miles west of Canton. He was killed in a car accident in 1953, and Hannah died in 1957.

Curt's mother, Olive Amanda, and her twin sister, Omie Abigail, were born March 4, 1888 in a dugout on their father's homestead near Onida, South Dakota. When Olive was twenty she took the train to visit her sister, Hannah, newly married to John Jacobs and living on a farm in Kansas. She stayed until her nephew Jesteen was born in April of 1907.

Olive decided to go west and find a homestead of her own. She found her homestead in Old Stanley County near the tiny town of Top Bar, 25 miles north of Philip. William Anderson was her neighbor and began courting the young lady homesteader.

On February 20, 1911, William proved up on his claim and went to Deadwood to work. Olive had a couple of years left to homestead, but they were married in Sturgis, South Dakota December 20, 1911. William was forty years old; Olive was twenty-three. She stayed on her homestead until she proved up January 28, 1913. They had three sons: Maurice Clair born June 23, 1913,

Curtis Seward born November 12, 1915 and Kenneth Wayne born August 21, 1921. In 1916, William bought an Overland car from Elrod and Bentley Auto Sales in Midland.

Olive's twin sister, Omie, changed her name to Oma and married Daniel Halkett at Onida in 1913. Her daughter, Isabella, was born in 1914. They moved to Old Stanley County in 1916 and lived on a farm southwest of Ottumwa near the Heeb's ranch.

William moved his family to a house in Midland three blocks north of Main Street on Russell Avenue. He hauled mail up the Mitchell Creek road to Ottumwa, driving a spanking team of bay mares on a spring wagon. At Ottumwa, Seth Southworth picked up the mail and hauled it to the Manila post office on Plum Creek.

Curt started first grade in Midland, climbing the hill to the school house with Maurice who was in third grade. Kenneth "Kink" was a tiny baby. One day Curt was dressed in a black suit and put in a Tom Thumb wedding with petite Ione Davidson. When picture taking time arrived, Curt could not be found. Robert Grady was dressed in a suit and posed beside Ione for the wedding picture instead.

When winter snow covered the hillsides, Curt and Maurice went sliding with Elsie and Harvey Madsen who lived next door. Elsie and Harvey were good to their small neighbors. The Victor Fergusons lived in the next house north. Vic worked in the State Bank and had a barn back of his house for his driving horse. Alex McCloskey and his wife lived on the south end of the block in a two-story house. Mrs. McCloskey gave Curt an Indian Runner duck. The duck followed Curt around like a dog, running with him when he played with other boys.

When Curt and Maurice played with their friends, one of their favorite tricks was sneaking up to Mrs. Bill Dunsmore's house with a wooden spool with cogs cut around the outer edge of one end. Using a pencil for an axle and a string wound around the spool for power, one boy held the spool against the window pane and pulled the string. The cogs screeched down the window, emitting a high-pitched scream that would raise one's hair. The unearthly noise brought Mrs. Dunsmore out of the house madder than a wet hen. Laughing, the boys ran away, waiting for another chance to annoy Mrs. Dunsmore.

In late summer when the watermelons were ripening, Curt and Maurice liked to jump on Charley Myrland's watermelon wagon and ride around town with him as he delivered melons to the housewives.

Lakota Indians often passed through Midland or came to town for celebrations. When they came from The Rosebud Reservation, they crossed Bad River with their horses and wagons south of the stockyards. The women set up their tipis in a large bend of Bad River on the flat South of the railroad track.

Young Pete Elrod matched races between a white boy and a Lakota boy and took bets on the race. The starting gun fired, and the boys were off, streaking for the finish line. If the Lakota boy was ahead, he ran like an antelope, but if he got behind, he sat down and let the white boy run alone.

The spring of 1922, William Anderson moved his family to a farm four miles north of Ottumwa. That fall Curt and Maurice went to the Matthews School, a mile south of their farm. Curt was in second grade, Maurice in fourth. Curt was doing well in school until he got pnuemonia in March. William took him to St. Mary's Hospital in Pierre and left the frightened little boy in that strange place until he recovered weeks later.

When William went after Curt, he took him to the South Dakota capitol building to watch "The Human Fly" walk all over the outside walls of the state house. Curt watched in awe. When he went home with his father, he didn't go back to school. Because of absences he didn't pass the second grade.

Oma, husband Dan, and little Isabella lived south of Ottumwa west of Mitchell Creek, which ran past the Heeb's ranch. They headed to Ottumwa in a buggy one day, and the team spooked and ran away. The horses tore down into the creek, splashing muddy water high. They loped up the bank with Dan hauling on the reins, shouting "Whoa!"

He finally got the team slowed to a walk. Mud splattered everyone from head to foot. He drove to the Heeb's house where they went inside and got cleaned up. While washing the mud off her face, Oma discovered that she had lost her wedding ring. They walked back to the creek and searched, but couldn't find the ring. The Halketts left South Dakota in 1926 and settled on a farm near Poplar, Wisconsin.

The summer of 1923, William Anderson moved his family again, this time to the farm vacated by Oma and Dan Halkett. By the time they had loaded up and ridden in the wagon five and a half miles to the new place, tired two-year-old Kink was crying. His mother carried him into the house and put him on the floor. William carried a mattress into the house and dumped it on the sobbing child. Curt thought that was a terrible thing to do to his little brother.

Curt and Maurice went to school that fall at the Ottumwa #3 school south of their home. Vesta Johnson, the teacher, put Curt back into first grade. With many small farms and a passel of kids on every farm, the school had many students. Besides Curt and Maurice, there were Brady kids, Gillaspie kids, Maeder kids, Buchholtz kids, Simpson kids, enough kids so two school busses ran to take the students to school.

William Anderson drove one bus; Carl Stinson drove the other. The buses were Model T trucks with the box covered. The kids sat on benches that ran the length of the box on either side. Curt and Maurice rode in Carl Stinson's bus. One afternoon the bus tooled down the road, hauling the kids home from school. The bus crested a hill and ran into a herd of Friday Simpson's fat hogs. Hogs scattered in every direction. The bus plowed into a large hog, tipping the bus up on two wheels. Screaming kids bounced off the seats and rolled on the floor. The bus roared along on two wheels, then settled back on all four. The kids scrambled back on their seats, and the pig ran off.

Brady's lived in Ottumwa where Liz Brady ran the hotel. The Brady kids put the run on some of the other kids. Pat Brady was older and bigger than Curt. The smaller boys, angry at Pat, decided that if they stuck together, they could whip Pat. Curt, Eddie Heeb and a couple of small friends took after Pat. Pat ran for the barn with the small boys on his heels. He stopped behind the barn and backed against the wall, fists ready.

The little boys worried him like pack of young coyotes, but every time one got close enough, Pat knocked him down. They finally gave up and left him alone.

Tom Gillaspie and Lowell Maeder spent noon and recess time in the school house to keep from getting beat up by the Brady and Heeb boys. The fuss started because of the range horses. Acres and acres of open range stretched between the fenced farms. Hundreds of horses ranged there. The Heeb's outfit raised cavalry horses. They owned a large herd of mares and kept a Thoroughbred remount stallion named Hidalgo. The herd ran on the open range. In spring, horses shed their heavy, itchy coat. A horse will back up against any handy post and rub its itching rear against the post.

The Heeb horses rubbed against Thomas Gillaspie Sr.'s fence posts, and the posts worked loose. Staples popped. Fences grew slack, and Thomas Sr. grabbed his shot gun, dashed out of his house and shot offending horses in the rear with loads of buck-shot.

To get even, the Heeb's boys beat up on Tom Jr. There was Davy, Jim, Earl and Eddie, a formidable outfit. The Brady boys might help. Lowell Maeder was Tom's friend. Tom and Lowell were no match for four Heeb's boys and two Brady boys. Besides there were three Brady girls who would rather fight than watch, so Tom and Lowell prudently stayed in the school house until the school bus came to take them home, thereby avoiding black eyes.

Curt went easily from first grade to second. Esther Martin, his second grade teacher, passed him into third grade with high marks. Then William Anderson moved his family again. In 1925 they settled on a farm on Plum Creek near the Manila post office. They were in a new country with new adventures.

The Anderson boys had geese so fierce they chased the horses, and a buck lamb that grew into a huge buck with curling horns. The buck loved to chase the boys and knock them flat, if they didn't lie down quickly before he got to them. John Gates brought a small Jenny to the Anderson farm one day. He gave Curt all the change in his pocket to care for her until he returned. Curt looked at the collection of quarters, dimes, nickels and pennies and was happy to oblige. He liked the small donkey and in due time she had a Jenny foal so he had two donkeys. Mr. Gates never came back for them.

The Anderson boys were happy with the pesky donkeys, but their mother was not. The little pests pulled the clean clothes off the line and dragged them in the dirt. When Andersons moved to a farm north of Ottumwa, the donkeys hiked two miles north and rolled in Mrs. Bill Lee's freshly plowed garden. Mrs. Lee tore out of her house, hopping mad, and chased the critters away.

William Anderson liked to play cards, and there were numerous card parties around the neighborhood. He hitched his team to the buggy and, with a reluctant Olive on the seat beside him, headed for a party. Little Kink didn't like to have his mother leave him alone with his older brothers, who were ten and twelve. Curt said, "Kink bawled till they came home."

Kink said he cried because Clarence Halvorson, a friend of Curt and Maurice, told him to go into the house and when he went inside, he fell down the stairs into the cellar because someone had left the cellar door open.

Olive gathered cow chips from the prairie to fuel her cook stove. In the evening she would take her bushel basket and head out across the peaceful prairie, gathering brown coal. Olive's sense of direction was poor. If she got over a hill and couldn't see her house, she tended to get lost and wonder off in the wrong direction. William teased her about getting lost every time she got a quarter of a mile from home. He said, "I never get lost."

That provoked her. "Well," she said, "a pig always know its way home."

Curt and Maurice were learning to harness and drive the teams by the time they moved to the Manila country, although Curt was only ten and Maurice twelve. William had a small team of mules as well as his team of mares. One of the mules kicked when they put her tail through the crupper on the driving harness, so Maurice would back her into a stall and hold her while Curt stood in the manger and put her tail through. The mules were fast, but untrustworthy.

They ran away whenever they got a chance. If William came to a gate, and had no one along to open it, he had to tie the mules to the fence, open the gate, get in the buggy, drive through and tie the mules to the fence again while he shut the gate.

Maurice and Curt liked working with horses, but one day a horse kicked Curt below the left knee, splitting it open. The pain was extreme. He couldn't walk. His mother poured hydrogen peroxide on the wound three times each day and left it open to the air so it would heal faster. Curt lay on his bed and suffered the pain. He had no aspirin, no pain killers of any kind, but his knee heeled completely.

The Brady family moved from the hotel in Ottumwa to a house in Nowlin. When summer came, Curt and Maurice went to visit Pat and Mike Brady. At that time, Nowlin, a small town eight miles up Bad River from Midland, had several residences, a school, a store, The Van Cleve Hotel, a post office, bank and a wonderful huge water tank. The wooden tank stood on four legs beside the railroad track and was filled with water from an artesian well. The train engine got water from the tank to make steam to pull the railroad cars. A ladder nailed to the tank went from the ground to the top of the tank.

Pat and Mike climbed the ladder and found a wonderful place to swim. They dived in. The water was deep, clear and just right for a swim on a summer day. The Brady boys took Curt and Maurice to the water tank. The boys climbed the ladder and dived in. They had a great time, cavorting in the water until the railroad engineer found out they were using the tank for a swimming pool. He boarded the ladder up for about thirty feet, ending the swimming excursions.

They found other mischief. The Van Cleve Hotel had a large dinner bell on a pole outside. When the bell rope was pulled, a melodious sound pealed out and could be heard all over Nowlin. The boys knew that Mr. Van Cleve always napped after dinner. When they figured he was asleep, they slipped up to the bell and jerked the rope, hard. The bell clanged mightily. Mr. Van Cleve roared out of the hotel, cussing. The boys were already far down the street, running like coyotes chased by hounds. Mr. Van Cleve went back to his hotel, mumbling to himself. Pat, Mike, Maurice and Curt hid, laughing, behind the store. They waited until they thought Van Cleve was asleep and sneaked up and rang the bell again. Some days poor Mr. Van Cleve never got his nap.

Mr. Van Cleve's pet hen laid eggs in a wooden barrel beside the fence in his corral. Van Cleve filled the barrel almost full of hay, making a lovely nest for his hen. Henry Brady, father of Pat and Mike, had a saddle horse roaming the streets of Nowlin. The horse found the barrel of hay inside Van Cleve's corral. He stuck his head over the fence and gobbled the delicious hay. Van Cleve hit the horse over the head with a broom. Brady came running and lit into Van Cleve for hitting his horse.

"He's eating my hay, " Van Cleve said.

Brady tried to be reasonable. "It's only normal for a horse to eat hay. Your hay is too close to the fence."

Van Cleve climbed the fence and swung a big fist at Brady and the fight was on. Liz Brady whipped out of her house with a broom and whapped the men until they ran away in opposite directions.

Brady's old horse was his means of transportation. Brady and Old Hicks, who also lived in Nowlin, liked to drink whiskey now and then, but there was prohibition. They made a batch of whiskey and went on a drinking spree. When they were pretty well lit up, they decided to go visiting. Brady caught his little saddle horse and put a rope around the animal's neck. They both climbed aboard, and Brady guided the horse with the rope as the little animal moseyed down the road.

All of William Anderson's brothers came to South Dakota except Oliver. Oliver settled in Canada. William's brothers brought their wives with them. Jim and Rachel, with children George and Verdie, homesteaded near Hayes. Jess and his wife had one daughter, Marie. Pearl and Liddy had five children, Cyrus, Opal, Vern, James and Orville.

Christmas of 1925 Jim and Rachel, and George and Verdie, drove to William Anderson's for dinner in their new black Model T. The Anderson boys thought the Model T was a wonderful car with its canvas top and side curtains with icinglas windows. William Anderson's Overland was worn out.

Curt and Maurice liked to visit Uncle Jim and Aunt Rachel and George and Verdie who were older than they were. Sometimes they stayed for several days. Once Aunt Rachel gave them each a chicken. Curt got a proud, little brown Leghorn rooster. The strutting cock fit right in with the Anderson's flock of brown leghorns. A flock of guineas ran with the chickens and warned the flock if a coyote was near or a hawk flew overhead. If danger threatened, the guineas streaked for the chicken house with the chickens close behind.

Aunt Rachel gave Kink some Brahma chickens. Kink loved his huge chickens with the feathers clear to their toes. When rain fell, the Brahmas strutted around in the mud and got mud balls on their feathered legs and feet. Kink hauled his huge chickens around in his little wagon, and they seemed to enjoy it as much as he did.

Jim and Rachel liked to sing "Redwing." With a little encouragement, they would rear back and belt it out, shaking the rafters. Curt thought it strange that Rachel and Jim talked to their cat and dog. Aunt Rachel thought it was terrible for a woman to smoke a cigarette. She smoked a clay pipe as did Uncle Jim. If either of them awoke in the night, they got up, lit the kerosene lamp, filled their pipes and smoked companionably, then blew out the light and went back to bed.

The Manila school was smaller than the Ottumwa school. Curt went into third grade there with Cora Lewis teaching. Maurice was in seventh grade. Manila had been a roadhouse and post office in pioneer days, but now had only a post office with a school nearby. The post office was discontinued in 1928. Inez McDonald taught at the Manila school the next year. Curt liked Inez. She went out at recess and played volleyball with the students. Maurice graduated from eighth grade that year.

The next year Eva Schumacker was the teacher, and Kink started school. She said Curt could mold a piece of clay into a horse or cow that looked exactly like the animal portrayed. There were eight students: Curt and Kink Anderson, Gladys and Bessie McKillip, Billie and Roy McKillip, Clarence Halvorson, Willie Drew and Aletha Engleman. When Curt was in sixth grade, Pearl Halvorson was the teacher. She passed Curt into seventh grade.

The summer of 1927 when the big flood roared across the land, Curt stood on a hill high above Plum Creek and watched the water come. The small creek ran half a mile wide, roaring and rolling on its way to the Cheyenne River. Ed Ferguson's eight-year old-son was drowned when the bank he was playing on gave way, plunging him into the angry water.

That summer Rollie Schumacker who lived in the Manila vicinity sold a herd of cows to Henry O'Neill. The cattle were to be delivered to the Bar N ranch some fifteen miles south. Curt's father said he could go on the cattle drive. Excited, Curt ran to the barn and saddled his pony. He mounted and took his place behind the slow moving herd.

The England and England Construction Company was building a huge dam on the Bar N, the largest dam in the country at that time. Curt watched fascinated as the crew moved dirt, using horses and mules to work the heavy machinery. The dump wagons were pulled by three mule teams. An excavator with a dozer pushed by eight horses loaded the wagons. As one wagon dumped its load of earth, another was being filled. One of the England boys was an expert mule skinner. He could snap a harness line out like a black snake whip and break a beer bottle.

The Andersons lived near Manila for four years. In 1929 William Anderson loaded his family once more and moved to the farm four miles north of Ottumwa. Kink said every time a house was vacant, their dad moved into it. Curt said he changed schools so much he couldn't learn anything.

Curt and Kink enrolled in the Mattison #29 school with Mrs. Edythe Wright, who lived on a farm near the school, teaching. Maurice was gone, working wherever he could find a job. Curt was in seventh grade; Kink in fourth. Curt passed into eighth grade without problems.

The next year Mrs. Wright was still teaching at Mattison school. There were eight grades and one year of high school. Lyle Stinson was in high school and was ornery to first graders Vern Foland and Walter Van Tassel. Curt's cousins, Vern and Opal Anderson and Lyle Stinson's sister were in school and Kink who was in fifth grade.

Lyle liked to promote fights between Vern and Walter. The little boys, fists flying, fought like a pair of tom cats when you push them nose to nose. Curt was nicer to the small boys. He drew a picture of a bucking horse for Vern Foland. Walter wanted a picture, too, so Curt drew one for him. The little boys were proud of their pictures and wondered how Curt could draw horses that looked exactly like the horses running on the range.

Maurice made enough money to buy a Model T, but he wasn't a very good driver. He wrecked it and sold what was left to Otis Foland. Otis hired him to work on his farm for a year. Maurice went to a dance in Ottumwa one Saturday night and drank too much kickapoo joy juice with his friend Bud Stalley. They got into a disagreement and went outside to have a bare knuckle duel. Maurice was bigger, but Bud was tough. Maurice went back to work all skinned up.

The spring of 1931 Mrs. Wright told Curt he had failed the eighth grade. He had missed too many days of school due to illness. Spelling and geography were his downfall, so he said he wasn't going to school anymore.

Both his father and his mother tried to persuade him to go back to school and finish the eighth grade, but Curt refused. He had had enough of school and enough of living with William Anderson, so one fall day Curt went to the barn, saddled his horse and rode to the house. His clothes were tied in a meagre bundle on the back of his saddle. He was fifteen-years-old and small for his age. Kink said, "He was a pitiful looking little thing, sitting up there on that big horse."

Curt said good-bye to his mother and Kink and headed his horse north, breaking his mother's heart.

Curt on a black pony, ready to go.

Olive and William Anderson.

Oma and Daniel Hackett.

Bud Stalley, Maurice Anderson, Kink Anderson, Curt Anderson, William Anderson and Joe Phillips. 1933.

Maurice and Curt Anderson up a tree on Lone Tree Ranch.

CHAPTER 24
A Job On The Cheyenne Reservation

Curt rode north into unknown territory for thirty miles, crossed the Cheyenne River and rode on until he came to the Jack Hunt ranch on the Cheyenne River Reservation. The Hunts welcomed the travel weary young cowboy. Jennie Hunt, Jack's wife, was Lakota. She didn't mind having another hand to feed. At Hunt's, Curt found a place to live, food to eat and a job for the coming winter.

One day, he rode with the Hunts to a Lakota celebration. He stood in the crowd, watching a large circle of dancers do the bunny hop. Two women and one man, arms linked, hopped and skipped around the circle. Curt was enjoying the show when two large Lakota women slipped up beside him. One grabbed his right arm, the other his left. They hopped him protesting into the circle.

"No, no," he said, "I don't know how to dance." The ladies laughed and said they would show him, and show him they did. They bunny hopped the little white cowboy around the circle until he was bunny hopping too.

During those years of drought and depression, Curt worked on ranches wherever he could find a job. He worked for a time for State Senator Ned Wilkenson on his ranch on the Cheyenne River north of Philip. Every morning that winter, the cowboys rode down the river to feed the cattle. The team waited in the stack yard. The boys loaded a huge load of hay and fed the cattle, then put the team back in the stack yard and went up the river.

At night a sly neighbor with about forty cattle slipped into the stack yard, hitched the Wilkenson team to the hayrack and fed his cattle a load of Wilkenson's hay. The cowboys figured the hay was going too fast and hid by the haystack to catch the thief. The wily thief apparently was warned and didn't come back to feed his cattle that night.

About a quarter of a mile down from Wilkensons, was the large Cheney spread. Cheney and Wilkenson were brothers-in-law. Mrs. Cheney seemed to think she was a cut above the cowboys. Curt sometimes milked the cow which was kept at the Cheney barn. When he took milk to the Cheney house, Mrs. Cheney opened the door, took the milk and closed the door without saying a word.

Mrs. Wilkenson was different. The cowboys ate with the family. Narciss Widow, a young Lakota, worked there, until he got angry one day and quit. He went up the river and stayed with Red Bulls in their tiny cabin. After a few days on short rations, he wandered back down the river. Mrs. Wilkenson asked him if he'd had breakfast.

"Yah," he said, "we had bread and coffee and then the bread ran out."

One day Mrs. Willkenson served the new Jello dessert with whipped cream. Narciss ate his dessert in about two gulps. When they were outside, he told Curt, "I could eat a washtub of that stuff."

Cowboys working on the Cheyenne often had to swim the flooding river horseback in spring and summer. Curt didn't worry about high water. He rode his horse into the river and let the animal head for the far bank. He had one horse that swam low with his head barely above the roiling water. One spring day he rode into the flooding river when ice cakes floated on the water. The horse was halfway across when he swam into a heavy flow of ice and snow blocks. Caught in the ice field, the horse dodged the blocks and swam for his life. That time Curt was afraid.

The Wilkenson cowboys gathered a large herd of cows and

calves from north of Cherry Creek and trailed them south to the flooding Cheyenne to cross and drive the herd into the Bar N pasture about twenty miles north of Midland. The cows didn't like the rolling, dirty water. Bawling calves ran back. Cows bellowed and ran after their calves. The cowboys shoved a bunch of cows into the water and galloped after another bunch. Crossing the river took all day.

Curt was in the river most of the day. Along toward sundown, the last cow and calf struggled onto the far bank, and the hungry cowboys rode to the cook wagon. Curt's boots were so tight he couldn't pull them off. He considered taking his jackknife to cut himself free but they were brand new, made-to-order Bluchers that cost a month's wages. He decided against cutting them to pieces. By morning his feet were swollen, and he still couldn't get his boots off. He wore them until they were dry and worked around enough so he could yank them off.

Wilkenson and Cheney drove luxury Buicks and threw large parties in the Alex Johnson and Harney Hotels in Rapid City. In the early thirties, when the dark days of the stock market crash overwhelmed the nation, they were worse than broke.

A loan company from Nebraska foreclosed on Senator Wilkenson. Curt helped deliver his cattle to the stock yards in Powell on Bad River. When Senator Wilkenson paid off his cowboys, he said, "I'm tickled to death to have my debt cleared." The huge ranches were gone. Wilkensons moved to Rapid City where Ned got a job as a guard in one of the same hotels that had hosted his parties in his affluent days.

Curt never went home again except to visit until he was eighteen-years-old. He went home then to drive his ailing father's team, helping to build the WPA dam at Ottumwa, to keep his family from starving. Maurice drove Miles Connor's team. They walked all day behind the teams pulling scrapers full of sod in the heat of summer and the cold of fall.

Miles and Alice Connor and two daughters lived northwest of Ottumwa across the draw from the Walt Stalley ranch. Miles smoked a pipe with a curved stem and a lid. He filled his pipe with Kentucky twist, stuck a wad of chewing tobacco so big it swelled his cheek like a pocket gopher's and smoked and chewed at the same time.

Stalleys didn't have many cattle, but they had a huge herd of horses running on the open range. Bud and Tom Stalley were friends of Curt and Maurice.

Curt traveled around the country on horseback unless he found a friend with a car. He ran around with the Heeb boys, who had cars, especially Eddie, who died of pnuemonia when he was very young.

Some cowboys had never driven a car, but, if they got the chance, they hopped behind the wheel and roared down a prairie trail until they came to a gate. The first time Curt drove up to a high prairie gate, he tromped on the low pedal instead of the brake and sashayed right through it. He broke his lower jaw in a car accident, and a doctor wired his jawbones together. He told Curt to come back in a month to have the wires removed. Curt didn't want the doctor fooling around with his jaw anymore. He took a pliers and removed the wires himself while blood ran down his chin.

During those days of depression, when money was scarcer than hen's teeth, young men did many things to make a buck. Curt broke horses and trapped when he didn't have a job. Sometimes he stayed at the Heeb ranch where Mrs. Heeb cooked for all those hungry boys and mothered them all, too.

Coyote hides were worth about $14.00 and skunks brought a dollar or two. Curt set traps for coyotes. He caught one, but the wily coyotes seldom snapped a trap. The Heeb boys got most of the coyotes. They ran the beasts down with hounds and fast horses.

Curt had better luck getting skunks. He and a friend would find a culvert where skunks were denned and plug one end of the culvert. They ran a pipe from a car exhaust into the other end of the culvert and gassed the skunks. Then a barbed wire was tangled in a skunk's fur and the dead skunk was dragged from the culvert.

Naturally, the men smelled like skunks when they got through.

They went home, bathed and put on clean clothes. If a neighborhood card party was in the offing, they went. When the heat warmed the skunk hunters, the skunk odor emerged. People sniffed and shifted in their chairs.

Some men, in those days of prohibition, made whiskey to sell. Lawrence Olam, a young man living in the Ottumwa country, bought whiskey from a man who lived and made whiskey in The Badlands, an excellent place to hide a still. The whiskey was so strong a man couldn't drink it straight, so Lawrence stopped at a stock dam and filled his gallon jugs half full of water, then filled them with whiskey. He stored his whiskey in pint bottles and sold it at dances. He had more money than any young man around.

One cold winter day, Lawrence backed up to the wood stove in Decker's Store at Ottumwa with a pint of whiskey in each back pocket. The heat felt good until one of the bottles exploded. Whiskey splashed everywhere. Mrs. Decker was angry, but she wasn't the only lady angry at the bootleggers. One of the Stearns boys had a still north of Ottumwa. His mother said if she found his still, she would turn him in, even if he were her son.

Lawrence hid a gallon of whiskey in a stack of bundles on the Joe Phillips' farm northwest of Ottumwa. When Curt and some of his friends were visiting someone mentioned that gallon of whiskey. All the guys said, "I didn't drink it." The whiskey must still be in the bundle stack. Joe got a fork and the bundles flew. They found the gallon of whiskey at the bottom of the stack, still full, still corked. Joe let out a whoop, grabbed the jug, and the party was on.

Curt and Bob Stearns rode horses around the country looking for skunks and coyotes. One day they stopped at a vacant school house to rest. Ten hundred pound sacks of sugar, a bootlegger's delivery for making whiskey, were piled on the floor. Curt and Bob tore out of there and went after a pickup to get the sugar, but when they returned the sugar was gone.

Jim Heeb made quality beer at his father's ranch. He measured all the ingredients precisely and used a thermometer to get the temperature exactly right. One Saturday night, he loaded his car with bottles of beer and invited Curt and Stanley Martin (not related to me) to ride to the dance in Ottumwa with him. Jim pulled up at the Ottumwa Hall prepared to make some money selling beer.

The boys stepped out of the car and were arrested by Federal Agent Mitchell. While Agent Mitchell was shuffling through his papers, Jim escaped into the dark. Curt and Stanley watched, too scared to move. Agent Mitchell took them to Philip and locked them in jail overnight. When he figured out that they didn't even know how to make beer, and that the beer didn't belong to them, he let them go.

In 1935 William and Olive Anderson moved from the farm north of Ottumwa to Midland. William's health was failing. Kink was a sophomore in high school. In 1937 William and Olive moved to Newberg, Oregon where her sister, Myrtle, lived. Maurice worked in a sawmill at Lakeview, Oregon. Kink stayed with his Uncle Pearl Anderson and finished high school.

The spring of 1937 Curt couldn't find work anywhere. His cousin, Cy Anderson, and Pierre Martin couldn't find work either. They decided to head for Montana. Curt had an Oldsmobile, but they didn't have money for gas. They caught a ride to Midland and hopped a freight going west. They learned to catch the front end of a boxcar, not the back. If you caught the front end, the motion of the train slammed you back against the car. If you caught the back end, you were apt to slam back against nothing and fall under the train.

Many desparate people rode the rails, looking for a place to earn a living. Men with wives and small children cowered in a boxcar while the cold wind blew through the cracks. Shivering on the hard boards, they rode west. They had no money and no food, but they hoped for a better life than the one they had left behind.

When the train stopped for water, fuel or cargo, the bums walked uptown to beg for food. They knocked on doors and asked for anything edible. They stopped at bakeries for old bread and grocery stores to get vegetables and anything else the stores were going to throw away because it would spoil before the next day. They carried the food to the hobo jungle to make a big stew. At one place the jungle was beside a small creek. Someone had scoured a scoop with a broken handle in the sandy creek, set it on rocks and built a fire underneath. He fried pancakes on the scoop for everybody. Curt said, "They sure tasted good."

Pierre Martin's girl friend lived in Dillon, Montana. When they hopped off the freight in Dillon, Pierre went to his girlfriend's home. They never saw him again. Curt and Cy walked up town to look for work. They passed cafes and saw people eating strawberry pie wih whipped cream. They wished they had the money to buy some, but they were flat broke. They went into the first bar they came to and asked if there were any jobs to be had. The Gilbert Livestock Company hired Curt.

They ran cattle, horses and sheep, mainly sheep. They claimed to have 90,000 head of the wooly critters. Curt was hired to pack supplies to the sheep herders. According to Montana law, a herder couldn't be sent into the mountains alone. The Company got around the law by hiring a packer to carry in supplies for the herders who ran the sheep on the high mountain meadows up on the Ruby River. Riding a horse and leading a pack-laden mule, Curt packed in food and clothing, stayed a couple of days with the herder, then moved on to the next man.

The first time he got paid, he went to a cafe and ordered strawberry pie with whipped cream, but the pie didn't taste as good as he thought it would. During haying time, Curt cut hay with a team and a six-foot mower. The crew had six teams, eleven horses and a mule. In winter he went into the mountains with two men and cut logs and posts. They lived in a frame shack, with two tents thrown over the rafters for a roof. The house had neither wallboard nor insulation, but they had plenty of wood to burn, wood they chopped each day. The small shack was cozy as long as the fire lasted. When the fire went out, the cold seeped in on every side.

Nearby was a spring that never froze. They got water from the spring and sunk a hundred pounds of potatoes into it where they kept until spring. They hung their bread in a tree until the camp jacks began stealing it.

The other men cut the logs from trees stamped by the ranger with the initials U.S. Curt drove a team and skidded the logs to the Livestock Company mill with its roaring steam engine. He broke teams to work and horses to ride and his boss considered him to be a good hand with horses. While in Montana, Curt registered for the draft in a small school house in Alder.

William Anderson died April 14, 1938. Maurice and Olive had no money to pay funeral expenses. Curt had sold a team of mares for $200.00. He sent his mother $100.00 to pay for the funeral. She wanted him to come, but he didn't have enough money. Kink didn't go either. Curt sold a horse and bought Kink a suit to wear his senior year in high school. Kink said the horse was his anyway.

The summer of 1938, Kink and Willie Drew, fresh out of high school, borrowed Curt's Oldsmobile and drove to Oregon. Aunt Myrtle was happy to see Kink and have the boys stay with her. Olive Anderson had returned to Midland and found work, cooking for the Chicago and Northwestern Bridge Crew, going with the train wherever the cook car traveled.

Kink and Willie picked apricots and hops and, when the season was over, hopped a freight for a sight-seeing trip around Oregon. Riding the rails was a rough life, they soon found. They tried to slip into a railroad washroom and were caught by a railroad guard. He chased them out and told them to stay away. Willie was indignant. "They treat us like bums," he said.

"What do you think we are?" Kink asked.

When they got back to Newberg, they hopped into the Oldsmobile and headed for South Dakota. On the way home, Willie scrounged corn from cornfields they passed. They roasted the nubby ears for supper. Willie got so sick of their adventure that he told Kink, "I'm never going any place with you again," and he never did. He settled in Philip and stayed there. Kink nursed the Oldsmobile to Midland and was glad to step on familiar sidewalks again. He got a job clerking in the Midland Co-op Store.

Curt worked for the Gilbert Livestock Company about three years. He came back from Montana the first part of December and went to work on the Elmer Stearn's ranch north of Ottumwa. In late December, he and Kink enlisted in the Marines, but were not accepted.

The spring of 1942, Curt went to Oregon and worked for Bob Were, herding sheep on the desert. It was a miserable job. He lived in a tent with nothing but desert, sheep, sheep dogs and an occasional snow storm. When Maurice drove out and told him there was an opening in the sawmill, he went to Lakeview where he worked in The Goose Lake Box Factory.

He hated to go to work in that strange place where he didn't know what to do and screeching, howling, buzzing machinery pounded in his ears. He just got settled in when his draft number came up. The foreman offered to get him deferred, but he said he was going to the army, anything had to be better than working there. He went back to Midland and boarded the train for Fort Snelling, Minnesota with Martin Schofield and Eddie Seidler from Midland and a bunch of other Haakon County recruits. He was inducted into the US Army September 10, 1942.

Curt said everybody gathered round for mail call, and the Sargeant would yell, "Martin Shofield, Hakon County." It made Martin angry to have his name mispronounced. He'd say "My name is Martin Scofield from Haakon County." Next time, same thing, until Martin wanted to twist that sargeant's neck three quarters of the way around and let it snap.

Curt wanted to be in the ski patrol although he knew little about skiing. Instead, he became a combat crewman, about as dangerous a place as a man can be in the army. He was sent to Camp Walters, Texas and from there to Camp Behl, California. He was paid $50 per month and had to borrow $25 from the U.S. to come home on furlough before going overseas. He paid it back $10 per month from his pay. Camp Behl was on the desert. Curt helped serve the Officer's Mess. The California desert was hot. No air conditioners cooled their barracks. The sweat ran down their faces.

Curt was put in the 13th Armoured Division. He was sent to Camp Bowie, Texas and shipped overseas on a huge luxury liner that had been converted to a troop carrier. He slept on a hammock swung among many in the swimming pool. A storm raged for two days. Gigantic waves rocked the boat. The soldiers got sick. They were too sea sick to do anything, except be miserable the first half of the trip. By the time they reached London, Curt was feeling sea worthy.

Kink enlisted in the United States Air Force and worked on guns. He married Marie Roseth February 23, 1943 in Atlantic City, New Jersey. He shipped out to Scotland on the Queen Elizabeth and came home on the Queen Mary, the largest luxury liners on the ocean.

While waiting for the invasion of France to begin Curt and his buddies went sight-seeing. They saw Windsor Castle in all its glory. At night London was completely blacked out. People carried a tiny flashlight about the size of a pencil when they walked around London at night. The tiny lights were like a flock of fireflies flitting about.

Curt made the rank of Private First Class, then Corporal, then he committed an infraction and was busted back to private. He didn't want to be an officer and he didn't allow them to make him one. He was beginning to wish he had stayed at the noisy sawmill.

At dawn on D-Day June 6, 1944, the Allied Forces began landing on Normandy Beach. The invasion of France was underway. The American Forces, including Curt's battalion, landed on Omaha Beach under heavy fire from the German soldiers entrenched in the cliffs high above the beaches, German resistance that was supposed to have been knocked out by bombers before the invasion began. Heavy fog had stopped the bombers, but the German enforcements were alive and deadly.

Shells rained down on the landing barges and the soldiers storming the beaches. The barges ran as close to shore as possible and let down the ramps. Soldiers, laden with about sixty pounds of gear, jumped into waist deep water and plunged ashore. Some soldiers jumped into the choppy seas too soon and, unable to swim with their heavy equipment, drowned in the deep water.

The German Army had littered the beaches with huge concrete structures that looked like the jacks from a child's game. The armoured vehicles couldn't land with all the concrete obstructions in the way. Caterpillar tractors came in to move the obstructions. The Germans rained fire down on the American soldiers. Curt jumped into the ocean and waded ashore with a wave of American troops. He ran for a concrete jack and hid behind the huge structure while all around his comrades fell, hit by the murderous fire from the cliffs. Soldiers crawled under the caterpillars and under the concrete obstructions to escape the deadly shelling. Soon the beaches were littered with dead and wounded American soldiers.

After eight days of fierce fighting, the beaches were secure. In the face of withering fire, the American soldiers climbed the cliffs. The soldiers on Omaha Beach suffered the highest casualties of any outfit in the Normandy invasion. The crosses in American Cemetaries in France stood row on row like the long straight rows in a field of corn.

The Armies began the long and deadly march across Europe. A tank came and picked up Curt and four buddies and hauled them through the night, then unloaded them. Each tank hauled five soldiers farther into the German lines and left them to press the stubborn German Army back across France to Germany.

In one town in France, the Army requisitioned a home and set up mess for the soldiers. They went into the house by companies, ate and came back outside. Curt's company was about to go in when they heard a mortor shell screaming toward them. The men dived for a stone fence and lay as close to the rocks as they could. Scared almost senseless, they waited for the shell they knew would hit right in their midst. The shell homed in on the fence, lit among the rocks and fizzled out. No explosion. Nothing. The shell was a dud. The men began to breathe again.

When the artillery leveled one town in France, the soldiers were told to hide in the woods. They were tired of hiding. Instead, they went into town and snooped through the rubble. They found a wine cellar with rows and rows of bottles of pink and white champagne with tin foil over the corks and wire wrapped around the cork to hold it in the bottle. One soldier found some tall glasses. They unwrapped the wire and removed the tin. Corks popped and foam ran. The aroma tickled Curt's nose. They had a rip roaring party with the best wine they had ever drank.

Curt spent the winter of 1944-45 with an infantry unit in France in a hole they dug under the railroad tracks. The Germans were dug in a short distance away. If an American soldier looked out of a foxhole, a German soldier blew his head off. A soldier sometimes lit a cigerette and held it in his hand and thought about home while the cigerette burned down until it singed his fingers. He didn't even realize he'd been scorched until he smelled his burning flesh.

The bunker wasn't bad until the spring thaw. Clothes got wet. Some soldiers had frozen feet. Everybody had wet boots. They were supposed to take off their boots and rub their feet periodically to keep the circulation going otherwise the feet turned purple, and, if circulation wasn't restored, the foot had to be amputed. Some soldiers were so desperate that they shot their own feet so they would be sent back to a hospital.

The German resistance crumbled. The Allied Armies swept into Germany, pushing across the country. Curt's unit entered cities where ragged, dirty children lived in holes in the bombed out buildings. The children came out of their nests among the ruins, carrying small baskets. They fell in behind the American soldiers in the chow line, holding up their pitiful baskets to get whatever was left after the soldiers were fed. They scampered back into the ruins to share their food with whomever they had back in those awful holes.

Curt's outfit was in Austria when the war in Europe ended May 7, 1945. Curt was a machine gunner, sometimes called the "suicide brigade," yet he fought across France and Germany and into

Austria and was never wounded. His buddies died beside him, but he wasn't hit.

An Austrian woman said to Curt, "Hitler, Mussolini, Roosevelt, all capute." "Then," he said, "she laughed like hell. She thought it was a helluva joke. Roosevelt died from a massive cerebral hemorage in April of 1945. Hitler killed himself eight days before VE Day. Two days before Hitler died, Mussolini was hung by Italian partisans. They were indeed all capute.

The Austrian dairy farms fascinated Curt. The farmers tied their cattle in the barn all winter and fed, watered and milked the cows without letting the animals outside. When spring arrived, the cattle were turned out and began a wild scramble of running, butting, fighting and kicking up their heels.

The herdsmen put the cattle from all the farms into one large herd and drove them to the high mountain pastures. A cable car ran to the high meadows each day. The herdsmen sent milk down on the car and got groceries and supplies sent back. They spent the summer in the high mountains with the cattle and drove them back down the mountain trails before winter came again.

Curt's unit was sent to Switzerland for a short furlough before they were to be shipped home and sent to Japan. From Switzerland they went to La Havre, France to wait for the ship that would take them home.

One day Curt was sent to guard a bus load of German POWs going to a large quonset they were renovating into an Officers Club. Curt watched the POWs work and listened to them talk. Their English was as good as his. Then he got tired. He grew sleepier and sleepier. Finally he crawled into a cubby hole under the stage and went to sleep. The POWs worked until evening, then one of them tickled Curt's feet to wake him, and they got on the bus and returned to camp.

When their ship arrived, Curt's outfit went to England and came home on The Queen Elizabeth. Nobody got seasick. Curt came home to Midland on furlough, and on August 14, 1945, Japan surrendered. He was sent to Camp Chaffee, Arkansas to await separation from the Army. He said whenever a Sargeant or a young Lieutenant told one of the battle-hardened veterans to dust, sweep, or pick up trash and they didn't feel like doing it, they told him to "go to hell." They landed in the guard house where they looked out the barred windows and laughed at the soldiers working or passing by. When a man has been to hell and back, spent a winter in a muddy foxhole and watched his friends die every day, the threat of a few days in the guard house must have seemed like a big joke. Curt said the officers soon gave up and left the war veterans alone.

Curt was discharged November 12, 1945, his thirtieth birthday. He got $300.00 mustering out pay and $50.85 travel pay. He was in the Army three years, two months and three days. He was glad to be home.

Curt on dark horse in front. Thurman Rank on the Buckskin. They were wintering horses in The Badlands in the1930's.

CHAPTER 25
A Cowboy's Life

Curt hired out to the Bar N ranch north of Midland on the gravel road. The Bar N had been purchased by *Western Farm Management*, based in Chicago. He called it *The Chicago Outfit.* Ike Benson was foreman. Old Billie McKillip had worked on the ranch for years. Other cowboys came and went.

When haying time came, the Outfit bought one of the new fangled hydraulic stackers and mounted it on a John Deere tractor with narrow front wheels. Billie was going to run the stacker building hay stacks while the younger guys got sweaty, manning the pitchforks. Billie roared up with a load of hay and pulled the up lever. The fork raised up, up, up. Billie forgot to pull the stop. The safety stops malfunctioned. The load kept going. Excited, Billie tipped the teeth back, instead of lowering the basket. The loader arms tipped the basket backward and bent right down over the back of the tractor. Billie found the hay basket behind him, and he was trapped between the bent stacker arms. Hay was scattered about.

Billie climbed out of his trap and jumped to the ground. "I'm not going to drive that contraption anymore," he said. Ike Benson took over and stacked the hay.

Curt was working for the Outfit during the terrible winter of 1949. The Western Farm Management usually gave their men a sizable bonus at years end, but in 1949 they struck a gold colored medal for each man. The medal had a skinny cow, tail to the blizzard, head down, and a legend that read, *"The Blizzard of '49"* on the front and *"From Western Farm Management to Curtis Anderson 'For Loyalty And Outstanding Service'"* on the back. Curt was disgusted. He would rather have had his bonus money in hard, cold cash.

In the spring Curt and Francis Murphy rode around looking for cows trapped in bogholes. They each led a harnessed horse, and, when they found a cow stuck in the mud, they hitched the team to the cow's head and pulled her out of the boghole.

Western Farm Management sent Curt to the Rudy Creek country north of the Cheyenne, and he went to work for Wagon Boss, Albert Lopez. Albert ran the last round-up wagons that rolled on the Cheyenne Reservation. A way of life was passing. Albert, his wife, Luvisa, and three children Annabelle, Effie and Lee lived on the Rudy Creek ranch.

Albert had been wagon boss of The Diamond A Cattle Company, the largest cattle outfit in South Dakota during the open range days, leasing a million acres on the Reservation, running from Rattlesnake Ridge near Faith, South Dakota to the Cheyenne Agency on the south side of Fox Ridge.

Albert Lopez was raised in Colorado. When he was twelve, he ran away from home and got a job working for the Adams Cattle Company in New Mexico. It took his mother a year to find him. When he was fifteen, he went to work for The Diamond A in Colorado. This huge outfit branded 15,000 calves that fall and over 6,000 horses.

When the Diamond A moved part of its operation to South Dakota, Albert Lopez went along. They unloaded three train loads of cattle at Mossman, South Dakota. Albert had eleven cents in his pocket, a saddle and a bedroll. The cowboys went to the small shack that was the bunkhouse and threw their bedrolls on the floor. The cabin had no tables and no chairs.

The depression hit Albert hard, like it did other farmers and ranchers. In 1943 he was just getting back on his feet. He rented some land on Goose Lake Creek near Mossman, moved a house there and settled his family in the house. He built a "nice little barn" amd bought his wife a new Maytag washer so she wouldn't have to wash clothes by hand anymore. Luvisa bought Christmas presents for the kids. It was the first time since they had been married that they had any extra money.

Albert went to Joe Hiett's to help gather some horses. Luvisa and the kids went to bed. Outside six inches of snow promised a white Christmas. In the night, the acrid smell of smoke woke Luvisa. She went into the kitchen and discovered that the house was on fire underneath the floor. She ran to three-year-old Lee's bed, grabbed him, wrapped him in a blanket and carried him outside where she laid him on the snow. She ran back in and woke the girls, Annabelle, ll, and Effie, 8.

She took the children to the barn and dumped a barrel of oats on the barn floor. They lay down in the oats and snuggled together until morning. As soon as light began to show, Luvisa saddled Blondie and put Annabelle on the pony. Annabelle rode five miles to a neighbor, a bachelor named Melkey.

Melkey cranked his Model A, jumped in and drove to the ridge above the Lopez place and parked. He was afraid if he drove down the hill, the car wouldn't make it back up. He walked down the hill and found Luvisa, Lee and Effie huddled in the barn, shivering with cold.

They went outside and looked at the house, now a smoldering pile of ashes and the twisted remains of the new Maytag washer. Melkey put his arm around Luvisa and said, "Oh, Mrs. Lopez." Then, for the first time, she broke down and cried. Melkey took the Lopez family to Joe Hiett's place, where they stayed until spring.

Albert went back to work for The Diamond A. When they lost their lease, Western Farm Management took it up. Albert Lopez became their wagon boss. Curt got acquainted with the Lopez family when he went to work north of the Cheyenne River in 1949.

Albert was a great horseman. He owned a large herd, and loved to trade horses. Curt said Mrs. Lopez lived in a small house, had a garden and a white milk cow that provided milk, cream and butter for the family. One day Albert came home and led the milk cow away. He had traded her for horses.

By 1951 Curt had quit cowboying and was skinning cat for Western Farm Management. He drove a Caterpillar, building and repairing dams until winter shut him down. When the blizzard of 1952 hit, he had a winter job, working for Ralph Jones. He and Frank Cvach lived at the Tom Jones ranch.

Curt and Frank hitched up a team and went out to feed cattle. The sun shone bright, the snow squeaked under the horses hooves. They heard the train whistle in Midland eight miles north. When the blizzard dropped suddenly over the land like a white blanket, they couldn't see where to go. They could barely see the horses. They let the team go, and the horses unerringly fought their way to the corral. Richard Doud and Clinton Harry were saddling up to ride to West Fork and cake the cattle there. Fortunately the blizzard hit before they started.

Ralph Jones had a bunch of three-year-old steers wintering on Brave Bull Creek that were caked every day. The steers were thin, but tougher than whang leather. Curt and Ralph would each put a hundred pound sack of cake on a shoulder and run with the cake dribbling to the ground. Those big steers stampeded after them, bucking, kicking and snorting. Curt said he wondered what would have happened if he stumbled and fell.

The winter of 1956 while Curt was visiting Maurice and Helen and children, Kirk and Karen in Oregon and the Thode brothers in Arizona, I wintered cattle on the Bertelson ranch and worked at The Midland Grain and Lumber Company. I missed him, but I was busy. The winter was not extremely cold. The cattle ranged over the breaks and found plenty of grass. Some snow fell, but not a lot. Cattle were wintering well.

My tan Chevy wasn't. It was falling apart, making sounds a good car shouldn't make. Midland's night watchman, Officer Murphy, watched Midland's streets at night and sold cars for The Burns Ford Garage in the day time. He brought me a late model Ford to try out. The lovely blue Ford purrred like a contented lioness, but I didn't trust second-hand cars. I could ruin a brand new one. The tan Chevy was five-years-old and had about as much get up and go as a dead horse. I drove the jeep to work. That little green giant took all the punishment I dished out and asked for more.

I gave the Ford back to Officer Murphy and went to Philip to buy the black Ford stationwagon that Curt and I had admired in the showroom at the Burns Ford Garage. I walked into the show-room and told a salesman I wanted to look at the stationwagon.

"Go ahead, look it over," he said and walked off down the hall. I watched his retreating back for a moment, turned and walked out without a glance at the black Ford. I drove back to Midland, stopped at Aunt Amanda's house and called Pete Elrod. Pete sold cars for *Dorothy Brothers*.

"Will you sell me a car, Pete?" I asked.

"I sure will," Pete said. "I'll be right over." Pete took me to Philip and sold me a 1957 Chevrolet Bel Aire with aluminum tail fins. The regal blue Chevrolet was much prettier than the black Ford. The 1957 is one of the most beautiful automobiles ever made. I gave *Dorothy Brothers* $2,000.00 and my tan Chevy and drove the new car home.

The first time I parked on Main Street, Officer Murphy came over. "Hey, why didn't you buy a Ford?"

"I tried to buy a Ford," I said. "They wouldn't even talk to me."

"I would have," he said.

I took Aunt Tina for a ride in my new car. She had loved speed since the long ago days when she beat everybody on the roads with her horses and buggy. Aunt Tina was 85-years-old. Like a true smart aleck, I decided to see how fast I would have to go before she said, "This is too fast. We better slow down." On a long stretch of straight highway, I revved the Chevy up to 84 miles an hour.

Aunt Tina looked at me, her brown eyes sparkling. "Isn't this fun," she said. I slowed to sixty miles an hour. The only person I scared was myself.

One afternoon I pulled up to the gas pump at Oscar's Service Station and told Sunny Merkle to fill the car with gas and check the oil. Sonny was in high school and worked for his dad part time. I went inside the station while he serviced the car. He put in the gas and came inside. He had a foolish grin on his face. "I'll have to drain the radiator and refill it with water," he said.

"How come?" I asked.

"Well-um, I poured oil in the radiator instead of the motor." I wonder what he was thinking about.

Mom and Dad moved from the farm to a house two blocks north of Main Street in Midland. Buddy and Bonnie and children, Scott, Jeannie and Mike, now lived in the house on the farm.

Curt came home from his winter vacation and went to work for Clarence Petoske building dams. He didn't drive past my house anymore, but he remembered where I lived. We often attended movies at the Drive-In Theater east of the Philip Sales Barn or at the Gem Theater in downtown Philip, both long since closed. Midland's Legion Theater was also closed.

We were married that summer in Martin, South Dakota. As the petals of a rose open before the sun, a door opened before us, a path beckoned, a path we would no longer have to walk alone.

Thelma Martin Anderson holding daughter, Faye. Curtis Anderson holding daughter, Deanna.

To order additional copies of **GUMBO LILIES**, complete the information below.

Ship to: (please print)
Name ______________________________
Address ______________________________
City, State, Zip ______________________________
Day phone ______________________________

_____copies of **GUMBO LILIES** @ $16.95 each $ _______

Postage and handling @ $2.00 per book $ _______

South Dakota residents add 5% tax $ _______

Total amount enclosed $ _______

Make checks payable to **Thelma Anderson**

Send to: Thelma Anderson
P.O. Box 211 · Midland, SD 57552

To order additional copies of **GUMBO LILIES**, complete the information below.

Ship to: (please print)
Name ______________________________
Address ______________________________
City, State, Zip ______________________________
Day phone ______________________________

_____copies of **GUMBO LILIES** @ $16.95 each $ _______

Postage and handling @ $2.00 per book $ _______

South Dakota residents add 5% tax $ _______

Total amount enclosed $ _______

Make checks payable to **Thelma Anderson**

Send to: Thelma Anderson
P.O. Box 211 · Midland, SD 57552